Praise for
Friends of the Law:

For more than a century, each generation of scholars has produced a definitive study that redefines our understanding of Luther's signature teaching on the "uses of the law." Edward Engelbrecht's impressive new title is the definitive study for our generation. It reflects a masterful command of all of Luther's writings on point, and of the place of Luther's teachings on all three uses of the law in the classical and Christian tradition. Crisply written, meticulously documented, and conveniently presented in short chapters, with useful tables and appendices, this is now the go-to book for scholars, students, and pastors alike.

—John Witte, Jr., J.D.
Jonas Robitscher Professor of Law, Emory University
Author, *Law and Protestantism: The Legal Teachings of the Lutheran Reformation*

In this tour de force Engelbrecht leaves no stone unturned as he shows that Luther maintained a third use of the law, even if he did not always use that specific phrase. For Luther, the law not only provides order and accuses sinners but also instructs us in Christian life and witness. Those familiar with the literature on antinomianism will discover new material here, while first-timers entering the debate on the role of law will find an accessible overview of the discussion. Advancing on previous studies, this book situates Luther's thinking within previous apostolic and medieval traditions. Engelbrecht offers a fine scholarly contribution with significant ramifications for pastoral ministry.

—Mark Mattes, Ph.D.
Professor of Religion and Philosophy
Grand View University, Des Moines, IA

The book is excellent. First, there is the attention that Engelbrecht gives to the history of the problem. I dare any contemporary interested in the issue of the third use of the law to come up with a better genealogy in the record of Western theology going back to the early church. Second, the references to Luther regarding third use are so many and so concentrated, I don't see how anyone who cares about Luther could continue to claim that Luther taught only two uses of the law. Third, the book is timely. The unmistakable tendency in mainline Protestantism today is to equate the gospel with subjective freedom and personal desire. Engelbrecht forces the reader to face the fact that this destructive tendency has been aided and abetted, however unintentionally, by a modernist confessional theology that dismisses the law as oppressive.

—Walter Sundberg, Ph.D.
Professor of Church History
Luther Seminary, St. Paul, MN

Throughout the centuries the use of the Law has raised many questions for theologians. *Friends of the Law* provides an excellent start at answering the questions with Martin Luther as a key. As each generation has to work out its own image of Luther, this book makes an important contribution to the revision of the common Luther image as it shows the historical Luther's positive connection to the exegetical tradition, in particular to the late-medieval Scripture scholar Nicholas of Lyra. The author takes the seminal contribution to this subject by the Catholic Luther scholar Heinrich Denifle (1905) into serious consideration and thus offers with *Friends of the Law* an eminent ecumenical study.

—Franz Posset, Ph.D.
Roman Catholic Historian
Author of *The Real Luther*

Swimming against the mainstream of contemporary Luther scholarship, Engelbrecht presents a plausible interpretation of an aspect of Luther's thought that does not receive the attention it deserves. His identification of medieval sources that had an impact on Luther is a particular strength of the book. Thoroughly researched and written in a style that will make it accessible to a wide range of readers, *Friends of the Law* will be of interest to Luther scholars, parish pastors, and parishioners. The book will be an excellent addition to church libraries, as well as to seminary and university libraries.

—Daniel E. Lee, Ph.D.
Professor of Ethics
Director, Augustana Center for the Study of Ethics
Augustana College

This wide-ranging historical survey demonstrates convincingly that Luther taught the so-called third use of the law, even though his terminology and emphases varied according to the occasion. It is a useful response to those in contemporary Lutheranism who advocate a form of antinomianism which denies the third use of the law as a guide or rule for the Christian, and who attempt to claim Luther as their ally. It shows, to use Luther's phrase, that Christians are friends of the Law.

—John Brug, Ph.D.
Professor of Systematic Theology
Wisconsin Lutheran Seminary

Friends of the Law is a clearly written, thorough, and comprehensive treatment of the functions of the Law in Christian history and theology. Engelbrecht's systematic examination of the uses and usefulness of God's Law is a tremendous resource for those who would understand this essential aspect of Christian theology, and especially its role in the Lutheran Church. A corrective to often unbalanced understandings of Law and Gospel, Engelbrecht has done a great service to the Church with the publication of this book.

—Jeffrey K. Mann, Ph.D.
Department Head, Philosophy and Religion
Associate Professor of Religion
Susquehanna University
Author, *Shall We Sin? Responding to the Antinomian Question in Lutheran Theology*

This book is an important contribution to the longstanding debate about whether Luther taught a third use of the Law. It can serve as an accessible introduction to the topic for those who are not deeply familiar with prior argumentation, but also presents a sophisticated rebuttal to the interpretation that has dominated scholarship for the past sixty years. Engelbrecht draws attention to the fact that Luther was not the first theologian to discuss various functions of the law. In addition to offering extensive background about the development of thought about this issue, he backs up his analysis of Luther's perspective with a rich array of quotes from the reformer's writings.

—Eric Lund, Ph.D.
Professor of Religion
St. Olaf College, Northfield, MN
Editor of *Documents from the History of Lutheranism, 1517–1750*

Engelbrecht has presented us with a comprehensive and compelling challenge to the conventional wisdom that Luther employed no Third Use of the Law in his construal of the Christian life.

—Robert Benne, Ph.D.
Author, *Ordinary Saints: An Introduction to the Christian Life*
Director, Roanoke College Center for Religion and Society

Lutheranism has needed a book like this for decades. Calling into question the "only-two-uses [of the law] consensus," Engelbrecht has done the most essential homework. Against the backdrop of theology's preceding centuries, he carefully reads Luther at the basic level of terminology. This important book shows that Luther not only taught the law's third use in substance, but also that the reformer even spoke of three uses. The emperor of regnant scholarship has no clothes!

—Rev. Ken Schurb, Ph.D.
Pastor, Zion Lutheran Church, Moberly, MO
Editor, *The Anonymous God*

All interpreters of Luther agree that in the Reformer's eye, the law has two uses. All further agree that the law restrains sinners and exposes sin. But has it *only* two functions? Can it *only* bring death? Might it not have a third use—the purpose of instruction *for life*? In this far-reaching, compendious text, Edward Engelbrecht—in great detail and in grand scope—offers a persuasive case for finding truth in the "at least three uses" camp. Students, pastors and scholars alike will find reliable guidance and provocative suggestion in these pages.

—Rev. Derek R. Nelson, Ph.D.
Associate Professor of Religion
Co-Director of Thiel Global Institute
Thiel College, Greenville, PA

Engelbrecht mounts an imposing case against the prevailing interpretation of Luther on the law. Well researched and carefully argued, *Friends of the Law* introduces us to a Luther whose nuanced understanding of the moral life surpasses many a Lutheran. This book will be a thorn in the flesh of all who insist Luther had no use for a "third use of the law."

—H. David Baer, Ph.D.
Associate Professor of Theology and Philosophy
Department Chair
Texas Lutheran University

With aplomb that is brazen yet respectful, Pastor Engelbrecht takes on the establishment of contemporary Luther interpreters in arguing for Luther's sustained affirmation of three uses of the law. Even those who might disagree with some of his claims will learn from his wide-reaching consideration of the use of law in the long history of Christian theology and in the lives of Christians today.

—Rev. Curtis L. Thompson, Ph.D.
Professor of Religion
Thiel College, Greenville, PA
A member of the clergy of the
Evangelical Lutheran Church in America

The mid 20th century consensus that Luther—and thus Lutheran theology—has no third use of the law has been seriously and carefully challenged! This monograph should create earthquakes in historical theology circles. Edward Engelbrecht traces the early church's problematic use of "new law," as well as the medieval church's introduction of "third use" language. Engelbrecht has set forth clear third use affirmations in Luther's writings. These are found before, during, and after the antinomian controversies. Luther's references to "uses" of the law in the life of the Christian are many (though not always with the "third use" term.)

—Ralph W. Quere, Ph.D.
Professor emeritus
History and Theology
Wartburg Theological Seminary
Dubuque, IA

This book provides a well-researched argument for a more nuanced interpretation of Luther's teaching on the law. Even those who disagree with its conclusions will benefit from its comprehensive case for why the law is not only an accusing force but also the means the Holy Spirit uses to enable us as forgiven sinners to praise God and to live righteous lives in joyous service to others.

—Lois Malcolm, Ph.D.
Associate Professor of Systematic Theology
Review Editor, *Journal of the Society of Christian Ethics*
Luther Seminary

Friends of the Law

FRIENDS OF THE LAW

LUTHER'S USE OF THE LAW FOR THE CHRISTIAN LIFE

EDWARD A. ENGELBRECHT

Peer Reviewed

CONCORDIA PUBLISHING HOUSE • SAINT LOUIS

Peer Reviewed

Published 2011 by Concordia Publishing House

3558 S. Jefferson Ave., St. Louis, MO 63118–3968

1-800-325-3040 · www.cph.org

Copyright © 2011 Concordia Publishing House

All rights reserved. No part of this publication may be reproduced, stored in a retrieval system, or transmitted, in any form or by any means, electronic, mechanical, photocopying, recording, or otherwise, without the prior written permission of Concordia Publishing House.

Scripture quotations are from The Holy Bible, English Standard Version, copyright © 2001 by Crossway Bibles, a division of Good News Publishers. Used by permission. All rights reserved.

Every effort has been made to contact all copyright holders. In the event of any omissions or erros the author asks the copyright holders to inform him so that the correct credits may be included in future editions.

Manufactured in the United States of America

Library of Congress Cataloging-in-Publication Data

Engelbrecht, Edward.
 Friends of the law: Luther's use of the law for the Christian life / Edward A. Engelbrecht.
   p. cm.
 Includes bibliographical references (p.   ) and index.
 ISBN 978-0-7586-3138-1
 1. Law (Theology)--History of doctrines. 2. Luther, Martin, 1483-1546. I. Title.

BR333.5.L3E55 2011
241'.2--dc23   2011026260

---

2 3 4 5 6 7 8 9 10   20 19 18 17 16 15 14 13 12

Contents

Tables	vii
Abbreviations	ix
Preface	xi
Acknowledgements	xvii
Part One: Background	**1**
1. Introduction	3
2. Biblical Wisdom and Natural Law	13
3. Jesus, Philo, and Paul	21
4. Early Christian Apologists	27
5. Early Western Theologians	35
6. Medieval Theologians	53
Part Two: The Reformation	**71**
7. Luther's Earliest Teaching (1515–22)	73
8. Regard for Moses (1522–25)	91
9. Luther's Early Interpretation of 1 Timothy (1525–28)	99
10. The Catechisms (1529–30)	121
11. Enumeration in the *Lectures on Galatians* (1531, 1535)	127
12. The Smalcald Articles (1536–38)	139
13. The *Antinomian Disputations* (1537–39)	147
14. Later Editions of the *Church Postil* (1540, 1543)	163
15. The *Lectures on Genesis* (1535–44)	171
16. Consistency in Luther's Teaching	175
17. Melanchthon on the Use of the Law	187
18. Calvin on the Use of the Law	201
19. The Council of Trent (1545–63)	209
20. The Formula of Concord VI	217
Part Three: Toward a New Consensus	**225**
21. Current Questions and Answers	227
22. Conclusions	247

CONTENTS

APPENDIX A: THE LAW OF MOSES IN EARLY JUDAISM AND CHRISTIANITY   **257**

APPENDIX B: LUTHER'S PHRASES FOR THE USE OF THE LAW   **259**

APPENDIX C: VARIETY IN LUTHER'S DESCRIPTIONS OF THE LAW   **261**

APPENDIX D: COMMENTARY ON FORMULA OF CONCORD VI   **263**

APPENDIX E: THE MODERN DEBATE ON THE USE OF THE LAW   **275**

BIBLIOGRAPHY   **279**

SCRIPTURE INDEX   **297**

TOPICAL INDEX   **303**

TABLES

Table 1: Only-Two-Uses Consensus	6
Table 2: Uses of the Law, Standard Terms and Definitions	10
Table 3: Status Change and the Teaching of the Law	25
Table 4: Biblical Roots of the Term *Use of the Law*	26
Table 5: Law and Gospel in the Two Testaments	51
Table 6: The Christian and the Law	65
Table 7: Medieval Terms for the Usefulness of the Law	70
Table 8: Divine and Human Uses of the Law (1522)	82
Table 9: Luther's Pattern of Teaching on the Law (1522)	87
Table 10: Luther's Pattern of Teaching in the *Preface to the Old Testament*	95
Table 11: The Stages of Man and the Use of the Law	105
Table 12: Luther's Pattern of Teaching in the *Lectures on 1 Timothy* (1528)	110
Table 13: Luther's Uses or Offices of the Law	113
Table 14: Luther's Enumeration	133
Table 15: Luther's Pattern of Teaching in the Smalcald Articles (1537)	142
Table 16: Theses and Disputations against the Antinomians (1537–39)	149
Table 17: Development of the *Church Postil*	165
Table 18: Development of Melanchthon and His *Loci Communes*	189
Table 19: Lutheran Dogmatic Terms for the Uses of the Law	197
Table 20: The Summary of the Law	257

ABBREVIATIONS

LW   Luther, Martin. *Luther's Works*. American Edition. Gen. eds. Jaroslav Pelikan and Helmut T. Lehmann. 56 vols. St. Louis: Concordia, and Philadelphia: Muhlenberg and Fortress, 1955–86. Vols. 56–75: Edited by Christopher Boyd Brown. St. Louis: Concordia, 2009–.

ANF   *The Ante-Nicene Fathers: Translations of the Writings of the Fathers down to 325 A.D.* Ed. Alexander Roberts and James Donaldson. Grand Rapids, MI: Eerdmans, reprint 1980–87.

BKS   *Die Bekenntnisschriften der evangelischen-lutherischen Kirche.* Göttingen: Vandenhoeck & Ruprecht, 1979.

CR   Corpus Reformatorum. Vols. 1–28: *Philippi Melanchthonis Opera Quae Supersunt Omnia.* Halle and Brunswick: C. S. Schwetschke, 1834–60.

CTQ   *Concordia Theological Quarterly*

Ep   Epitome of the Formula of Concord

FC   Formula of Concord

LC   Large Catechism

LCC   *Library of Christian Classics*

Lenker   *Sermons of Martin Luther.* Ed. John Nicholas Lenker. 8 vols. Grand Rapids, MI: Baker Book House, reprint 1989.

NPNF1   *A Select Library of the Christian Church. Nicene and Post-Nicene Fathers*, Series 1. Ed. Philip Schaff. Grand Rapids, MI: Eerdmans, reprint 1986–89.

PL   *Patralogiae cursus completus: Series Latina.* Ed. Jacques-Paul Migne. 221 vols. Paris & Turnhout, 1859–1963.

SA   Smalcald Articles

ABBREVIATIONS

SD   Solid Declaration of the Formula of Concord

WA   Luther, Martin. *D. Martin Luthers Werke: Kritische Gesamtausgabe. Schriften.* 73 vols. in 85. Weimar: Böhlau, 1883–.

WABD Luther, Martin. *Luthers Werke: Kritische Gesamtausgabe.* Bibel. 12 vols. in 15. Weimar: Böhlau, 1906–.

PREFACE

I have not come to destroy the Law but to fulfill it.

—Jesus of Nazareth

This book investigates one of the thorniest issues of Reformation theology: the use of the Law for the Christian life. It is not simply a history of the doctrine of the Law, nor is it a systematic treatment. It is a pathway, tracing the thoughts and steps of earlier believers to explore their views on the use of the Law.

The book focuses especially on the thoughts and life of Martin Luther whose views of Law and Gospel have been the subject of nearly limitless study and debate, which has in turn affected parish practice. In the course of this book, you will learn much about Luther on the topic of the Law but you will also see that Luther did not walk alone in his views. He had a host of companions to set him on the course of reformation for theology and for life, a reformation in which the use of the Law played a central role.

My prayer as a researcher and writer is that you will find along the way new insights and topics to explore but, most importantly, an opportunity to see your life and the Law of God differently, to pray with the psalmist, "Let Your mercy come to me, that I may live; for Your law is my delight" (Ps 119:77).

GETTING STARTED

Normally I do not set out to read all the way through a theological journal. I usually pick out an article or two that most interests me. A new journal usually comes before I find time to read all the articles in the previous edition. However, in 2005 I eagerly read a collection of conference essays published in volume 69 of the *Concordia Theological Quarterly*. The essays focused on the use of the Law and Scott Murray's book *Law, Life, and the Living God: The Third Use of the Law in Modern American Lutheranism*.

The published articles and internet articles mentioned in that edition of the CTQ grasped my attention for two reasons: (1) the looming decisions about sexuality in the Evangelical Lutheran Church in America and other mainline Protestant churches, and (2) my personal reading of Martin Luther's writings. I was especially struck by Larry M. Vogel's little sentence, "Luther had no Third Use of the Law" (CTQ 69:192). I immediately thought, "Really? Why are you so sure? With so many volumes of *Luthers Werke* available, what are the chances that Luther *never* wrote about a third use of the Law?"

The informed reader may immediately conclude that I was unaware of the broad, scholarly consensus that Luther had only two uses of the Law. I was marginally aware of this consensus, having read Timothy J. Wengert's *Law and Gospel: Philip Melanchthon's Debate with John Agricola of Eisleben over* Poenitentia (Grand Rapids: Baker Books, 1997) and having read Werner Elert's caveats about the idea that there could be a use of the Law that did not accuse but only instructed.

The Search for Consensus

The only-two-uses consensus replaced an earlier scholarly consensus that Luther taught the threefold use of the Law. Werner Elert described this earlier consensus, which he helped displace. In the following quotation, Elert names four prominent theologians who supported a threefold use consensus at the beginning of the twentieth century: Kawerau, Seeberg, Loofs, and Aner. Their view of the history supported the traditional opinion about agreement between Luther, Melanchthon, the Formula of Concord, and the long catechism tradition of teaching three uses of the Law in the Lutheran Church.

> Luther also is said to have "clearly espoused" the *usus triplex legis* (threefold function of the law), hence also a third function, at the conclusion of his second disputation Against the Antinomians held on January 13, 1538. . . . Thus Gustav Kawerau in his article on the Antinomian controversies in the *Realenzyklopaedie für die protestantische Theologie und Kirche*, of the disputation in his volume *Disputationen Dr. Martin Luthers* (Göttingen, 1895), the more prominent scholars adopted this view: e.g., Reinhold Seeberg, *Lehrbuch*

der Dogmengeschichte, Vol. IV (4th ed.; Leipzig, 1933), p. 261; Friedrich Loofs, *Leitfaden zum Studium der Dogmengeschichte* (4th ed.; Halle an der Salle, 1906), pp. 860 f.; Karl Aner, in the article "Gesetz und Evangelium, dogmengeschichtlich," *Religion in Geschichte und Gegenwart* (2nd ed.; Tübingen, 1927 ff.), II, 1133.[1]

By the middle of the twentieth century, Werner Elert was rejecting the threefold use consensus and teaching that Luther had only two uses of the Law. Other theologians adopted Elert's position to form a new scholarly consensus. The American scholar, William Lazareth, has characterized the current consensus in view of Wilhelm Maurer, an Erlangen theologian and colleague of Elert. In the following quotation, Lazareth lists ten scholars who supported the only-two-uses consensus by 1965.

> The international scholarly consensus on Luther and the Law was summarized in 1965 by Wilhelm Maurer. In contrasting Luther's approach with the title and parts of the later Formula of Concord (1577), Maurer judged: "In Article VI, however, the Gospel is actually subordinated to the Law. . . . Recent Luther research has adduced the evidence that the doctrine of the third use is foreign to Luther; nor is it set forth in the Augsburg Confession [1530] or the Apology [1531]" (Bodensieck II:873). This authoritative evaluation covered the published research of such celebrated Luther scholars as Paul Althaus, Heinrich Bornkamm, Gerhard Ebeling, Werner Elert (Germany); Ragnar Bring, Anders Nygren, Lennart Pinomaa, Regin Prenter, Gustaf Wingren (Scandinavia).[2]

Lazareth also listed Karl-Heintz zur Mühlen, Oswald Bayer, Bengt Hägglund, Lauri Haikola, Gerhard Heintze, Wilifried Joest, and Martin Schloemann as supporters of the current consensus for a total of seventeen Luther scholars. A most impressive list! The American

---

[1] "The Question of the Law's 'Third Function.'" In *Law and Gospel*, Edward H. Schroeder, trans. (Philadelphia: Fortress Press, 1967). Elert originally delivered the essay in 1948.

[2] "Antinomians: Then and Now," *Lutheran Forum* (Winter 2002). Available at www.elca.org. The Maurer citation is from *The Encyclopedia of the Lutheran Church*, vol. II, Julius Bodensieck, ed. (Minneapolis: Augsburg Publishing House, 1965).

scholars Kolb and Arand review the matter somewhat differently. They note that some Lutheran theologians are uncomfortable with the theological use of the Law standing together with the idea of the Law as instruction.

> They believe that new obedience is necessary but that the instructions for it should be called "God's commands" or "the imperative of the gospel" to distinguish them from the killing function and power of the Law. Others argue that God's plan is the law regardless of how it functions. So with Melanchthon they speak of a third use of the law, a term that Luther did not use even though he often preached the law of God to instruct his hearers in Wittenberg.[3]

Today, the weight of scholarly opinion stands very heavily on the side of only two uses. In this book I will call into question the only-two-uses consensus on the basis of the history of doctrine. As a student of Lutheran theology, I certainly appreciated Elert's insight and emphasis on "The Law always accuses" (*Lex semper accusat*; Ap IV 38), which fits so well with my confessional training as well as my personal and pastoral experience. However, as I have read more of Luther, I have doubted that he *never* taught about a third use of the Law. After reading some of the articles in the 2005 CTQ, I pulled down my copy of *Geist aus Luther's Schriften* (Darmstadt: Druck und Verlag von Karl Wilhelm Leske, 1828–31) and quickly strengthened my suspicion about the only-two-uses consensus.

Unfortunately for this topic, I had to spend my available time on other matters, especially the development of *The Lutheran Study Bible*, which was an all-consuming task, though one that had me reading ever more of Luther's writings on biblical interpretation.

Over Christmas in 2008 I was able to return to my research on whether Luther taught a third use of the Law. It was then that I made many of the historical discoveries of this book. My experience with the history of biblical interpretation guided my strategic search of Luther and other interpreters. The more I read Luther's teaching about the Law, the more apparent it became to me that he was indebted to and responding to the ideas of earlier theologians.

---

[3] *The Genius of Luther's Theology: A Wittenberg Way of Thinking for the Contemporary Church* (Grand Rapids: Baker Academic, 2008), 157–58.

PRESENTATION OF RESEARCH

At this point I should share something about my method and presentation of research. There is a mountain of secondary literature on Law and Gospel and on the use of the Law in the New Testament and in the sixteenth century. Researchers have traced and retraced these paths so often that deep ruts abound in these areas of the history. I have included a list of this literature in Appendix E and in the bibliography. Unfortunately, scholars have written very little on the use of the Law for the ancient and medieval eras. This is because many, perhaps most, twentieth century scholars assumed that Luther invented the idea of use or uses of the Law, as I illustrate in the introduction. Because the secondary literature is so heavily weighted toward the New Testament and the sixteenth century, this book will not include a lot of interaction with secondary literature. I have focused on presenting a survey of primary sources that will clarify the relationship between the ancient and medieval eras and the sixteenth century. When English translations of texts were available, I cited them with occasional comments on the translation. Where no translation was available, I provided a rough translation and placed the original text in a footnote. I hope that scholars will investigate the broader history of doctrine so that the Church may have a fuller account of how God's people have understood and benefited from studying His Word as Law and Gospel.

Chapters one and twenty-one are topical; chapter two includes topical elements as I present the interrelationship between biblical theology of the Law and ideas of natural law described in other cultures. Otherwise, the presentation is in chronological order from the Old Testament to the Reformation.

What emerges from the history of the doctrine of the use of the Law is, I believe, a significant correction to the current consensus. The discoveries are possibly the basis for an entirely new consensus that sees the leading Protestant theologian properly not as an innovator of doctrine but as one who renewed the importance of the Law and its use in the doctrine of justification by grace alone, through faith alone, on account of Christ alone. This new understanding and description of the broader historical context, if upheld, would also place Luther, Melanchthon, and the Formula of Concord nearer one another in their teaching about the Law and its use. Indeed, there may even be a shorter distance between Luther and Calvin than previously

PREFACE

imagined, though in the end one must agree that their doctrine of the Law differed. An unresolved historical and doctrinal matter is why the doctrine of the use of the Law is not more prominent in Roman Catholicism, a matter that I hope others will investigate.

FURTHER INVESTIGATION

I should emphasize that this little book is only the beginning of a history. There are many, many more theologians and resources to be explored. In chapter twenty-one, I suggest other paths of investigation that should be pursued if we are to have a full account of this enduring, controversial question about the role of the Law in the believer's life. I have also included a series of questions that illustrates just how much remains for historians and theologians to explore in this neglected topic, which has significant implications for theology today, church fellowship, and the day-to-day lives of Christians.

I believe that the history of Martin Luther's teaching has been misunderstood and that this misunderstanding encourages a false doctrine of the Law and of the Gospel with grave implications for individuals and even whole denominations. In this matter we see how historical theology influences modern dogmatics and modern dogmatics can distort our understanding of history. Lord, have mercy.

REV. EDWARD A. ENGELBRECHT, STM
Senior Editor for Professional and Academic Books
and Bible Resources
Concordia Publishing House

NOTE FOR THE SECOND PRINTING: As I finished the book, an earlier example of Luther's terminology came to my attention. I am adding to a footnote on p. 75 a cross reference to the epilogue on p. 255 so that readers may catch this earliest example from Luther at that point. If the book ever goes to a second edition, I will fold the information of the epilogue into the body of the book. I have also discovered some interesting passages in Josephus that may contribute to chapter two or three. More on that as God grants opportunity.

Acknowledgements

I would like to thank my peer reviewers, who read an earlier draft of the manuscript and provided numerous and helpful suggestions for improvement:

Rev. Dr. Carl L. Beckwith, Assoc. Prof. of Divinity, History, and Doctrine at Beeson Divinity School, Samford University in Birmingham, AL

Rev. Dr. Scott R. Murray, Senior Pastor at Memorial Lutheran Church and School in Houston, TX; Fifth Vice President of The Lutheran Church—Missouri Synod

Rev. Dr. Jeffrey G. Silcock, Head of the Theology Department at Australian Lutheran College, Adelaide; Chairman of the Commission on Theology and Inter-Church Relations for the Australian Lutheran Church

They pushed me to think through the mass of material that I had collected and to draw more thorough conclusions. I bear sole responsibility for the final form of the content and for any mistakes.

I also want to thank my colleagues at Concordia Publishing House who reviewed and supported my book proposal through the peer review process, especially my editorial assistant, Sarah Steiner, who helped with formatting the manuscript, pulled books from the library, and finalized the text for publication.

As always, I give thanks to my Lord Jesus Christ for my dear wife, Susan, and our four children who listen and encourage. Susan read the manuscript in the final stages and helped me identify points that were not clear enough for someone who was new to the topic. This led to further explanation in the preface and introduction.

Part One

Background

CHAPTER ONE

INTRODUCTION

The Galatians are rebuked and the apostle, showing the imperfection of the Law of Moses, says that righteousness is by faith, though having to be bound with the usefulness of the Law.

—Martin Luther, 1516/17

On December 10, 1520, Philip Melanchthon posted an invitation and John Agricola organized a gathering for Luther's friends and students. They gathered outside Wittenberg's Elster gate and filled a pit with wood. A fire was lit and loaded with several editions of canon law and some volumes of scholastic theology. Luther arrived to add his contribution to the flames: a copy of the bull threatening excommunication signed by Pope Leo X. Their little fire responded to the news that detractors at Cologne and Mainz had burned Luther's books.[4]

The Law, in this case canon law, was of high concern for Luther and his friends. Luther's understanding of the Law was a key factor in the Reformation and thereby key to the future of western society. Those who opposed Luther and his friends regarded their actions as lawlessness. The Lutheran Reformation has always suffered such accusations. In fact, since the sixteenth century, some theologians have regarded Luther's theology as inherently driven toward

---

[4] See Martin Brecht, *Martin Luther: His Road to Reformation, 1483–1521* (Philadelphia: Fortress, 1985), 423–26. The bull was "Arise, O Lord" (*Exsurge, Domine*). See LW 48:186, n. 2.

antinomianism—a rejection of the Law. This charge extends also to the Geneva reformer, John Calvin, whose heirs erupted in an antinomian controversy early in the seventeenth century.[5] On the other hand, Reformation theologians and historians have counter-charged Roman theologians with legalism, while reminding everyone of the lawless excesses of the Renaissance popes. Everyone has had to take their lumps on the topic of the Law. The fires set in the sixteenth century continue to burn.

Because Luther's theology flows from the distinction between Law and Gospel, what Luther thought and wrote about the doctrine of the Law is at the center of his theology. What Luther said about the Law necessarily affected what he said about the Gospel. This same essential bond is found throughout Reformation theology and, arguably, western theology too. Under such circumstances, a weak or confused doctrine of the Law would possibly lead to a weak or confused doctrine of the Gospel. In other words, as we write about the Law and its role in the lives of people, we are at the same time anticipating the role of the Gospel. Although the title of this book shows that the doctrine of the Law is the focus, the reader must realize that the Gospel—the basis of our justification and everlasting life—is at stake.

To illustrate this relationship between Law and Gospel, consider the following example. If one teaches that sin is a sickness, then one would correspondingly teach that salvation is a cure. However, if one teaches that sin causes spiritual death, then one would teach that salvation is a spiritual resurrection from the dead. What one says about one side of the relationship affects what one says about the other side of the relationship. Though the two teachings are distinct, they are also connected and interrelated. I believe the same circumstances prevail with Law and Gospel. The doctrines are distinct and must be distinguished. Yet what you say about one of them affects what you say about the other. To have a full and clear doctrine of the Gospel, one cannot settle for a reduced or weak doctrine of the Law without introducing trouble, as I see taking place in the moral views of mainline Protestants today.

---

[5] See Eve LaPlante, *American Jezebel: The Uncommon Life of Anne Hutchinson, the Woman who Defied the Puritans* (New York: HarperOne, 2004).

This book will look carefully at Luther's theology of the use of the Law and the charges of forgery, heresy, immorality, and legalism that surround the doctrine of the use of the Law. To do so, it will provide a sweeping look at the history of doctrine so that we may see Luther's teachings in fuller context. Along the way, many new insights will come to light. To help us recognize what is new, this introduction will briefly rehearse what other historians have concluded about Luther's doctrine of the use of the Law. In particular, we will consider whether Luther taught a third use of the Law and what it means to be a friend of the Law.

THE CURRENT CONSENSUS

Students of Luther agree that the doctrine of the use of the Law is a cornerstone in his thought, laid early in the Reformation. However, current ideas about Luther's doctrine are not properly grounded in history. As you read through the statements of the scholars in the following paragraphs, watch for exclusive expressions such as "only" and "no." These little words have great weight in an argument and we must use them with great care.

In a 1522 postil on Galatians 3:23–29 and in the 1528 *Lectures on 1 Timothy*, Martin Luther taught a threefold use of the Law, a fact neglected by numerous modern researchers.[6] This neglect has led to an assumption by some dogmatic theologians that the "third use of the law" (Formula of Concord VI) does not stem from Luther and may be incompatible with Lutheran doctrine. For example, in a highly influential historical article originally published in 1950, Gerhard Ebeling wrote that Luther always spoke only about a twofold use of the Law, though Ebeling also noted that Luther introduced the wording about a threefold use of the law before anyone else.[7] In the

---

[6] There is another passage from Luther's second antinomian disputation (1538). Werner Elert concluded that this example was a later addition to Luther's text that did not reflect Luther's teaching but Melanchthon's teaching. See *Zeitschrift für Religions- und Geistesgeschichte* (1948): 168–70. See also ch. Thirteen where I discuss Elert's accusation of forgery.

[7] "On the Doctrine of the *Triplex Usus Legis* in the Theology of the Reformation," *Word and Faith* (Philadelphia: Fortress Press, 1963), 62, 64. This was originally published as "Zur Lehre vom *triplex usus legis* in der reformatorischen Theologie" in *Theologische Literaturzeitung* 75 (1950): 235–46. Ebeling continued, "The exposition of Gal. 3.23–29 in the

Oxford Encyclopedia of the Reformation, Karl-Heinz zur Mühlen argued that Luther rejected a third function of the Law because a Christian keeps the Law spontaneously through faith.[8] Gerhard Forde wrote in *Toward a More Radical Gospel*, "It is commonly agreed that Luther spoke explicitly of only two uses of the law: the political use—perhaps we could call it the ethical use, and the theological use."[9]

More recently and based on research by Maurer, Lazareth, and Wengert, Larry M. Vogel wrote, "Luther had no Third Use of the Law. . . . The history seems conclusive. Philip Melanchthon actually introduced the Third Use into Reformation theology."[10] Table 1 summarizes the consensus:

Table 1
Only-Two-Uses Consensus

First Use:	Civil, to restrain behavior
Second Use:	Theological, to accuse of sin

There are no other uses of the Law.

Weihnachtspostille of 1522 . . . is a different thing from the later doctrine of the *triplex usus legis*. The threefold use of the law which Luther speaks of here bears solely on the question of fulfilling the law. . . . Our conclusion therefore is, that the formula 'threefold use of the law' is indeed found in Luther for the first time, yet it only expresses a passing thought and is then dropped again" (pp. 62–64). Although many researchers base their commitment to the only two-uses consensus on Ebeling's research, they fail to note his observations about the *Weihnachtspostille* and how it anticipated the later doctrine of the Law.

[8] Vol. 2 (Oxford: Oxford University Press, 1996), 405.

[9] Mark C. Mattes and Steven D. Paulson, eds. (Grand Rapids: Eerdmans, 2004), 152. Note how Forde states the matter differently from Ebeling. The adverbial "only," which Ebeling used to qualify Luther's speaking, has become an adjective qualifying "two uses." In other words, Ebeling was describing a historical matter—how Luther talked about the uses of the Law; Forde is describing a doctrinal matter—what Luther taught about the Law.

[10] *Concordia Theological Quarterly* 69 (July/October, 2005), 192. See also Werner Elert's *Law and Gospel*, Edward H. Schroeder, trans. (Philadelphia: Fortress Press, 1967), 40. For our purposes, the most important article was "Eine theologische Fälschung zur Lehre vom *tertius usus legis*" in *Zeitschrift für Religions- und Geistesgeschichte* 1 (1949): 168–70.

In *Harvesting Martin Luther's Reflections on Theology, Ethics, and the Church*, Timothy Wengert described viewing the Law as "a guide to what we ought to do" as "the legalist's 'third use' of the law," a description that more or less characterizes earlier generations of Lutheran catechists as legalists.[11] The harshness of the accusation invites further investigation. In a more recent book, Wengert appeared to soften his opinion, allowing that the Law may be whispered to Christians.[12]

Researchers have even called into question the catholicity of the idea that the Law has uses. For example, Ebeling wrote:

> When we recall that from the year 1519 on Luther finds in the question of 'benefit and use' applied to the work of Christ, to the Sacraments, and to the Word of Scripture the method and means of bringing about the application of the Reformation's basic discovery to the whole field of theology, then that confirms the conjecture that in the section of the [*Christmas Postil*] *Weihnachtspostille* referred to we find ourselves very near the original source of the term [use of the Law] *usus legis*. For '*usus legis*' seems to me to be in fact a theological concept coined by Luther. So far as I am aware, the term is to be found neither in Augustine, where one would soonest expect it, nor in the scholastics either.[13]

Ebeling invites us to a mystery. He swept through the obvious places, lighted the corners, and found himself back with Luther minting Reformation theology, seemingly from ore to coin, stamping his thought upon the Church ever after. Luther, who is sometimes described as discovering the Gospel, appears here to have created the use of the Law.

In a statement similar to Ebeling's, Timothy Wengert wrote:

> The notion that the law has uses or functions is a peculiarly Protestant concept with origins deep within Martin Luther's

---

[11] Timothy J. Wengert, ed. (Grand Rapids: Eerdmans, 2004), 10. He writes less harshly in *A Formula for Parish Practice: Using the Formula of Concord in Congregations* (Grand Rapids: Eerdmans, 2006), 90.
[12] *A Formula for Parish Practice* 97.
[13] *Word and Faith* 72–73.

> theology. . . . In "De votis Monasticis" (1521) Luther spoke for the first time of an "officium legis."[14]

Wengert provides a different date and document but strikes upon the same conclusion, even isolating the first moment when Luther opens the treasury of his thoughts on the use of the Law.

Lowell Green explains in a conference paper that Luther taught two functions of the Law, the civil and the theological. He then questioned where the term *usus legis* came from. He had searched for an example in the medieval writers but did not find one. He consulted with the Melanchthon scholar, Ralph Keen, who also could not find the term in medieval theology. Keen concluded that Melanchthon must have created the term.[15] These scholars arrive at the same point in history as Ebeling and Wengert: the Reformation. However, they propose a different author. In any case, they credit the Reformers with special creativity, the Reformation as an enlightening moment.

The researchers appear to operate with a simple, evolutionary understanding of doctrinal development in the following sequence:

> Luther began with the medieval opinion that it was necessary to fulfill certain laws in order to obtain justification. The Gospel was a new law.
>
> Luther noted first that the Law had uses. He excluded the use of the Law from justification.
>
> Luther distinguished two uses: the political use and the theological use. He never developed further uses.
>
> Melanchthon added the third use of the Law in c. 1534/1535, which heralded his departure from Luther's theology. Melanchthon emphasized that it was necessary to keep the Law (Decalogue).
>
> The writers of the Formula of Concord, as students of Melanchthon, largely followed Melanchthon's teaching about the uses of the Law. They clarified their position against

---

[14] *Law and Gospel: Philip Melanchthon's Debate with John Agricola of Eisleben over* Poenitentia (Grand Rapids: Baker Books, 1997), 191.

[15] "The 'Third Use of the Law' and Werner Elert's Position." Paper for Symposium on the Lutheran Confessions, Fort Wayne, Final Version- January 25, 2005.

Melanchthon's statement that good works are necessary (Ap V [III] 227; FC Ep IV 3).

This book will demonstrate that neither Luther nor Melanchthon was the first theologian to describe the use of the Law. It will show that the doctrine and terminology are deeply rooted in biblical teaching and patristic theology.[16] It will show that Luther's unique contribution was to renew the distinction and to explain how it properly related to the chief article of the Christian Faith: justification. Also, this book will demonstrate that Melanchthon did not invent the idea of a third use as a doctrinal category. The idea and terminology of a threefold use of the Law came from medieval biblical interpretation and entered Reformation theology through Luther who early in his career described Christians as friends of the Law.

TERMS

Before proceeding with the history, some basic definitions are needed. The Lutheran catechetical tradition has typically included three uses of the Law, due to the influence of Formula of Concord VI. Catechisms usually refer to the uses by their enumeration ("first," "second," "third") or speak of the Law functioning as a curb, mirror, or guide. As a curb, the Law constrains sinners so that they do not destroy one another. This first use of the Law is based on fear of punishment. As a mirror, the Law shows sinners their flaws, the things they have done wrong. This second use of the Law speaks to the sensitive consciences who are not yet Christians and also to Christians, who remain sinners in need of repentance daily. In both cases the Law drives sinners toward repentance. As a guide, the Law shows repentant, reborn Christians what works are pleasing to God. This third use of the Law is like a path stretching out before the believer, who may joyfully walk in God's ways.

When considering these catechetical uses of the Law, it is important to remember that it is the same Law that has three different uses. Lutheran teachers have traditionally maintained that the unchanging will of God, the natural law that God wrote into human hearts at creation, the moral law taught by Moses, the prophets,

---

[16] A goal of Ebeling's article was to discover the beginning of the doctrine's "theological *terminus technicus*" (*Word and Faith* 73, n. 2).

Christ, and the Apostles is all one Law. Although points of this teaching may be worded differently in different parts of the Bible, the Law is one, while having different uses or functions depending on the state of those who hear it proclaimed.

The enumeration of the uses of the Law is not so simple historically and theologically since theologians have used a variety of enumerations over the centuries. Modern theologians call into question some of the historical terms and usages.

In order to simplify references to the uses of the Law of Moses, I will refer to the entries in Table 2, recognizing that these specific terms and definitions developed over centuries. The "civil" and "theological" uses are commonly found in the dogmatic tradition and histories describing the doctrine of the Reformation. These terms come from Luther's *Lectures on Galatians* of 1531/1535. I have drawn the name for "righteous man's use" from 1 Timothy 1:8 and the ancient and medieval commentaries on that text (e.g., the *Glossa Ordinaria*).[17] A fourth use appeared in the literature. It described New Testament fulfillments of future things prefigured or prophesied in the Law of Moses. Medieval commentaries often include this prophetic use of the Law. In chapter eight, I will explain how Luther described yet another use of the Law, which I have titled the "magistrate's use."

Table 2
Uses of the Law, Standard Terms and Definitions

Civil use	To restrain ("first use" or "curb")
Theological use	To reveal sin and accuse ("second use" or "mirror")
Righteous man's use	To instruct or guide oneself or others ("third use" or "guide")
Prophetic use	To announce beforehand the coming of Christ and New Testament teachings
Magistrate's use	To draw legal principles from the Law of Moses

For the sake of completeness, I mention here a few other terms found in the post-Reformation dogmatic tradition, which modern writers do

---

[17] Modern descriptions of the "third use" focus on God using the Law to instruct Christians on how to do good works. This is not always the use described in medieval and Reformation commentaries. I will address this matter in chapters six and seven.

not use widely.[18] The *usus politicus* is the same as the civil use of the Law. This term appeared in Luther's published edition of the *Lectures on Galatians* (1535) and in later writers. The *usus elenchticus* comes from the Greek term for "refutation." It corresponds to the theological use, emphasizing how the Law reveals sin. The term *usus paedagogicus* is drawn from Gal 3:24. It emphasizes the role of the Law of Moses in driving sinners toward Christ (cf. theological use). The *usus didacticus* describes the Law's power to teach (cf. righteous man's use above). The *usus normaticus* describes how the Law guides a Christian to perform good works (cf. righteous man's use above). Because of this variety of terms and distinctions, some post-Reformation writers have three or four uses of the Law. To simplify matters, I will stick with the terms in Table 2.

For a definition of *natural law*, Melanchthon's thought from the 1559 *Loci Praecipui* will serve: "The law of nature is the knowledge of the divine law which has been grafted into the nature of man."[19]

---

[18] I will provide further comment on these terms in chapter seventeen, "Melanchthon on the Use of the Law."
[19] *The Chief Theological Topics: Loci Praecipui Theologici* 1559, 2nd English ed., J. A. O. Preus, trans. (St. Louis: Concordia, 2011), 116.

CHAPTER TWO

BIBLICAL WISDOM AND NATURAL LAW

> In your offspring all the nations of the earth shall be blessed, because Abraham obeyed My voice and kept My charge, My commandments, My statutes, and My laws.
>
> —The LORD to Isaac (Gn 26:4b–5)

Before plunging into our topic, I will provide a few comments about the opening chapters so that readers know what to expect along the way. Chapters two through six will survey noteworthy passages and persons who contributed to the doctrine of the use of the Law prior to the Reformation. I do not intend that these chapters will provide a thorough history of the doctrine, but only the necessary background for understanding the teaching of Martin Luther, whose unique contribution is important for understanding church life and doctrine today.

This road offers many opportunities for side trips along the way, some of which I have explored. The footnotes will mention places I have looked that I found less helpful for our final destination or that turned out to be dead ends for the research. Such examples will show that the investigation of the history of doctrine is never as straight forward or obvious as one would like, yet there is great reward for those who will push aside the undergrowth and press forward.

THE LAW AS WISDOM

The dogmatic expression "use of the Law" (*usus legis*) and the Reformers' other expression, "office" or "function of the Law" (*officium legis*), do not appear in Holy Scripture. However, the idea is taught already in the Old Testament, especially in the wisdom literature that celebrated God's Law.[20] For example, a psalm attributed to David states:

> The law of the Lord is perfect,
> reviving the soul;
> the testimony of the Lord is sure,
> making wise the simple;
> the precepts of the Lord are right,
> rejoicing the heart;
> the commandment of the Lord is pure,
> enlightening the eyes;
> the fear of the Lord is clean,
> enduring forever;
> the rules of the Lord are true,
> and righteous altogether.
> More to be desired are they than gold,
> even much fine gold;
> sweeter also than honey
> and drippings of the honeycomb.
> Moreover, by them is your servant warned;
> in keeping them there is great reward.[21]

Note how the psalm describes various effects of the Law and its teaching: reviving, making wise, causing rejoicing, enlightening, and warning. When the Law is read or proclaimed, it brings about beneficial effects. Also, the reader or hearer may use the Law for beneficial purposes,[22] making the Law a desirable companion on life's way. Other passages from the first and second Books of Psalms

---

[20] Hebrew *torah* was first recorded by Moses in Gn 26 and became one of the most common nouns in the Old Testament.
[21] Ps 19:7–11; cf. Ps 25.
[22] Cf. e.g., Lv 6:4–7; Dt 6:24–25; Ps 25, 119. The most frequent use of *torah* in the wisdom literature occurs in Ps 119, the great psalm of God's Word.

highlight the benefit of friendship and counsel that come with a knowledge of God's Word (Ps 25:14; 32:8; 33:11; 37:3–4; 55:14).[23]

The Proverbs of Solomon express some of the same ideas. Consider the following insights from Proverbs 3 and 6:

> My son, do not despise the Lord's discipline or be weary of His reproof, for the Lord reproves him whom He loves, as a father the son in whom he delights.... For the commandment is a lamp and the teaching[24] a light, and the reproofs of discipline are the way of life to preserve you from the evil woman, from the smooth tongue of the adulteress.[25]

In family-style counsel, Solomon advises his readers about the benefits of God's Law and the love—even delight—that stands behind it. In a dark and difficult world, the Law is as necessary as a lamp for keeping one's way. Solomon may even speak of the law, command, and teaching as "the way of life," not for salvation but for preservation from false friends, great shame, and vice. Wisdom and insight are viewed as family or friends (Pr 1:30; 7:4; 22:20; 27:6; see also Ps 73:23–26 attributed to Asaph at the beginning of the third Book of Psalms). These themes are not so common in the later prophetic literature, though they do arise occasionally (e.g., Is 5:19).

When reading Old Testament wisdom literature, one must keep in mind the broader meaning of Heb. *torah*, which encompasses not only the commands and rebukes of God but also His instruction about life and salvation.[26] Nevertheless, the psalms and proverbs clearly teach that the Law has beneficial uses as command and rebuke. In the passages, the Law is celebrated rather than regarded as a matter of mere fear and dread. Historian John Bright wrote:

> The wisdom tradition in Israel is exceedingly old, reaching back at least to the tenth century. After the exile, however, it

---

[23] Many of the texts in the first two Books of Psalms are attributed to the era of David, son of Jesse (eleventh and early tenth centuries B.C.).
[24] Heb. *torah*.
[25] Pr 3:11–12; 6:23–24.
[26] On the broader history of the biblical terms, see *Theological Dictionary of the Old Testament*, G. Johannes Botterweck and Helmer Ringgren, eds. (Grand Rapids, MI: Eerdmans, 2006), XV:609–46; *Theological Dictionary of the New Testament*, G. Kittel and G. Friedrich, eds. (Grand Rapids, MI: Eerdmans, 1967), IV:1022–1085.

enjoyed a heightened popularity and, in the period of emergent Judaism, issued in a considerable body of literature setting forth the nature of the good life. . . . It is clear that Jewish teachers so adapted the wisdom tradition as to make it a vehicle for describing the good life *under the law*. To them, the sum of wisdom was to fear God and keep his law; indeed, wisdom was ultimately a synonym for the law.[27]

After the return from Exile, Judeans clung to the law with a new vigor. Years of subjugation in a foreign land, surrounded by idols and foreign ways, caused the Israelites to crave the close companionship of the Law. For example, in the fifth Book of Psalms, the Law is described as companion and counsel.[28] Having lived without the Law of Moses, among people without the Law, seems to have raised a devotion in the Israelites that perhaps we in well-ordered and familiar society find difficult to appreciate. Rather than regard these earlier believers as legalists because of their devotion to the Law of Moses, it is helpful to keep their experiences of suffering and deprivation in view.

THE APOCRYPHA

Jewish intertestamental books that show this torah-wisdom emphasis are Ecclesiasticus, Wisdom of Solomon, and Tobit. As in the earlier Old Testament writings, there is no systematic description of uses of the Law. However, Jesus son of Sirach described the Law filling a person's heart (Eccl 2:15; cf. Pr 3:1; Jer 31:31–34). Possession of the Law leads to possession of wisdom: "The one who holds to the law will obtain wisdom" (Eccl 15:1). The expression "the one who holds to the law" describes someone who is the master of something's power so that he is able to use it. One could translate more literally, "the master of the Law."[29]

The Seleucid emperor, Antiochus IV Epiphanes, again deprived Judeans of their Law during a persecution in the second century B.C. His troops captured the Jerusalem temple, made it a place of pagan

---

[27] *A History of Israel*, 4th ed. (Louisville: Westminster John Knox Press, 2000), 438.
[28] See Ps 107:11; 111:1; 119:24, 63. See also Ps 1:1, which was likely written or collected at a later date for introducing the books of the Psalms.
[29] Cf. the idea in Ecclus 39:1–4; 1 Tm 1:6–8.

sacrifice, required Jews to adopt Seleucid religious practices and culture, and even burned copies of the Law of Moses when the terrorized Jews turned them over.[30] This led to the Maccabean Revolt. After the death of Antiochus IV, the Jews received fairer treatment. In a letter sent on behalf of King Antiochus V Eupator (c. 164–162 B.C.) to the "senate of the Jews," one finds an explicit appearance of an expression that may be translated, "to use . . . laws" (2 Macc 11:31).[31] The passage is not doctrinal but practical. The king would grant a concession that the Jews could govern themselves according to the Law of Moses. After the experience of the exile and the suffering under Antiochus IV Epiphanes, the opportunity to use their own laws was doubtless great consolation.

USE OF NATURAL LAW

In view of 2 Macc 11:31, one should pause and carefully consider the assertion that the Reformation invented the idea of using the Law or uses of the Law.[32] The assertion seems unreasonable, given that the nations had natural law (as Paul taught in Rm 1:18–20; 2:14–15) and would likely ponder how to use it. Consider also the words attributed to Socrates in the *Republic* of Plato (c. 429–347 BC) when he stated that the laws were intended for the good of all citizens rather than any class in particular. The text speaks of the laws' effects, *persuading* and *compelling*[33] the citizens to get along with one another. In the mutual observance of the laws, citizens produce *benefits*[34] for one another. Through laws, the community *uses*[35] the citizens for the common good.[36]

---

[30] See the descriptions in 1 and 2 Maccabees.
[31] The LXX text has Χρῆσθαι τοὺς Ιουδαίους τοῖς ἑαυτων δαπανήμασιν καὶ νόμοις.
[32] See pp. 3–4.
[33] Πείθω means "to persuade" with the consequence that one becomes obedient. Ἀνάγκη means "force" or "constraint" and can describe punishment. The former term is more positive than the latter. They are often paired. See Plato, *The Republic, with an English Translation by Paul Shorey* in *The Loeb Classical Library* (Cambridge, MA: Harvard University Press, 1935), vol. II:140, n. d.
[34] Ὀφέλεια is "help," "profit," or "advantage."
[35] Καταχρῆται.
[36] Plato, *The Republic*, bk. VII ch. V.

The ancient Greeks clearly had the usefulness of their laws in view. In one of Plato's last dialogues, *Laws*, he explained that the term "law" was in his day a word for songs (IV:700).[37] Etymologically, the word refers to allotment of property.[38] Plato referred to this when he described law as "the distribution of mind" (IV:714; Kittel IV:1032). The mind that is true and free is in harmony with nature and has no need of laws to rule it (VIII:877).

However, human society requires laws that are wisely crafted in order to preserve society.[39] Plato described a twofold purpose for law: (1) the law persuades, and (2) it compels. These two purposes of law appear consistently in the treatise.[40] He also described the purpose of the laws as instruction for the sake of good order. In these passages, Plato's treatise commented on the use, practical usefulness, and functions of the laws.[41]

Aristotle, in his treatise on *Politics*, made frequent reference to the *Laws* of Plato, demonstrating the influence and importance of Plato's work. Aristotle defined Law as "reason unaffected by desire" (III:16; 1287a 32) and "order" (VII:4; 1326a 30).[42] His definitions were built from Plato's teaching about natural harmony and mind, from which good and useful laws derive.[43]

With reference to Plato's treatise, the Roman orator Cicero (106–43 BC) wrote that the laws were meant to persuade people of their benefits and, therefore, do not always compel or force.[44]

---

[37] Plato, *Laws*, R. G. Bury, trans. *The Loeb Classical Library* (Cambridge, MA: Harvard University Press, 1926).

[38] See Kittel IV:1023.

[39] See III:683, 686. Book IV 718B. See also II 660. IX: 880. Plato also describes the roles of law givers (III:701) and guardians of the law (νομοφύλαξ; VI:755).

[40] IV:721, 722, 733, VIII:839; X:890.

[41] IV:722; VIII:836. Note use of χρῆσθαι.

[42] *The Works of Aristotle Translated in English*, vol. X, W. D. Ross, ed. (Oxford: Clarendon Press, 1921).

[43] Cf. *Politica* VI:4; 1319a 7.

[44] "quos imitatus Plato videlicet hoc quoque legis putavit esse, persuadere aliquid, non omnia vi ac minis cogere." *Laws* Clinton Walker Keyes, trans. *The Loeb Classical Library* (Cambridge, MA: Harvard University Press, 1928), Book II V 14. The translator's choice of the words, "the function of the Law" is incidental and is not to be equated with the dogmatic expression found in Christian theology.

From these examples, we see that major figures in classical antiquity had established a consistent, twofold understanding of the law's effects: (1) the law persuades by its reasonableness and (2) the law compels by threat of force. The ancient Greeks even reflected on why people failed to keep the law.[45] However, they did not limit the use of the law to these two. Plato included a third benefit: the law instructs a good man about how to live with his neighbor.

Regarding the development of Roman law, Bruce W. Frier observed that Roman jurists defended legal decisions based on their practicality and fairness.[46] In his explanation, Frier used the term *utilitas*, which may be translated "practicality," "benefit," or "usefulness."

One sees an example of this thinking in the basic definition of "law" (Lat. *jus*) provided by the Roman jurist, Iuventius Celsus. In the early second century AD, he taught, "*Jus* is the art of what is good and fair."[47] Iulius Paulus, a Roman jurist of the third century AD, taught, "The word [*jus*] signifies that which is available for the benefit of all or most persons in any particular state, as in the case of the expression civil law."[48] In Roman law we see "usefulness" (*utilitas*, based on the verb *utor*), emerging as a significant term.

CONCLUSION

What are the chances that thousands of generations of humanity would have the Law written on their hearts, as Paul described, and not reflect on its use? The doctrine that the divine law has uses, whether

---

[45] Consider a speech attributed to Diodotus, the son of Eucrates in *Thucydides, with an English Translation by Charles Forster Smith* in *The Loeb Classical Library* (London: William Heinemann, 1930), bk. III ch. XLV. The speech presents ideas very like the doctrine of original sin and the powerlessness of the Law to prevent sin since penalties cannot drive mischief from the human heart.

[46] *Oxford Classical Dictionary*, 3rd ed., Simon Hornblower and Antony Spawforth, eds. (Oxford: Oxford University Press, 1996), 824.

[47] *The Digest of Justinian*, vol. 1, Charles Henry Monro, trans. (Cambridge: Cambridge University Press, 1904), bk. 1:1. "Jus est ars boni et aequi." *Digesta Iustiniani Augusti*, vol. 1, Th. Mommsen, ed. (Berlin: Weidmann, 1868), bk. 1:1.

[48] *Digest of Justinian*, bk. 1:11. "Altero modo, quod omnibus aut pluribus in quaque ciuitate utile est, ut est ius ciuile." *Digesta* bk. 1:1.

considered by the ancient Jews or other people, is clearly a common idea rather than a product of the sixteenth century as some historians have supposed.[49] It would seem to be a natural conclusion from experience in legal matters. Old Testament and intertestamental ideas about Law show important consonance with classical ideas.

With these points in place, one may proceed to consider anew the theology of the Law and a person's relationship to the Law before conversion and after one is in Christ. Of highest concern for this study is whether a Christian may regard the Law differently after receiving the forgiveness of sins and in setting out on the course of the Christian life.[50]

---

[49] See quotations from Ebeling and Wengert on p. 7.

[50] For more on natural law and its place in biblical and Lutheran theology, see *Natural Law: A Lutheran Reappraisal*, Robert Baker, gen. ed. (St. Louis: Concordia, 2011).

CHAPTER THREE

JESUS, PHILO, AND PAUL

> Why then the law? . . . Is the law then contrary to the promises of God?
>
> —the Apostle Paul

The Old Testament and intertestamental teachings about the Law are important background for understanding comments on the Law and its purpose in the writings of Jewish and Christian teachers of the first century A.D. The Lord Jesus raised the matter when He taught His disciples about the Law on the night when He was betrayed. In addition, the Gospel writers drew on the prophecy of Ps 41:9 about the circumstances of Jesus' betrayal by Judas, tapping into the wisdom themes of friendship. These themes will be our focus in this chapter.

On the night when Jesus was betrayed, He gave His disciples a new commandment about love (Jn 13:31–35). This commandment summarized the Old Testament teaching of the Law, making Jesus Himself the standard of what love should be. Jesus went on to emphasize the bond of love and friendship taught by His commandment (Jn 14:15; 15:12–13). He called His disciples His friends as they kept His command:

> You are My friends if you do what I command you. No longer do I call you servants, for the servant does not know what his master is doing; but I have called you friends, for all that I have heard from My Father I have made known to you

that you should go and bear fruit and that your fruit should abide, so that whatever you ask the Father in My name, He may give it to you. These things I command you, so that you will love one another. (Jn 15:14–17)

The Law, love, election, and friendship are bound up with one another in Jesus' teaching that night when His trial would begin. His friends would flee from Him and He would face the cross the next day forsaken by His Father. Yet even on this darkest path of human suffering and experience, Jesus was anticipating the role of the law of love for His wayward disciples whom He would befriend again after the resurrection.

As part of Jesus' teaching about friendship and the new commandment, He described a change in status for His disciples. Formerly, He could call them servants. But now that Jesus had taught them, He gave them the status of friends, which included a new relationship with Jesus and His Father. We shall see that other first century teachers also described a change in status with respect to God and His Law.

PHILO JUDAEUS

A contemporary of Jesus and St. Paul was Philo Judaeus of Alexandria (c. 20 BC–AD 50). In the treatise *On Mating with the Preliminary Studies*, Philo explained that God uses the Law's afflictions to correct people. He included an expression for the Law that has similarity to an expression used later by the apostle Paul, referring to the work or power of the law.[51]

The passage bears the marks of the Jewish wisdom literature tradition described in chapter two, including a quotation of Pr 3:11

---

[51] *Philo with an English Translation by F. H. Colson and Rev. G. H. Whitaker*, vol. IV in *The Loeb Classical Library* (London: William Heinemann, LTD, 1932), para. 179–80. The Greek expression is δικαιοσύνης καί νομοθετικῆς ἔργον. Cf. Romans 2:15, "They show that the work of the law [τό ἔργον τοῦ νόμου] is written on their hearts, while their conscience also bears witness, and their conflicting thoughts accuse or even excuse them." Rm 2:15 became a key passage for Christian theologians describing natural, moral law, and its connection to the revealed Law of Moses.

about the Lord's instruction or discipline.[52] In the passage, Philo's allegory on Gn 16:1–6 included a contrast between Hagar and Sarah, who embody different levels of education and virtue. He described how Sarah would use the Law to correct and instruct Hagar for her good; Philo insisted on reading the account in Gn 16 as an allegory about the effect of the Law upon someone's mind.

This counsel of Philo resembles Paul's allegory about Hagar and Sarah in Gal 4, where he contrasted the slavery of Hagar with the freedom of Sarah. These associations are tantalizing because the previous chapter in Galatians is one of the most significant passages in Paul's writings for describing the purpose of the Law, where Paul explicitly asks, "Why then the law?" (Gal 3:19). Likewise in Gal 3 Paul wrote that the Law was our "guardian," using a term related to Philo's term for "preliminary studies."[53]

There is yet another interesting expression to note in the passage from Philo above. He wrote that the mind "exercises itself in the preliminary studies." A similar idea appears in Paul's first letter to Timothy, "Train yourself for godliness" (1 Tm 4:7).[54] We shall see that other authors used the idea of exercise to describe the work of the Law.

Note that in Philo and in Paul there is also a change in status described in connection with the Law. Philo describes minds that are at first chastened but later become victorious. Paul describes a slave-like existence under the Law as guardian, followed by a status of sonship and freedom. These descriptions of changes in status form an interesting parallel with the teachings of Jesus above.

However, one should not conclude from these parallels that there is a direct dependence for this point among the teachers. Instead, it seems likely that scribes during the intertestamental period were considering how God's Law "worked" in people's lives and what the purpose of the Law should be. Jesus, Philo, and Paul likely built on this theme, which had important application for believers generally. The moral failures of Israel and Judah that caused the exiles under the

---

[52] Philo also exhibits strong influence of Stoic philosophy and other Greek philosophical traditions. His treatise is a reflection on the usefulness of the Greek gymnasium or "preliminary studies" (cf. the title of the treatise).

[53] Gal 3:24 has παιδαγωγὸς for the slave that takes a boy to school; Philo has προπαιδεῦμα for the studies a boy would pursue at the school.

[54] Both passages use forms of γυμνάζω.

Assyrians and Babylonians, as well as the suffering under the Seleucids, likely prompted this focus on the Law and its work, as appears also in wisdom psalms such as Ps 1 and Ps 119.

THE APOSTLE PAUL

In one of Paul's earliest letters he raised the question, "Why then the law?" (Gal 3:19) and provided answers about the purpose, function, or use of the law (3:19–29). Like Philo, Paul also used the expression "the work of the law" as illustrated in Rm 2:12–16.

> For all who have sinned without the law will also perish without the law, and all who have sinned under the law will be judged by the law. For it is not the hearers of the law who are righteous before God, but the doers of the law who will be justified. For when Gentiles, who do not have the law, by nature do what the law requires, they are a law to themselves, even though they do not have the law. They show that the *work of the law* is written on their hearts, while their conscience also bears witness, and their conflicting thoughts accuse or even excuse them on that day when according to my gospel, God judges the secrets of men by Christ Jesus.

The expression "work of the law" was an important step toward considering the use of the law. The passage is also one of the few places in the New Testament where the terms "Law" and "Gospel" appear together. For these reasons, Rm 2:15 would become a key passage in the early history of the doctrine of the Law, as will be seen in the next chapter.

The root of the expression "use of the law" is actually found in 1 Tm 1:3–11.[55] Paul wrote:

---

[55] Though not all New Testament scholars agree that the apostle Paul wrote 1 Tm, there is at least agreement that the letter is Pauline in its theology. See D. A. Carson and Douglas J. Moo, *An Introduction to the New Testament*, 2nd ed. (Grand Rapids, MI: Zondervan, 2005), 555. Ebeling wrote, "Although in I Tim. 1.8—*Scimus autem quia bonus est lex, si quis ea legitime utatur*—the way is already prepared for the phrase, yet it was Luther who first gave it a significance that goes far beyond the sense of the New Testament passage" (*Word and Faith* 73). Ebeling seems unaware of the broader consideration in ancient cultures, where people pondered the

The aim of our charge is love that issues from a pure heart and a good conscience and a sincere faith. Certain persons, by swerving from these, have wandered away into vain discussion, desiring to be teachers of the law, without understanding either what they are saying or the things about which they make confident assertions. Now we know that the law is good, if one *uses it lawfully*,[56] understanding this, that the law is not laid down for the just but for the lawless and disobedient, for the ungodly and sinners, for the unholy and profane, for those who strike their fathers and mothers, for murderers, the sexually immoral, men who practice homosexuality, enslavers, liars, perjurers, and whatever else is contrary to sound doctrine, in accordance with the gospel of the glory of the blessed God with which I have been entrusted.

1 Tm 1:8 is a vital source of western Christian teaching about use of the Law, as will be demonstrated in the following chapters. Like Rm 2:12–16, 1 Tm 1:3–11 is also one of the few places in the New Testament where the terms "Law" and "Gospel" appear together. As a consequence, these texts were bound to have an important role in the theological discussions about the relationship between the doctrines of Law and Gospel.

CONCLUSION

Jesus, Philo, and Paul note a contrast, a change in the lives of those who hear the Law. At first they are servants or slaves chastened by the Law. But after the discipline of the Law, there may be a new status as shown in Table 3 below.

Table 3
Status Change and the Teaching of the Law

Teacher	Old Status	New Status
Jesus (Jn 15)	servant	friend
Philo (Prelim. Studies)	Chastened mind	Victorious mind
	Hagar	Sarah

usefulness of laws. He did not investigate the history of the interpretation of 1 Tm 1:8.
[56] νομίμως χρῆται.

Paul (Gal 3–4)	Slave-like immaturity	Sonship
	Hagar/slavery	Sarah/freedom

Jesus speaks of friendship, Philo of victorious mind, and Paul of freedom and sonship. The domination of the Law ceases and a new life begins. The similarity in these analogies stems from the biblical and intertestamental teaching about the work of the Law in the history of Israel. God used the Law to chasten His people and call them back to faithfulness. Through the use of the Law, He prepares them for a new status and life.

More could be written on the teachings of Jesus, Philo, and Paul on the topic of the Law. Careful exegetical study of the passages in view of one another would be a welcome addition. However, as noted in the preface, this book is not a comprehensive treatment of all possible history or theology on the use of the Law. It is a survey providing examples that illustrate how the doctrine entered into the Reformation. We could pursue a more thorough overview of Jewish, classical, biblical, and patristic writings but that goal does not fall within the bounds of this study. We will press forward.

By tracing the history of interpretation from Rm 1–5, Gal 3, and 1 Tm 1—especially the key passages in Paul's letters, such as Rm 1:20; 2:15; 5:20; Gal 3:19–24; 1 Tm 1:8–9—one likewise traces the history of the doctrine of the use of the Law. Please note that it is not merely a doctrine of the Protestant Reformation but is biblical and apostolic, rooted firmly in Pauline theology. The following table provides the points that would become the focus of later theologians.

Table 4
<u>Biblical Roots of the Term *Use of the Law*</u>

Rm 2:15, "work of the Law" (*opus legis*).
    Early theologians adopted this expression to describe the theological use of the Law.

Gal 3:19, "Why then the Law?"
    Paul's question invited commentators to explain the benefits or uses of the Law.

1 Tm 1:8, "the Law is good, if one uses it lawfully."
    The Latin verb *utor*, when nominalized by ancient and medieval theologians, became the basis of the technical doctrinal term *usus legis*. The passage invited reflection on whether lawful use of the Law was for the sake of the repentant, the unrepentant, or for both.

CHAPTER FOUR

EARLY CHRISTIAN APOLOGISTS

This, we affirm, was the function of the law as preparatory to the gospel.

—Tertullian

The splendor of the Gospel flooded Israel and the Roman world the way dawn's radiant lavender, yellow, and white light dispells the deep blue and black of night. The old covenant's emphasis on the Law gave way to the new covenant's brilliance, causing the first Christians to see their lives and the lives of their neighbors as never before. Life in Christ changed one personally and this change upset the familiar ways. Life in Christ gave freedom and pilgrim-feet, leading one to pass through this life devoutly on a journey toward the heavenly, the holy, and a new home (Heb 12:18–24; 13:13–14). In the day light of the Gospel, Christians would see and would understand the Law of Moses differently from those who lived under the shadow of Sinai.

After St. Paul sorted through the differences between early Jewish views of the Law and the use of the Law in Christian churches, issues of applying the Law seem to have diminished. In A.D. 132–35 the Bar Kochba revolt clearly separated synagogue and church. The Apostolic Fathers and Christian apologists continued to appeal to the Old Testament to show their continuity with its teaching and to show that the Old Testament had prophesied the coming of Jesus as the

Savior.⁵⁷ But it appears that there were no great enquires about the use of the Law.⁵⁸

In the middle of the second century, the teachings of certain Gnostics renewed controversy about the Law. Early Gnostics, probably following the example of Jews like Philo, allegorized portions of the Old Testament that they found disagreeable to their views. (This is what the Greek philosophers were doing with Homer's writings—allegorizing them to explain away the odd behaviors of the Greek gods that Homer had described.) More aggressively, the Egyptian Gnostic Valentinus and the Syrian Gnostic Cerdon rejected the Old Testament completely.

At about the same time, Marcion of Sinope (d. c. 160) rejected the Old Testament as the work of an inferior god. He accepted only his own revised edition of the Gospel according to Luke and ten letters of the apostle Paul as canonical Scripture. From Luke and Paul he cut away any references to the old covenant. He sought to divide the "Law" from the "Gospel," that is, he drove a wedge between the Old Testament and New Testament teachings.⁵⁹ Marcion treated Sinai as foreign ground and not as the homeland of believers. Marcion would raze the mountain where Moses walked to receive the tables of the Law from the hands of God. He would declare the Old Testament an enemy, not a friend to the Christian.

Marcion, Valentinus, and Cerdon converged at Rome in the first half of the second century. But it was Marcion's teaching that drew the most attention since he organized his followers in ways similar to the Church and rapidly gained converts.

JUSTIN MARTYR

One of the first to respond to Marcion's teaching was Justin Martyr (c. 100–165), though his treatise on Marcion is lost to us. Justin's other writings show him defending the usefulness of the Old

---

⁵⁷ Cf. Justin's *Dialogue with Trypho, a Jew*.

⁵⁸ Victor Ernest Hasler, in *Gesetz und Evangelium in der alten Kirche bis Origenes* (Zurich/Frankfort am Mein: Gotthelf-Verlag, 1953), documents examples of the early Christians' enduring interest in biblical teachings about the Law.

⁵⁹ See Tertullian, *Against Marcion*, bk. I ch. XIX; ANF 3:285. Marcion's distinction is not the same as the Christian distinction between the doctrine of the Law and the doctrine of the Gospel as taught by Paul and others.

Testament, which is now fulfilled by the New Testament. But in doing so, Justin introduced a problematic way of speaking about the New Testament.

In some respects, we can hardly fault Justin for doing so. The terms *testament* and *covenant* are legal language. We call the primary section of the Hebrew Scriptures the *Law of Moses*. So we cannot be surprised that in conversations with a Rabbi, Justin began to describe the new covenant as a "new law."[60] However, speaking in this way, making the New Testament a new law, would have grave consequences for the doctrine of later Christians. Justin could appeal to the teachings of Jesus about "a new commandment" (Jn 13:34) to explain his views, but calling the New Testament a new law obscured the promise of grace and forgiveness for those who failed to keep the Law. He inadvertently took the teaching of the Church back into the long, cold shadow of Sinai, even while defending the goodness and blessedness of Jesus' fulfillment of the Law for our sakes.

IRENAEUS OF LYONS

Irenaeus (c. 130–c. 200) was also one of the first to respond in writing to Marcion's teachings and likely drew upon Justin's treatise against Marcion.[61] He did so in the work popularly called *Against Heresies*, which Irenaeus himself titled, "The Detection and Refutation of False Knowledge," a title that reveals his two-part outline for writing.

Irenaeus wrote five books for the treatise. The largest, book IV, deals with the relationship between the Old and New Testaments and is central to the refutation. Irenaeus melded together his argument that the same God inspired both testaments with his argument for the value and truth of both testaments. In other words, his argument about the nature of God parallels his argument about the nature of the Scripture. In this section, he repeatedly comments on the Law of Moses. In *Against Heresies*, Irenaeus summarized the character and use of the Law as follows:

> For the law, since it was laid down for those in bondage, used to instruct the soul by means of those corporeal objects which

---

[60] See *Dialogue with Trypho* ch. XIII; ANF 1:200.
[61] See Johannes Quasten, *Patrology* (Allen, TX: Christian Classics, 1996), 1:290.

were of an external nature, drawing it, as by a bond, to obey its commandments that man might learn to serve God.[62]

Irenaeus describes the Law primarily as instruction, especially bodily instruction through outward ceremonies. The Law was a "bond" that curbed Israel's behavior.

Irenaeus was repeating St. Paul's argument about the pedagogue in Gal 3, whereby the Law would train Israel. Irenaeus also emphasized that "certain precepts were enacted for them by Moses, on account of their hardness [of heart]."[63] In other words, the Law was given to restrain sinful Israel. Regarding the permanence of the Law, he wrote:

> Preparing man for this life, the Lord Himself did speak in His own person to all alike the words of the Decalogue; and therefore, in like manner, do they remain permanently with us, receiving by means of His advent in the flesh, extension and increase, but not abrogation. The laws of bondage, however, were one by one promulgated to the people by Moses, suited for their instruction or their punishment.[64]

Irenaeus noted that the moral law, the Decalogue, was permanent also for Christians. Patristic interpreters commonly emphasized this point in contrast with the ceremonies and national laws that would not carry over into the New Testament teachings. In this way Irenaeus distinguished what was permanent about Old Testament teaching, being in continuity with the nature of God Himself. The same God commands and blesses. The same God gives the Law and fulfills it in Christ. The same God punishes the wicked and rewards His elect.

CLEMENT OF ALEXANDRIA

Like Irenaeus, Clement (c. 150–c. 215) drew on Gal 3 for teaching about the use of the Law. His treatise, *The Instructor*, builds upon his earlier *Exhortation to the Heathen*, which had appealed for people to follow Christ. The title of *The Instructor*[65] seems to come directly

---

[62] IV XIII 2; ANF 1:477; cf. 1:478.
[63] IV XV 2; ANF 1:480.
[64] *Against Heresies* IV XVI 4–5; ANF 1:482.
[65] Ὁ παιδαγωγὸς.

from St. Paul. However, Clement also attempted to find a role for categories of Greek pedagogical practices in his treatise.

Clement's theme of an instructor drove the categories of his teaching. For example, in chapter VII, where Clement introduces the Instructor, he makes Jesus the pedagogue rather than the Law, as Paul taught in Galatians. The Instructor sought to train believers for a virtuous Christian life.

In the first book of the treatise, Clement explains how the Logos does this work of training, which naturally brings Clement to a consideration of the use of the Law. Toward the end of Book I, Clement introduced Paul's themes about the Law as pedagogue.

> The law is the training of refractory children. . . . On that account the law was given them, and terror ensued for the prevention of transgression and for the promotion of right actions, securing attention, and so winning to obedience to the true Instructor, being one and the same Word, and reducing to conformity with the urgent demands of the law. For Paul says that it was given to be a "schoolmaster to bring us to Christ."[66]

Like classical authors, Clement noted two uses of the Law: prevention of sin and promotion of right action,[67] which he described in terms of fear and exhortation. Clement joined Justin and Irenaeus in emphasizing the continuity between the two testaments. Though the Lord of all Holy Scripture punishes and disciplines, the same Lord works for our salvation, which for Clement is typically sanative: the Lord cleanses and heals those diseased by sin. The result is that new obedience and a virtuous life seem equal to justification and salvation in Clement's writings.

TERTULLIAN

Like other early apologists, Tertullian (c. 160–c. 225) defended the Law of the Old Testament against the opinions of Marcion. His treatise against the false teacher developed through three editions to become his longest extant work. *Against Marcion* is the richest source

---

[66] I XI; ANF 2:234.
[67] See "Use of Natural Law," pp. 17–19. "Promotion of right action" is comparable to Plato's comments about the persuasive effect of the law.

of information about the heretic's teaching since Tertullian so thoroughly refuted his views, even drawing on Marcion's editions of St. Luke and the Epistles of Paul. In Book II, when Tertullian explained that the Creator is the genuine and good God described in both testaments, Tertullian provided some chapters on God's purposes in giving the Law. He writes the following:

> The commission of wrong was to be checked by the fear of a retribution immediately to happen. . . . But even in the common transactions of life, and of human intercourse at home and in public, even to the care of the smallest vessels, He in every possible manner made distinct arrangement; in order that, when they everywhere encountered these legal instructions, they might not be at any moment out of the sight of God. For what could better tend to make a man happy, than having "his delight in the law of the Lord?" In that law would he meditate day and night. It was not in severity that its Author promulgated this law, but in the interest of the highest benevolence, which rather aimed at subduing the nation's hardness of heart, and by laborious services hewing out a fealty which was (as yet) untried in obedience: for I purposely abstain from touching on the mysterious senses of the law, considered in its spiritual and prophetic relation, and as abounding in types of almost every variety and sort. It is enough at present, that it simply bound a man to God, so that no one ought to find fault with it, except him who does not choose to serve God. [68]

In this passage, Tertullian referred to various purposes for the Law, such as restraint, instruction, and prophecy of future teaching. He saw in the minute details a preparation for the Gospel. Tertullian also referred to the Israelite wisdom tradition and its devotion to the Torah not as a matter of fear but of delight. For the believer, the Old Testament was not mere dread as Marcion complained. The discerning heart recognized God's purposes in the Law and through them was bound to God. In this way, Tertullian also refers to the Roman view of "religion," which derives from the term for binding

---

[68] ANF 3:311–312. He returned to a description of the Law's purpose in bk. IV chs. XVI–XVII. See again bk. V ch. IIff.

(Lat. root *lig*) and is related to the term for law (Lat. noun *lex* and verb *lego*).

In Book IV, while refuting Marcion from the Gospel according to Luke and showing the harmony between the testaments, Tertullian returned to a discussion of the purpose of the Law. For example, in the Old Testament principle of refusing to take interest on a loan, Tertullian saw the "inculcating of benevolence" as taught fully in the New Testament.

> Now this, we affirm, was the function of the law as preparatory to the gospel. It was engaged in forming the faith of such as would yearn, by gradual stages, for the perfect light of the Christian discipline, through the best precepts of which it was capable, inculcating a benevolence which as yet expressed itself falteringly.[69]

Tertullian's Latin phrase for "function of the Law" (*opus legis*, literally "work of the Law") stemmed from the Pauline terminology of Rm 2:15, which may stand as the first technical expression for what later writers would call the "use of the Law." In the passage, Tertullian omitted the teaching of justification and described the Law of Moses moving the sinner from loving less to loving more. The use of the Law seems more civil than theological and the "gospel" here means the teaching of the New Testament generally, not simply justification through Christ.

Before leaving Tertullian, it is fitting to cite one further text, which bridges us back to the opening comments about Justin. There we noted that Justin introduced the description of the New Testament as a "new law." In a moral treatise, *On Monogamy*, Tertullian took the matter a step further. After providing a series of arguments for monogamy from the Old Testament, Tertullian switched to write about the New Testament by stating, "Turning now to the law, which is properly ours—that is, to the Gospel . . ." (ANF 4:65). Tertullian bound here the word "Law" with "Gospel" in a confusing way that would reappear for centuries. Later thinkers would regard the Gospel as a uniquely Christian set of commandments, causing them to think

---

[69] "Hanc enim dicimus operam Legis fuisse procurantis Evangelio. Quorumdam tunc fidem paulatim ad perfectum disciplinae Christianae nitorem, primis quibusque balbutientis adhuc benignitatis informabat." PL 2:399. *Against Marcion* IV XVII; ANF 3:372–73.

of salvation as the consequence of one's personal righteousness rather than the righteousness of Jesus Christ.

Conclusion

Marcion's depiction of the Old Testament as the work of an unfriendly god brought the biblical doctrine of the Law back up for investigation. The early apologists wrestled with the relationship between the Old Testament and the New Testament. This issue would become a permanent topic of theology as Christians of each generation responded to critics and to the concepts of classical civilization based on natural law.

The apologists effectively refuted Marcion by demonstrating the unity of God from the Old and New Testaments. They also demonstrated the unity of the testaments themselves, which were good and served divine purposes. They noted that the New Testament fulfilled things promised in the Old Testament. Unfortunately, as the apologists built on one another's work, they introduced confusing terminology that described the New Testament—the Gospel—as a new law, thereby obscuring the graciousness of God.

The earliest Christian writers also described various uses of the Law, although they did not develop a thorough treatment of the topic or a consistent terminology. The doctrine of the use of the Law would receive greater attention during the inter-Christian debates about salvation. Paul's question, "Why then the law?" (Gal 3:19) would reemerge at that time, and with it, a more thorough doctrine of the Law.

As is so often the case in western theology, Tertullian's observations and his use of biblical terminology ("the work of the Law") laid a foundation for later Latin Christian writers.

CHAPTER FIVE

EARLY WESTERN THEOLOGIANS

How then is the law not made for a righteous man, if it is necessary for the righteous man too, not that he may be brought as an unrighteous man to the grace that justifies, but that he may use it lawfully, now that he is righteous?

—Augustine

The fourth century began with one of the bloodiest persecutions of Christians. The emperor Diocletian presented himself as a semi-divine ruler on a mission to reform and unify the empire. In 303 Diocletian set his attention upon the Christians with an edict that urged the burning of their churches and sacred books, punishing the dissenting pastors, and eventually also the laity. The lists of martyrs and commemoration of their suffering and devotion grew from 303–12 even after Diocletian retired from public service in 305.

W. H. C. Frend described the efficiency with which western imperial administrators carried out the persecution, following the new law "without fuss," driving people to sacrifice to the emperor or suffer the consequences.[70] Yet by the close of the fourth century, Christianity was not just an allowed religion of the empire, it became the official religion. Christianity had moved west and north, following the legions of Rome to reach the barbarous Celts, Brits, and Goths at the outer fringes of the empire. Church and state established a partnership—a friendship—that would become a model in western

---

[70] See W. H. C. Frend, *Martyrdom and Persecution in the Early Church* (New York: Anchor Books, 1967), 368.

civilization for centuries and which still exists in the state churches of Europe.

Also during this time, Christian emperors revised the imperial legal code and received the teachings of the Bible into the legacy of Rome. However, the empire would before long divide into east and west after the barbarian invasions. Yet the ubiquity of Christianity and the common legal foundation would guarantee interaction between east and west despite the administrative, cultural, and language barriers.

In the previous chapter, we saw how Tertullian described the function of the Law (*opus legis*) in leading to a Christian's life and discipline. Ebeling speculated about the origin of the term *use of the Law* (*usus legis*) when he wrote, "So far as I am aware, the term is to be found neither in Augustine, where one would soonest expect it, nor in the scholastics either."[71] Holsten Fagerberg suggested,

> Ebeling is of the opinion that it was Luther who coined the term [*usus legis*], but this judgment overlooks the obvious origins in Augustine's *De spiritu et littera* (10,16), where there is an analysis of how the Law is used by the unrighteous and the righteous (even though the term itself is absent).[72]

In this chapter we will test these suggestions and provide a more concrete history.

MARIUS VICTORINUS

The earliest Latin Christian commentaries on the letters of Paul were written by Marius Victorinus, a rhetorician who became a Christian in c. 355. In 362 Victorinus responded to an edict of emperor Julian, called the Apostate.[73] After this, Victorinus disappeared from view, though not without leaving the Church commentaries on Galatians, Philippians, and Colossians.[74] Unfortunately, the existing text of the commentary on Galatians skips over Paul's question at Gal 3:19.

---

[71] *Word and Faith* 73.
[72] *A New Look at the Lutheran Confessions, 1529–1537*, Gene J. Lund, trans. (St. Louis: Concordia, 1972), 82.
[73] Quasten 4:69.
[74] PL 8:1145–1294.

In view of the outcome with Marius Victorinus, I should note that I have not included treatment of every Church Father I investigated in the course of writing this history. Although the theologians commonly had something to say about the doctrine of the Law, I did not find all of them contributing significantly to the doctrine of the use of the Law. Theologians I investigated but did not include are Cyprian, Ambrose, Sedulius Scotus, and Gabriel Biel. I did not have access to the potentially helpful writings of Giles of Rome, Johannes de Caseli, and the earliest editions of Desiderius Erasmus's exegetical writings.

The alert reader will also note that I did not pursue research in the Greek, Syrian, or other Fathers since my goal was to trace the doctrinal terminology from the biblical literature toward Luther in the western, Latin tradition. One can readily see that many other paths of investigation remain open for those who would pursue the history of this doctrine and terminology more fully.

TYCONIUS

The *Book of Rules* is the first thorough Christian treatment of the topic of biblical interpretation. Tyconius (d. c. 400), a Donatist layman, wrote the book. Augustine carefully studied it, guaranteeing its lasting influence.[75]

Although the book largely focuses on allegory, in some cases Paul's insights guided Tyconius's thinking. This is most evident in Rule III, "The Promises and the Law," where Tyconius provided extensive comment on Paul's letters, especially Romans and Galatians. As one studies Tyconius's comments on the abrogation of the Law, it is essential to bear in mind that Tyconius and other theologians have the Law of Moses in view when interpreting these passages from Paul. He was not describing the abrogation of natural law—the moral law—that always stands and applies.

To start, Tyconius recognized Paul's emphasis on the Law's power to accuse. He wrote, "The purpose for which [the Law] was given was to multiply sin."[76] This was not a new insight but it is

---

[75] The *Book of Rules* dates from c. 380. See Augustine's critique in *On Christian Doctrine* III 30–37.
[76] *Tyconius: The Book of Rules*, William S. Babcock, trans. (Atlanta, GA: Scholars Press, 1989), p. 23.

important because, unlike earlier theologians we have studied, Tyconius saw and described the role of the Law in repentance. Tyconius further wrote:

> Anyone who fled to God for refuge received the Spirit of God. And when the Spirit of God was received, the flesh was mortified. When the flesh was mortified, the spiritual man was able to do the law, having been set free from the law since "the law is not laid down for the just" and again, "if you are led by the Spirit" of God "you are not subject to the law." In this light, it is manifest that our fathers, who had the Spirit of God, were not subject to the law. . . . And what held true before still holds true now. The fact that we are not under the law does not mean that the ban against coveting has come to an end; rather it has even more force. But we, through faith, take refuge in revealed grace, taught by the Lord to ask for his mercy in order to do the law and to say, "your will be done," and "deliver us from evil," while they, through the same faith, took refuge in unrevealed grace, compelled by fear of death which they saw stretched out against them with the law as its minister, its sword at the ready.[77]

Tyconius characterized the different experience with the law between the old covenant and the new. He saw a significant difference in the revelation of grace, which new covenant believers see more fully. They also have the gift of the Holy Spirit to mortify the flesh; under the old covenant the people experienced greater fear.

Note that Tyconius brought together teachings from Galatians and 1 Tm 1:8–9. He was exploring the role of the Law in the life of a believer, puzzling over Paul's comment that the Law was not laid down for the righteous man. He wrote:

> What still holds true is the moral law, which is natural and eternal. Each has held its own order. For just as the law has never cancelled faith, so neither has faith undone the law . . . we confirm it, for each confirms the other.[78]

---

[77] Tyconius 29, 31. He further wrote, "We endured the law as our guardian, compelling us to strive for faith, compelling us to Christ." Cf. Rm 5:20.
[78] Tyconius 25.

Just as the covenants both needed to be defended and preserved in Christian theology against the excesses of Marcion, so both the moral law and faith that apprehends the promised grace must hold their place in Christian teaching and the Christian life. In these ways, Tyconius moved the discussion of the Law more into the theological discussion of justification and sanctification.

Toward the end of Rule III, Tyconius brought together the interpretation of Gal 3 with 1 Tm 1:8–9. He came close in expression to what would later become a dogmatic term.

> Just as [Paul] called Ishmael a persecutor with respect to his play, so also he calls those people persecutors who fight to separate the sons of God from Christ and strive to make them sons of Hagar, their own mother by appealing to what is of common use, i.e., the discipline of the law.[79]

In this passage, Tyconius briefly described the usefulness of the Law, which is similar to the civil use of the Law described in later literature. In mentioning "common use," he acknowledged the ideas found in classical civilization about the usefulness of the law. But Tyconius's greatest contribution for this history was to highlight Paul's emphasis on the accusations of the Law against the sinners and the believer's changed relationship with the Law in view of grace and the gift of the Spirit.

AMBROSIASTER

A second early western writer of note has been called "Ambrosiaster," because his work was attributed to Ambrose of Milan, though no one knows this writer's real identity. In the late fourth century, Ambrosiaster wrote a commentary on the Pauline epistles, which is remarkable for its straightforward interpretation without the excesses of allegory. For Gal 3:19, which is a key verse for promoting consideration of the Law, he answered Paul's question, "Why then the Law?" by noting that the Law came after the promise and that the distinction between the Law and the promise was necessary. The Law would distinguish Israel from the Gentiles and

---

[79] Tyconius 52. The Latin text has, "... *per communem utilitatem, id est disciplinum legis.*"

prepare them to receive the promised Christ.[80] Ambrosiaster described the preparatory work of the Law as making one worthy, though he did not indicate precisely what he meant (e.g., is repentance in view or a civil righteousness?).

In Ambrosiaster's comment on Gal 3:19, we see that he noted the enduring nature of the promise, which preceded the giving of the Law of Moses. Like Tyconius, Ambrosiaster made it clear that the natural law also continued to apply. Regarding 1 Tm 1:8–11, Ambrosiaster wrote:

> Paul does not deny that the law given by Moses was good, but he wants its meaning to be understood and the purpose [Lat. *sensus*] for which it was given to be accepted. The person who understands the law and why [Lat. *causa*] it was given is the one who, once Christ has been preached, will abandon that part of it known as the law of works. Nevertheless, out of love for God, he will make use of it by proclaiming and confirming those things which are said of the savior in the law and the prophets.[81] The person who uses the law correctly is the one who can distinguish the things which were given for a time from those which are eternal. . . . Moreover the righteous . . . no longer live under it but have been delivered from it by the gift of God through faith in Christ, so that from now on they will keep the law of nature, which admits to a knowledge of the Creator and encourages people not to sin, and wait for the day of judgment when the righteous will be rewarded for keeping the natural law.[82]

Ambrosiaster envisioned the righteous man, not showing contempt for the Law, but keeping what is moral, natural, and enduring in it. God's forgiveness changes his relationship toward the Law. Whereas before he held the Law in contempt, now he would hold it to be a life-long companion. Moses had to write down the Law because people had held the natural law in contempt. The written text confirmed the

---

[80] *Lectures on Galatians—Philemon*, Gerald L. Bray, trans. In *Ancient Christian Texts* Thomas C. Oden and Gerald L. Bray, eds. (Downers Grove, IL: IVP Academic, 2009), 18. Cf. also p. 20.
[81] See Tertullian's comments about the prophetic character of the Law of Moses, p. 33.
[82] Ambrosiaster 121–22.

natural law and made it clear that God would judge those who did not keep the natural law. In Ambrosiaster's commentary on Romans 2:12, he provided a helpful way of expressing this thought. He described the one declared righteous through faith to be "a friend of the Law."[83]

Tyconius and Ambrosiaster show considerable agreement in their understanding of the Law. Both writers affirmed the enduring character of the moral Law and its importance to all people as well as the righteous. Ambrosiaster emphasized the temporary character of the Law of Moses as well as its enduring proclamation of the coming Savior (cf. Heb *torah* as instruction rather than as simple command and rebuke; p. 10). Both of these writers were important contributors to the views of Augustine, who used their writings.

PELAGIUS

Like other western theologians, a British layman who took up residence in Rome, Pelagius, had special interest in the Pauline epistles. He was born c. 354 and known to be active through 419. He is most famous for his sharp reaction to Augustine's teaching about the power of the will and divine predestination; his name is ever associated with the heresy of Pelagianism, which teaches that man can take the first steps toward salvation apart from divine grace. Today, scholars recognize from Pelagius's writings that he saw grace as something adhering in mankind perhaps naturally or from Baptism.[84]

Because Pelagius's doctrine was condemned, scribes did not preserve his writings with diligence. However, a version of his commentary on Paul survived under the name of St. Jerome.[85] The British scholar, Alexander Souter, identified manuscripts of Pelagius's commentary and created a critical edition.[86]

---

[83] PL 17:67. See also his comments on Rm 5:4. Ambrosiaster is the earliest theologian I have found using this expression, though I wonder whether it has roots in earlier writers of the classical or Christian tradition.

[84] See Gerald Bonner, *St. Augustine of Hippo: Life and Controversies* (Norwich: The Canterbury Press, 1986), 318.

[85] Pelagius's commentary survived in a rewritten form attributed to Jerome (PL 30:645–902; original in PL Supplement I, ed. By A Hamman in 1958, cols. 1110–1374).

[86] *Pelagius's Expositions of Thirteen Epistles of St Paul*, vol. II (Cambridge: Cambridge University Press, 1926).

Pelagius's comment on Gal 3:19 shows that he was familiar with traditional ideas about the effects of the Law. He wrote, "It was given so it might either compel or teach that we not transgress, until Christ should come."[87] This brief observation has similarities with the comment from Clement of Alexandria, who seems influenced most by the classical tradition on this point. In Pelagius's comments on 1 Tm 1:8–9, he noted that the Law was given conditionally and temporally for believers. "It was not necessary for Christians, who are justified through Christ."[88] Pelagius wrote here specifically about the Law of Moses and, like other early Christian authors, would see the natural, moral law as permanent.

JEROME

Jerome (c. 342–420) also wrote a commentary on Galatians, which was widely influential though not especially helpful for a history of the doctrine of the use of the Law. In commenting on Galatians 3:19, he emphasized that God gave the Law to restrain transgression. He wrote,

> For after the offense of the people in the wilderness, after worshipping the calf, and murmuring against the Lord, the Law followed for the intention of prohibiting transgressions. Surely the Law is not appointed for the righteous, but for enemies/sinners—not for slaves—for the impious and sinners (1 Timothy 1:9).[89]

Jerome strongly emphasized the civil use of the Law in his interpretation. Israel did not have the Law of Moses while in Egypt. As slaves who were already restrained, they did not yet need it. Only when they were free in the wilderness and rebelled did they need the Law of Moses.

Notice that Jerome, like Tyconius, brought Gal 3 and 1 Tm 1 together explicitly to explain one another. Here is perhaps Jerome's

---

[87] "Data est, ut [nos] non transgredi vel cogeret vel doceret, usque dum Christus veniret."
[88] "Ergo Christianis opus non est, qui [sunt] iustificati per Christum."
[89] PL 26:365–366. "Post offensam enim in eremo populi, post adoratum vitulum, et murmur in Dominum, Lex transgressionis prohibitura successit. *Justo quippe lex non est posita, iniquis autem et non subjectis, impiis et peccatoribus* (I Tim. I, 9)."

most significant contribution. Because later interpreters would constantly consult his commentary, Jerome guaranteed that western theologians would read these two passages in light of one another. Jerome may also have indirectly provided for an analogy of friendship when he described the civil use of the Law as applying to "enemies" (*iniquis*). We shall see that, like Ambrosiaster, other writers took the step of describing the righteous man's use of the Law as a matter of friendship with the Law.

AUGUSTINE

As anticipated by Ebeling and Fagerberg, Augustine (354–430) was an important contributor to the doctrine of the use of the Law. Throughout his career, he referred to passages from Paul regarding the work of the Law and the use of the Law.

Among Augustine's earliest attempts to explain Scripture are propositions of St. Paul's letters to the Romans and Galatians. That Augustine should focus on these letters is no surprise, given the instrumental role Paul's letters played in his conversion.[90] Also, other people were asking for his help in interpreting Paul and a variety of biblical texts.[91] One of the approaches he developed for helping others understand Paul was to outline from the beginning of Romans his "four stages of man," listed below:

(1) Before the Law

(2) Under the Law

(3) Under grace

(4) In peace[92]

Augustine used these categories for explaining the purpose of the Law of Moses in expounding key passages such as Rm 3:20, 5:20, and 1 Tm 1:9.[93] The distinctions correspond to the uses of the Law. The first refers to the time before God gave the Law to Moses. The second describes Israel's history after they received the Law from

---

[90] See Confessions bk. VIII ch. XII; NPNF1 1:127–28.

[91] See Quasten 4:369.

[92] See *Augustine on Romans*, Paula Fredricksen Landes, trans. (Chico, CA: Scholars Press, 1982), 5.

[93] See *Augustine on Romans* 5. See also Eric Plummer, *Augustine's Commentary on Galatians* (Oxford: Oxford University Press, 2003), 149.

Moses. The third describes the coming of the Gospel, which changes the believer's relationship to the Law of Moses, as seen in the New Testament. The fourth describes the bliss that lasts eternally.

These four stages of history could also be applied to the life and conversion of anyone reading Romans and Galatians. The experience of Israel would then serve as a model for the role that the Law would have for each Christian so that under grace the righteous man rejoices in the permanent goodness of the Law and "is living the law itself."[94] Augustine sees the grace announced in the Gospel changing the believer's relationship to the Law.

Another early reference to the role of the Law is in *Confessions* XII XVIII 27, dated AD 397.[95] This appears in the latter part of the *Confessions*, where Augustine wrote about the outcome of his life and the interpretation of the Holy Scripture. While considering the allegorical interpretation of the Books of Moses, Augustine wrote, "The law is good to edify, if a man use it lawfully; for the end of it 'is charity out of a pure heart, and of a good conscience, and of faith unfeigned'" (NPNF1 1:182). In this passage Augustine has the Christian life in view, how a Christian learns from and uses the Law appropriately. He sounded a theme about use of the Law that would appear throughout his writings: the general purpose of the Law is to edify us about love, i.e., the righteous man's use of the Law in showing love for others.[96]

In the same year Augustine wrote what would become a controversial passage in the first book of *On Christian Doctrine*. Augustine opened the work with the goal of explaining how to interpret the Scripture (Preface and bk. I, ch. 1). He then began the explanation with a chapter on what something is and what is a sign. He next provided a contrast between *enjoying* someone or something and *using* someone or something (Latin terms *frui* versus *uti*; I 3–4; NPNF1 2:523).[97] Augustine did not provide these terms in a negative sense of taking advantage of or abusing another person. He meant

---

[94] Plummer 149.
[95] This is not long after he was ordained bishop of Hippo.
[96] Cf. NPNF1 1:186, 188.
[97] See the overview by Raymond Canning, "Uti/frui" in *Augustine through the Ages: An Encyclopedia*, edited by Allen D. Fitzgerald et al. (Grand Rapids: Eerdmans, 1999), 859–61. The idea of using people has been much discussed in philosophical literature.

appropriate joy and interaction that was mutually beneficial. Both *enjoying* and *using* are important terms that appear persistently in Augustine's teaching above love. When Augustine wrote about using the Law or the usefulness of the Law, he was relating the Law to his central teaching about appropriate and inappropriate love, about proper use and misuse/abuse. The prominent place that the matter of "use" has in this treatise illustrates how foundational it was to Augustine's thought. He proceeded as though running through a series of questions: What is it? How is it signified (spoken or written about)? How is it used or enjoyed? In this way Augustine provided a catechism approach for everything, culminating in the Triune God Himself as the true object of enjoyment. All things, including the Law, would be used on the journey home to Him so that it would be quite natural for a thinker like Augustine to reflect more on the use or usefulness of the Law than those who came before him. And indeed, that is what one finds.

In c. 397–98, while replying to Faustus the Manichaean, Augustine described the doctrine of the Law more thoroughly. Faustus was supposed to be an expert at interpretation and doctrine. But even while living as a Manichaean, Augustine found Faustus wanting. After Augustine became a Christian, he wrote a refutation of Faustus's teaching about the Scriptures.

Note well that when Augustine replied to Faustus, he wrote about the Law in a threefold way, taking a step beyond the twofold descriptions found in classical authors and also among early Christians.

> There are three laws. One is that of the Hebrews, which the apostle calls the law of sin and death. The second is that of the Gentiles, which he calls the law of nature. "For the Gentiles," he says, "do by nature the things contained in the law; and now having the law, they are a law unto themselves; who show the work of the law written on their hearts." The third law is the truth of which the apostle speaks when he says, "The law of the spirit of life in Christ Jesus hath made me free from the law of sin and death."[98]

Augustine's characterizations of the Law may be related to the uses of the Law as follows: (1) natural law in the heart regulates human

---

[98] NPNF1 4:239.

behavior generally (civil use), (2) the law of the Hebrews condemns sin and brings death (theological use), and (3) the third kind of "law" has to do with the gift of New Testament teaching (cf. prophetic use). The use of the Law changes with different users of the Law who are at different places on the journey home to God, as described in his four stages of man.

In the *Reply to Faustus*, Augustine also introduced an allegory about unlawful use of the law, which he would repeat in later writings. The allegory, like that used by Paul in Gal 4, drew on an Old Testament story: the immorality of Lot and his daughters (Gn 19:30–38). Lot represented the Law, which the daughters misused to the shame of all.

> Lot seems to prefigure the future law; for those who spring from the law, and are placed under the law, by misunderstanding it, stupefy it, as it were, and bring forth the works of unbelief by an unlawful use of the law. "The law is good," says the apostle, "if a man use it lawfully."[99]

Misunderstanding and unbelief lead to abuses of the Law, yet a man with understanding and faith may come to use the Law properly, as we shall see Augustine argue.

The Donatist controversy may have deepened Augustine's interest in 1 Tm 1:8. In *Against the Letters of Petilian* (c. 398–401) there is a record of Petilian citing 1 Tm 1:8 in a letter against catholic doctrine (NPNF1 4:562). Petilian cited the passage rhetorically to attack the way the catholics cited Scripture against the Donatist's teachings and practices. He mocked the presupposed holiness and purity of the catholics and asserted that they have a Cain-like devotion. Augustine's reply to this charge is short and weak, little more than: we do not do what you have charged and you do no better than we do. The circumstances of this weak reply cry out for further reflection on how the passage speaks about the Christian life. The Pelagian controversy would provide Augustine with another occasion to explore the uses of the Law and expound the key passages of 1 Tm 1 and Gal 3.

In *On the Spirit and the Letter* (c. 412), Augustine provided several long passages about the Law's use. As described in 1 Tm 1, he noted that the Apostle's wording introduced "two seemingly

---

[99] NPNF1 4:288. See also NPNF1 4:466; 8:247, 398.

contradictory statements" (ch. 16) and that the appropriate conclusion was that only a righteous man lawfully uses the Law, while setting out to attain this conclusion from the passage. Here is an excerpt where he distinguished among the Law's various uses to show that the Law cannot justify or lead to lawful use of the Law, which can only happen through God's grace and Spirit.

> The law, indeed, by issuing its commands and threats, and by justifying no man, sufficiently shows that it is by God's gift, through the help of the Spirit, that a man is justified; and the prophets, because it was what they predicted that Christ at His coming accomplished.[100]

Augustine's reflections are very like those of Tyconius, who elevated understanding of the theological use of the Law to make the role and use of the Gospel clear. In the passage, Augustine referred to what we call the civil and theological uses of the Law of Moses, then followed with prophecy of Christ's appearing (cf. prophetic use of the Law). Therefore, the passage presented three uses of the Law, though without designating them explicitly or enumerating them. Augustine continued by expounding 1 Tm 1:8–9 with Gal 3 in what may be regarded as the culminating insight of the treatise.[101] He described how the righteous man "lawfully uses the law" (ch. 16; NPNF1 5:89). He concluded:

> The law was therefore given, in order that grace might be sought; grace was given, in order that the law might be fulfilled. Now it was not through any fault of its own that the law was not fulfilled, but by the fault of the carnal mind; and this fault was demonstrated by the law, and healed by grace.[102]

In referring to the fulfillment of the Law, Augustine referred to the righteous man's use of the Law, introducing a fourth use. One sees then a rather full accounting of uses of the Law as Augustine expounded 1 Tm 1 and Gal 3 in view of one another in an effort to

---

[100] NPNF1 5:89.
[101] See Quasten 4:387.
[102] NPNF1 5:97; cf. NPNF1 5:220–21.

resolve the question of why the Law was not given for a righteous man even though he is the one who may fulfill it.[103]

In a letter to Asellius (AD 418) and a Sermon on Rm 8:12–17 (AD 419), Augustine finally struck upon the specific term for the "benefit" or "usefulness of the Law," which he began to use in a consistent way.

> This, then, is the benefit of the law,[104] namely, that it reveals us to ourselves in order that we may know our weakness and see how the prohibition increases carnal concupiscence rather than heals it. . . . The benefit of the law, then, is that it convinces human beings of their weakness and compels them to beg for the medicine of grace, which is found in Christ.[105]

Augustine visited the same theme in a sermon of this time in his ministry.

> What's the use of the law,[106] then, and how does it help? . . . So when he's [Paul] discussing this point, he has made this objection to himself: So why the law?, as though to say, "What is the law?" He answers, it was laid down for the sake of transgression (Gal 3:19).[107]

Augustine's term, *utilitas Legis*, in these passages described the theological use of the Law as preparatory to the proclamation of the Gospel. The term would become standard in theology only at a later time when medieval theologians would study Augustine's writings and build upon his insights.

---

[103] We do well to remember, however, that Augustine derived his observations about the Law while reading St. Paul.

[104] "utilitas Legis." One may see in Augustine's expression the basis of the "theological *terminus technicus*" that Ebeling sought. The development of this expression likely stemmed from 1 Tm 1:8–9 and from Roman law (see pp. 17, 25–26).

[105] Letter 156:2, 5–6. *The Works of Saint Augustine: A Translation for the 21st Century, Letters (156–210)* (Hyde Park, New York: New City Press, 2004. © Augustinian Heritage Institute), 312–13.

[106] Also "utilitas legis." PL 38:851.

[107] Sermon 156:3. *The Works of Saint Augustine: A Translation for the 21st Century, Sermons (148–183)* (New Rochelle, New York: New City Press, 1992. © Augustinian Heritage Institute), 98–99.

One further observation is needed with regard to Augustine's teaching. Earlier we noted that Ambrosiaster spoke of a Christian as a "friend of the Law." The same expression comes up with Augustine but in an unusual way. The expression occurs on the lips of Faustus the Manichaean, who refered to a catholic as a friend of the law in one of his rhetorical appeals before launching an attack on the Old Testament teaching.[108] Augustine himself used a similar expression in his treatise *On the Grace of Christ*[109] and the precise expression in tractate XLI *On the Gospel of St. John*.[110] Augustine embraced the description of the Christian as a friend or companion of the Law, preparing the way for this view in later teachers.

REVISION OF ROMAN CIVIL LAW

There was also at this time another stream of influence that would be important for the later development of terminology of the use of the Law, though its importance could only be recognized much later. In the fifth and sixth centuries, Roman emperors made significant revisions of the civil legal code. In 435 Emperor Theodosian II commissioned a special effort to prepare a new legal code for the empire. Publication of further revisions and additions began in 529 under the Emperor Justinian. The last document, the "Institutes of Justinian" was published in 553. The complete collection of work would become known as the *Corpus Juris Civilis*. This work set an important precedent for the further development and organization of church law known as the *Corpus Juris Canonici*, which began with the *Decretum Gratiani* in the twelfth century.[111]

ISIDORE OF SEVILLE

At the end of the Patristic era, Isidore of Seville (c. 560–636) wrote his encyclopedic work, the *Etymologies*. He drew together and organized much of the learning available to him. He brought the

---

[108] NPNF1 4:272–73. These circumstances add to my suspicion that the expression "friend of the Law" is not something Ambrosiaster created but borrowed from earlier thinkers. See n. 83.
[109] NPNF1 5:223.
[110] NPNF1 7:235.
[111] See pp. 57–58.

classical tradition about the civil law together with the biblical tradition.

In an entry "On Law," Isidore wrote about the usefulness and the benefit of law in keeping with the interests of Roman jurists.[112] He later traced the historical background of Roman imperial law by beginning with the Law of Moses.[113] He distinguished divine laws, which endure, from human laws that fade into disuse.[114] Isidore provided this definition, "What is law? Law is an arrangement of the people where those of noble birth ratify something with the masses."[115] Yet, all such human law depended upon the divine, natural law.

Under the heading, "What the law is able to do," Isidore wrote,

> Every law either permits something, such as "an honest man seeks a reward"; or it forbids, such as "No one is allowed to seek marriage with consecrated virgins"; or it punishes, such as "Whoever has committed a crime shall suffer punishment," Indeed, human life is governed by reward or penalty.[116]

In this passage, Isidore listed ways that individuals and societies use the law to their benefit. Isidore's verbs provided an inventory of actions: law demands, forbids, punishes, and governs. Medieval scholars would study these works or effects of the Law as they commented on Scripture, as we shall see in the next chapter.

CONCLUSION

At this point, we may draw together observations from both chapter four and chapter five, which build upon the earlier insights. The early apologists and the early western theologians faced a common problem in combating false teaching: how to explain the two testaments or covenants in view of one another. Their solution had to do with

---

[112] Bk. II X 6. PL 82:131. "utilis . . . utilitate." See p. 19.
[113] Bk. V I 1. PL 82:197.
[114] Bk. V II.
[115] Bk. V X 1. PL 82:198. "Quid lex. Lex est constitutio populi, qua majores natu simul cum plebibus aliquid sanxerunt."
[116] Bk. V XIX. PL 82:202. "Quid possit lex. Omnis autem lex, aut permittit aliquid, ut vir fortis petat praemium; aut vetat, ut, Sacrarum virginum nuptias nulli petere liceat; aut punit, ut, Qui eaedem fecerit capite plectatur, ejus enim praemio, aut poena vita moderatur humana." Cf. list at bk. II X 4–5.

answering the question of the usefulness of the Law of Moses and why the one good God would give two testaments, which were at once similar and different from one another. What was unique and common to them both? Drawing on St. Paul, the early Church Fathers provided helpful observations, which the following chart summarizes.

Table 5
Law and Gospel in the Two Testaments

	OLD TESTAMENT	NEW TESTAMENT
ETERNAL LAW:	Natural/moral law	Fulfilled & enduring
TEMPORAL LAW:	Ceremonial & civil law	Both fulfilled & ended
ETERNAL GOSPEL:	Promised	Fulfilled & enduring

What endured were the natural/moral law and the Gospel as promised and fulfilled. The Law of Moses filled a temporary role in preparing Israel and others for the new covenant. Unfortunately, in explaining this the Fathers introduced the misleading distinction between the old law and the new law, terminology that would characterize the Gospel as law in subsequent teachers, which obscured the biblical doctrine of grace.

The early western theologians provided increasing focus on the purpose and usefulness of the Law as distinguished from the Gospel. They described the Law's use to restrain sinners (Irenaeus, Tertullian, Tyconius, Ambrosiaster, Jerome, Augustine, Isidore; cf. civil use), the Law's role in convicting sinners (Tyconius, Augustine; cf. theological use), the Law's role in showing love or obedience (Tertullian, Augustine; cf. the righteous man's use of the Law), and the prophetic use of the Law, which pointed to the coming of Christ (Tertullian, Ambrosiaster, Augustine).[117] Writers such as Tyconius, Jerome, and Augustine are important because they brought together Galatians and 1 Timothy to expound one another.

It appears that these early writers did not enumerate the uses of the Law nor did they standardize the terminology. However, note that Augustine, who was a diligent student of Pauline theology driven by a series of controversies with Manichaean, Donatist, and Pelagian teachings about the Law, described or referred to all four of the uses

---

[117] This survey is based on the citations in chapters four and five. It is not comprehensive for all the views of the theologians noted.

of the Law. He related the doctrine of the Law to his central teaching about love for one's neighbor and love for God. Augustine also appears to have settled on the expression "usefulness of the Law" (*utilitas Legis*).

Ambrosiaster introduced us to the idea that the righteous man may view the Law as a friend. The origin of the expression, "friend of the Law" (*amicus legis*), may come from a source earlier than Ambrosiaster since it occurred in the writings not only of Church Fathers but also in Faustus the Manichaean. For example, one wonders whether this was an expression used in Roman civil law or used by Christians to defend themselves against detractors, though these possibilities are not yet established. Whatever the case, Ambrosiaster's expression leads one back to Jesus' statements to His disciples in Jn 15. Jesus called those who received the fullness of His teaching "friends," indicating a change in status from *servants* who did not understand the will of their master to *friends* who understood and shared in the interests of Jesus and His Father. Ambrosiaster's expression could describe this change in status that a Christian experiences with respect to the Law.

Augustine also took up this expression. His influence guaranteed that later theologians would discuss this way of thinking about the Law and the Christian life. To draw on Augustine's four stages of man, our lives before Christ are "under the Law," under its threat and condemnation. But after Christ has freely redeemed us by His grace and instructed us in the teaching of His Father—who becomes our Father—we live the Christian life *with* the Law as a companion. We see clearly its value and its shortcomings. We may use it for bearing the fruit of righteousness (Jn 15:16). While "under grace," we are with the natural/moral law, which endures as an element of God's will alongside His gracious and good will in the Gospel.

This way of seeing the Law would allow the Christian to continue using both the Old Testament and the New, which the Church Fathers held as an important goal over against the false teachers who rejected the Old Testament. In this little phrase, "friend of the Law," one may see and hear a culmination of biblical and early Christian reflection on the Law. Whether this vision should inform our lives today, we shall explore in chapters to come. Medieval interpreters would provide further contributions, as the next chapter will show.

CHAPTER SIX

MEDIEVAL THEOLOGIANS

> Here [Paul] responds to the question and shows the threefold usefulness of the Law.
>
> —Nicholas of Lyra

Our English word *clerk* depicts the intimate relationship between church and state, secular law and canon law that developed from the ancient church down to the Reformation era. In the early years of Greek and Latin Christianity, a *cleric* (Greek *klerikos*; Latin *clericus*) was a priest or pastor, as mentioned in Justinian's legal code.[118] Over time, the word was used for other offices in the church, such as parish clerks who acted as readers at church services.

The ability of the clergy to read made them most valuable servants not only to the church but also to the state, which employed clerics in support of governance. Christian rulers naturally became involved with clerical appointments of all kinds, which led to an increasing struggle between the popes and kings as each sought to make decisions that affected one another.

Dionysius Exiguus (c. 500–50) created the earliest widely used collection of canon law, which included decrees of councils (canons), papal decretals, and church court decisions. Overtime, more and more laws were written, which required more and more clerics to read them until the medieval universities were filled with students of canon law,

---

[118] *Codex Justiniani* bk. I. I.3 distinguishes bishops and clerics.

a major topic of study in Italy where the western church was headquartered.

About 1500 the English word *clerc* gained independence from Latin and gave birth to all manner of clerks in businesses as well as families of Clarks, a most common English surname. The advantages of a thorough legal system had been many. Yet ultimately, the increasingly technical system exasperated people in the late medieval period, due to the endless number of lawyers and suits. The Reformation would propose new standards to address these medieval concerns.

Just as some scholars suggested that the doctrine and terminology for "use of the Law" (*usus legis*) stem from Augustine, others suggested that they stem from the medieval era.[119] This chapter will explore the writings of some medieval theologians and provide specific examples of their teaching about the use of the Law. Once again, among other texts and streams of thought, we will see the importance of Gal 3 and 1 Tm 1:8–9 for the doctrine and terminology.[120]

RABANUS MAURUS

The next significant commentator on the Pauline Epistles was Rabanus Maurus (d. 856), a leader during the Carolingian Renaissance who served as abbot of Fulda and Archbishop of Mainz. Rabanus wrote concerning 1 Tm 1:8–9 that the Law was established to prohibit iniquity and instruct people so that they would sin less (cf. civil use of the Law). However, he also wrote that the Law was not necessary for the righteous. Believers grow less willing to sin and so finally do not require the boundary of the Law. They abide in the pattern of their Baptism and so abstain from sin. In this way, they

---

[119] Kolb and Arand 150. The comment may describe *usus* in medieval theology, leading to the term *usus legis*. However, it more likely refers to the research of Erik Herrmann, "'Why then the Law?' Salvation History and the Law in Martin Luther's Interpretation of Galatians 1513–1522," PhD Diss. (St. Louis: Concordia Seminary, 2005), 255, n. 557.

[120] As I continued my research, I found that these two texts from Paul were most instrumental in shaping the doctrine and terminology. Therefore, I focus on them rather than describing the interpretations for Rm, Gal, etc. more broadly.

could teach others what ought to be imitated (PL 112:584; cf. righteous man's use of the Law).

ANSELM OF LAON

One finds similar ideas in the *Glossa Ordinaria*, a biblical commentary that developed with the renewed interest in biblical studies at the University of Paris. Modern scholars attribute the glosses for St. Paul's epistles to Anselm of Laon (d. 1117), who lectured on the Bible at the cathedral school of Laon. He drew together the Father's earlier thoughts on the biblical text and introduced more careful investigation. Anselm's work laid the foundation for the *Glossa Ordinaria*, though the glosses passed through many hands and changed over the centuries.[121] At Gal 3:19, one finds:

> [The Law] was appointed between the promise and the seed, about whom the promise was made. That is, [it was appointed] between Abraham and Christ, so that it might instruct the people of God in the fear of God. Thus, the people would be made worthy to receive the promise, which is Christ.[122]

With the verb "instruct," the gloss focused on the theological use of the Law as one would find in Augustine and earlier writers. It

---

[121] According to tradition, Walafrid Strabo wrote the marginal gloss and Anselm of Laon wrote the interlinear gloss. This is apparently incorrect. Modern scholars believe that Anselm of Laon was the organizer and responsible for the Psalter, John, and the Pauline Epistles. His brother Ralph compiled the gloss for Matthew. Gilbert the Universal worked on the Books of Moses and perhaps other Old Testament books. The entire commentary was complete in about the 12th century. See Margaret Gibson, "The Latin Apparatus," in *The Eadwine Psalter: Text, Image, and Monastic Culture in Twelfth-Century Canterbury*, Margaret Gibson, T. A. Heslop, Richard W. Pfaff, eds. (University Park, PA: The Pennsylvania State University Press, 1992), 108–109. See also *Cambridge History of the Bible* (Cambridge: Cambridge University Press, 1969), 2:205–207. PL 113–114 includes only the marginal gloss, though in the medieval era the two forms of glosses always appeared together.

[122] PL 114:576. "Posita est in medio, inter promissionem et semen: cui facta est promissio, id est, inter Abraham et Christum, ut populum Dei erudiret sub timore Dei: ut dignus fieret excipere promissionem quae est Christus."

included the idea of merit ("made worthy") in connection with redemption. The following is commentary on 1 Tm 1:8–9, which includes only the marginal glosses.

> *But we know.* Lest he should appear to find fault with the Law, he adds: But we know, etc. But lest he should appear to reintroduce [the Law], he places afterward: *Knowing this, that the law is not made for a righteous man*: because one is not righteous by the law, but by faith. Why, then, is the law necessary for him? For this reason it was given, either to punish the guilty, or that it should restrain the one who wants to sin. However, the righteous man—even if he does not need it—uses [the Law], so that it may be in authority toward others, and the future may be attested with deeds. *A man uses it lawfully.* He knows that the law was given temporarily and it ceases under Christ. Now for those who are righteous through remission there is no need for the Law, from which they are free through Christ. Now, there are many ways of using the Law lawfully, so that the righteous one way, and the unrighteous another correctly is said to use the law lawfully. For the unrighteous uses it lawfully when, knowing why it was given, he is led to grace by its threats as by a pedagogue, and through grace he is made righteous. But the righteous also uses it lawfully when, by keeping it, he imposes it upon the unrighteous, so that when the sickness of implanted lust begins to be increased in the unrighteous by means of the incentive of the prohibition, and the increase of violation, they may flee for refuge to justifying grace, and through it, by the sweetness of righteousness, they may avoid the penalty of [the Law's] threatening letter.[123]

---

[123] PL 114:625. "*Scimus autem.* Ne videretur legem incusare, addit: Scimus autem, etc. Sed ne iterum videatur eam inducere, subjungit: *Scientes hoc,* quia justo non est lex posita: quia non ex ea est justus, sed ex fide. Ad quid igitur ei necessaria est lex? Ideo data est, ut vel reum puniret, vel peccare volentem coerceret. Justus tamen, et si ea non eget, utitur, ut sic esset in auctoritate aliis, et futura attestaretur factio. *Legitime utatur.* Qui scit ad tempus datam esse legem et sub Christo deserit. Jam justis per remissionem non est opus lege, a qua liberi sunt per Christum. Lege autem legitime utendi multiplex est modus, ut secundum aliud justus, et secundum aliud injustus recte dicatur legitime uti lege. Injustus enim ea ligitime utitur, quando

The gloss taught first that the Law was given to punish the guilty and to restrain the one who wants to sin, the civil and theological uses of the Law. These applications are not necessary for the righteous man who instead uses the Law for the sake of others. In this way the gloss included the righteous man's use of the Law in which the believer takes up the Law and uses it for the benefit of others. Then the gloss further defined how both the righteous and the unrighteous may appropriately use the Law for the benefit of others or for personal benefit. The gloss presented a well-developed understanding of some uses of the Law and provided multiple reasons to use it, even though it did not include a specific enumeration of uses.

GRATIAN

In the first half of the twelfth century, an Italian monk and legal consultant compiled a foundational work on canon law, which came to be known as *Decretum Gratiani*. It became a standard textbook and the basis of university lectures, though medieval writers preserved very little information about its author. Gratian's work sparked renewed interest in the importance of Law for governing church and society.

The first pages of the work drew extensively on Isidore's *Etymologies*, including Isidore's list of verbs that defined the abilities of the law.[124] However, Gratian gave this passage from Isidore a new heading. He titled it: "What the office of the law should be."[125] The term *officium* is often translated "function," akin to the idea of "use."[126] It derives from *facio* ("to do") and *opus* ("work").[127] It

---

intelligens quare data sit, ejus comminatione tanquam paedagogo perducitur ad gratiam, per quam justus fiat. Justus vero et illa legitime utitur, cum eam tenendo injustis imponit, ut cum injustis coeperit inolitae concupiscentiae morbus incentivo prohibitionis, et cumulo praevaricationis augeri, confugiant ad justificantem gratiam, et per eam suavitate justitiae delectati poenam litterae minantis evadant."
[124] See p. 51.
[125] "Quid sit officium legum." Decreti pars prima, distinctio III, ch. IV. PL 187:34.
[126] Gratian, *The Treatise on Laws (Decretum D.D. 1–20) with Ordinary Gloss*, Augustine Thompson, O. P. and James Gordley, trans. (Washington, D. C.: The Catholic University of America Press, 1993), 11. Cf. translations

describes service done for another person whether done freely or due to obligation. In classical Latin *officium* could describe favor or help.[128] In the Vulgate it often described tabernacle/temple service or a person's duties. Gratian's legal term "office of the Law" (*officium legis*) did not become a theological term right away, though the way was prepared for this adoption as a myriad of canon lawyers studied the *Decretum*.

PETER LOMBARD

Peter Lombard (c. 1100–60) taught at the cathedral school of Paris. He is famous for his *Sentences*, a theological textbook that drew together the statements of Church Fathers (especially Augustine) and the achievements of scholastic learning. Peter used the *Glossa Ordinaria* to create what is known as the *Magna Glossatura* (PL 191–192), in which he rewrote and expanded the earlier glosses. At Gal 3:19, Peter explained that Paul's question, "Why then the Law," is rhetorical. The first answer is that the Law was given on account of transgressions. He further asked, "Why is it that the Law was given by God? What is its use?"[129] He recognized in Paul a second answer, "The Law was applied in the meantime, namely between the promise and the seed who had been promised" (cf. v. 19b).[130] So, in Paul's one question, Peter began to see multiple reasons for why God gave them the Law of Moses. He concluded that there are four: (1) To humble the stubborn so that they desire healing and justification, (2) to conquer their pride and weakness, (3) to whip the obstinate, and (4) to bear witness to the future fulfillments in Christ. He wrote,

---

of the later dogmatic term *officium legis*, which became interchangeable with *usus legis* in sixteenth century theology.

[127] Cf. *opus legis* in Table 3 and Tertullian's *opus legis*, p. 34.

[128] *Dictionary of Medieval Latin from British Sources*, Fasc. VI, D. R. Howlett et al., eds. (Oxford: Oxford University Press, 2001), 2012. In Gratian's *Decretum*, the common spelling is *offitium*. See *Wortkonkordanz zum Decretum Gratiani*, Timothy Reuter und Gabriel Silagi, bearb. (München: Monumenta Germaniae Historica, 1990).

[129] PL 192:127. "Id est cur a Deo data est lex? Quae est ejus utilitas?" The text includes bracketed and parenthetic references to Augustine and Ambrose from whom Peter drew his insights.

[130] PL 192:127. "Lex *posita est* in medio, scilicet inter promissionem et semen cui facta est promissio."

Behold, you have four gifts of the Laws, causes briefly distinguished, which in the Epistle to the Romans are fully explained, where it says, "The Law entered in," etc. (Romans 5[:20]).[131]

Peter's four uses of the Law do not correspond directly to Isidore's four verbs about the actions of the Law.[132] Isidore likely drew his thoughts from Roman civil law. Peter drew his thoughts from Scripture and theology. His first use of the Law is the theological use. His second use may correspond to the theological or civil use. His third use is a civil use of the Law. The fourth is the prophetic use of the Law.

Peter's careful examination of Gal 3:19 led to a flowering of fuller understanding about the Law. As in the writings of earlier theologians, he used the theological and philosophical terms "usefulness" (*utilitas*) and "cause" (*causa*) with the Law.[133] In his comments on 1 Tm 1:8–9, he again wrote of multiple ways to use the Law by building on the points in the earlier gloss. Like Ambrosiaster and Augustine, Peter added a fascinating description of the Law as "a friend of the righteous man."[134] If someone obeys out of fear, he acts as an enemy and not as a friend. But the righteous man does not sin because the Law is his friend, whom he does not want to violate. In this we see further reflection on the idea of Ambrosiaster and Augustine, including the idea of status change whereby the believer has a different relationship to the Law. Peter believed that "The Law is good and the righteous man uses it lawfully" though not for justification, which takes place through "the rule/law of faith" (*ex lege fidei*).

THOMAS AQUINAS

Peter Lombard's observations appear to have influenced the views of Thomas Aquinas (c. 1225–74). Thomas was a Dominican who taught philosophy, theology, and biblical studies at the University of Paris.

---

[131] PL 192:127. "Ecce habes quatuor datae legis causas breviter distinctas, quae in Epistola ad Romanos plenius explicantur, ubi dicitur; *Lex subintravit*, etc. (Rom. v)."
[132] See p. 50.
[133] Cf. Augustine (p. 48) and Ambrosiaster (p. 40).
[134] PL 192:330.

He was one of the most prolific writers of the medieval era and the sum of his thought has greatly influenced Roman Catholic theology; his views have great significance beyond the medieval era. In his comments on Gal 3, lecture 7, Thomas provided four answers about the purposes of the Law. The following is an extensive quotation that will illustrate just how thoroughly medieval theologians were thinking about the role of the Law in society and church. Note that the purpose of the Law that receives the most attention and explanation is the theological use of the Law.

> [Paul] sets down the purpose of the Law;[135] . . . With respect to the first [purpose], it should be noted that the Old Law was given for a fourfold purpose, corresponding to the four consequences of sin enumerated by Bede, namely, because of wickedness, weakness, passion, and ignorance.[136] Hence the Law was given first of all to suppress wickedness, since by forbidding sin and by punishing, it restrained men from sin. This he touches on when he says, The law was set because of transgressions, i.e., to prevent them. On this point it is said: "The law is not made for the just man but for the unjust" (1 Tim 1:9). The reason for this can be taken from Ethics IV of the Philosopher.[137] For men who are well disposed, are inclined to act well of themselves, so that fatherly admonitions are enough for them: hence they do not need a law; indeed, as it is said, "They are a law to themselves who show the work of the law written in their hearts" (Rom 2:14).[138]
>
> But men who are ill disposed need to be kept from sin by penalties. Hence with respect to such men it was necessary to set down a law which has power to constrain.
>
> Secondly, the Law was set down in order to disclose human weakness. For men gloried in two things: First, in their knowledge; and secondly, in their power. Hence God left men without the instruction of the Law during the period of the

---

[135] The Latin has "legis utilitatem."
[136] The source of this is not yet known, or whether Bede expounded uses of the Law in connection with his doctrine of sin.
[137] Aristotle.
[138] The correct reference is 2:15.

Law of nature, during which time, as they fell into errors, their pride was convinced of its lack of knowledge, even though they still presumed on their powers. For they said, "Many are willing and able, but there is no one to lead," as a Gloss says on Exodus (24:8): "All things that the Lord hath spoken we will do. We will be obedient." And therefore the Law was given which would cause a knowledge of sin, "for by the law is the knowledge of sin" (Rom 3:20). But it did not give the help of grace to avoid sin, so that man, bound by the Law, might test his strength and recognize his infirmity. Finding that without grace he was unable to avoid sin, he would more ardently yearn for grace. And this cause can also be derived from these words, if they are taken to mean that the Law was set for the sake of filling up transgressions, in the sense in which the Apostle speaks when he says: "Now the law entered in that sin might abound" (Rom 5:20). This is to be taken not in a causal but in a sequential sense; for after the Law entered in, sin abounded and transgressions multiplied, because concupiscence, not yet healed by grace, lusted after that which was forbidden, with the result that sin became more grievous, being now a violation of a written law. But God permitted this in order that men, recognizing their own imperfection, might seek the grace of a mediator. Hence he says significantly, It was set, i.e., interposed, as it were, between the Law of nature and the Law of grace.[139]

Thirdly, the Law was given in order to tame the concupiscence of a wanton people, so that, worn out by various ceremonies, they would not fall into idolatry or lewdness. Hence Peter says: "This is a yoke which neither our fathers nor we have been able to bear" (Acts 15:10).

Fourthly, the Law was given as a figure of future grace in order to instruct the ignorant, according to Hebrews (10:1): "For the law, having a shadow of the good things to come."[140]

---

[139] Thomas has three Laws in mind: (1) law of nature, (2) Law of Moses, (3) and law of grace. Regarding the latter, cf. his fourth use below and his doctrine of the New Testament as a new law in the *Summa*.

[140] Thomas Aquinas, *Commentary on Saint Paul's Epistle to the Galatians*, F. R. Larcher, trans. (Albany, NY: Magi Books, Inc., 1966), 95–97.

Thomas based his enumeration on Bede's doctrine of the four consequences of sin, though the enumeration also corresponds to some points made by commentators such as Peter Lombard (cf. pp. 59–60). He provided a well-developed and enumerated view of the use of the Law, though his first use and third use appear to overlap.

Thomas began with the civil use of the Law, confirmed from St. Paul and Aristotle, including reference for the biblical expression "work of the Law" noted earlier by Tertullian. He secondly described the theological use of the Law, distinguishing the time before the Law of Moses when mankind had only the natural law, from the time of the Law when people were confronted with their transgressions (cf. Augustine's four stages of man). Thomas's third use described the effects of the ceremonial law in restraining Israel. This is most likely a civil use of the Law rather than the righteous man's use since the passage emphasized restraint and burden rather than joyful learning or use. Lastly, Thomas included the prophetic use of the Law.

In the *Summa Theologica* (1265–1274), Thomas wrote about the "effect of the law,"[141] dealing with both human and divine laws. He raised two questions and interacted with the four abilities of law provided by Isidore:

> We must now consider the effects of law; under which head there are two points of inquiry: (1) Whether an effect of law is to make men good? (2) Whether the effects of law are to command, to forbid, to permit, and to punish, as the Jurist states?[142]

Thomas noted points from Aristotle on whether law makes a person good while also noting from Augustine that obedience based on servile fear does not lead to genuine goodness. These topics anticipated the issues of righteousness or justification that would arise in the Reformation.

THE BEGUINES AND BEGHARDS

To understand the reception of Luther's doctrine of the Law, it is helpful to note the views of some lay mystical groups that may have

---

[141] Prima Secunda, Questio 92. St. Thomas Aquinas *The Summa Theologica*, Fathers of the English Dominican Province, trans. (Benziger Bros., 1947).
[142] See p. 50.

begun around Liège, c. 1170.[143] The groups became controversial in the thirteenth and fourteenth centuries because they did not have approved religious orders, did not take vows, and some members of these groups taught pantheistic, perfectionist, and antinomian ideas.[144] Antinomian controversies are commonly known from the Early Christian conflict with Gnosticism and the Reformation conflict with Johannes Agricola.[145] Medieval antinomians receive less attention.

The lay mystical groups of Beguines and Beghards spread broadly from the region of France to Poland. Schaff noted:

> In the fourteenth century, the number of houses increased very rapidly in Germany and by 1400 there was scarcely a German town which had not its beguinage.... In 1368 Erfurt had four hundred Beguines and Beghards.[146]

Schaff described a specific example of a person who has been regarded as an antinomian:

> To the general class of free thinkers belonged such individuals as Margaret of Henegouwen, usually known as Margaret of Porete, a Beguine, who wrote a book advocating the annihilation of the soul in God's love, and affirmed that, when this condition is reached, the individual may, without qualm of conscience, yield to any indulgence the appetites of nature call for. After having several times relapsed from the faith, she was burnt, together with her books, in the Place de Grève, Paris 1310.[147]

---

[143] "Beguines and Beghards," by Robert E. Lerner in *Dictionary of the Middle Ages*, Joseph R. Strayer, ed. (New York: Charles Scribner's Sons, 1983), 2:157–62. See also Walter Simons, *Cities of Ladies: Beguine Communities in the Medieval Law Countries, 1200–1565* (Philadelphia: University of Pennsylvania Press, 2001) and Ernest W. McDonnell, *The Beguines and Beghards in Medieval Culture, with Special Emphasis on the Belgian Scene* (New York: Octagon Books, 1969), especially the chapter, "Tares in the Vineyard."
[144] See Schaff V:489–93.
[145] See "Antinomianism" in *Oxford Dictionary of the Christian Church*, 3rd ed. (Oxford: Oxford University Press, 1997).
[146] Schaff V:492.
[147] Schaff VI:500.

Robert E. Lerner provided a critical review of charges against the lay mystical groups, noting that many of the complaints about them were typical, general complaints or stories used to characterize a wide variety of heretical groups. Although Lerner provided helpful caveats against accepting such reports, he also showed that there are better-documented descriptions of extreme teachings. Some literary works from these mystics survive, which illustrate how the ideas of these groups could lead to misunderstanding and heresy.[148]

The Council of Vienne (France, 1312) condemned eight errors with which the Beguines and Beghards were charged. These included views about perfection freeing a person from virtue so he could pursue carnal acts. Teachers cited, "Where the Spirit of the Lord is, there is freedom" (2Co 3:17) to defend their freedom from civil and ecclesiastical rules.[149]

LEGALISM AND ANTINOMIANISM

At this point, we will take a break from the history of the terms and teachers to reflect briefly on the implications of the teachings. The extreme doctrinal positions of legalism and antinomianism force one to consider the role of the Law in the Christian life. Theologians commonly hold that legalism is the idea that some form of obedience to the Law merits justification before God. Antinomianism is more difficult to describe doctrinally and historically. Scholars apply the term to numerous groups and individuals, beginning with the Gnostics of the early Christian era, eventually followed by medieval groups such as the Beguines and Beghards.

According to *The Oxford English Dictionary*, the term *antinomian*, comes from medieval Latin (*antinomi*) though obviously based on Greek terms for "opposed to the Law."[150] However, the earliest specific example of the term that I have seen is in Luther's

---

[148] See *The Heresy of the Free Spirit in the Late Middle Ages* (Berkeley: University of California Press, 1972).

[149] See J. D. Mansi, *Sacrorum Conciliorum Nova et Amplissima Collectio*, vol. XXV (Paris: Hubert, 1782), 410. According to Henry Charles, a similar group—the Brethren of the Free Spirit—resorted to passages such as Rm 8:2; Gal 5:18; 1Tm 1:9. However, he did not provide any references to concrete examples. See *A History of the Inquisition of the Middle Ages* (New York: Harper & Brothers, 1887), 2:357.

[150] Oxford: Oxford University Press, 1989.

1539 treatise *Against the Antinomians*, which we will examine in chapter thirteen. The classical rhetorician, Quintilian, wrote about *antinomia* in ancient times, which referred to conflict between laws.[151] Quintilian's term could have suggested the creation of the term *antinomian* since Quintilian was one of the classical thinkers reintroduced during the Renaissance whose writings were studied in the curriculum at Wittenberg.[152] As this paragraph shows, the history of the term itself requires further investigation.

The following table provides a list of descriptive statements about the Law, which may be helpful for considering issues of legalism and antinomianism. I have arranged the list by obligations under the Law, uses of the Law, and responses to the Law. The statements appear in Scripture and other theological writings about the doctrine of the Law, which I offer here as examples. No doubt there are other statements that could be introduced and perhaps better arrangements that could be considered.

Table 6
The Christian and the Law
The Christian is:

A. Condemned by the Law	F. Unable to use the Law
B. Bound by the Law	G. Free from the Law
C. Curbed by the Law	H. Indifferent to the Law
D. Guided by the Law	I. Opposed to the Law
E. Able to use the Law	

At what point along this list of options does one become a legalist or an antinomian? Legalism might reside at point B. But does it extend into points C through E? The matter is greatly complicated by views of sin, mankind, and the Law itself. For example, the medieval thinkers continued to write about the New Testament as a *new law*, placing their teaching under the shadow of legalism. The medieval antinomian views that the Council of Vienne condemned declared their freedom from the Law (point G on the list), which they based on

---

[151] *Institutio Oratoria* bk. 7.
[152] See *One True God: Understanding Large Catechism II.66* (St. Louis: Concordia, 2007), 51.

statements of the apostle Paul. Does orthodoxy stand somewhere between points B and G? If we were to distinguish appropriate statements about the Law and the Christian life, which ones would we choose?

The very thorough treatment of the uses of the Law provided by Thomas Aquinas does not work out these issues. One sees then some of the shortcomings of the doctrine of the Law in the medieval era, which explains why the topic of the use of the Law would become so important in the Reformation.

PETRUS AUREOLI

With Petrus Aureoli (c. 1280–1322) began a more concise way of describing the usefulness of the Law. Petrus, like Thomas Aquinas, taught at the University of Paris. He distinguished himself from other biblical interpreters because he focused on the literal sense of the text of Scripture in his *Compendium Biblie totius*.[153] In his commentary on Gal 3, Petrus introduced us to a threefold use of the Law, which he derived from and attributed to the teaching of the apostle Paul.

> Therefore he sets forth a threefold usefulness of the Law: first, for example, on account of punishment of transgressors and sinners; second, in truth, concluding all men under sin, so that by this all men would be longing for that Son of Abraham concerning whom it was promised, "In your seed all nations will be blessed," [that] is Christ; third, also introducing man to faith in Christ, because unless the Law would appear they would not have knowledge concerning Christ's coming.[154]

Petrus saw the first use in Paul's answer to the question in Gal 3:19. He saw the second use in Gal 3:22–24 where Paul used the language of imprisonment to describe how the Law declares everyone guilty.

---

[153] Argentinae: [1514].

[154] "Idcirco po[n]it tres utilitates legis. Prima[m] quide[m] / propter punitione[m] transgressor[um] & peccator[um]. Secundam v[er]o / coclusione[m] omniu[m] ho[m]i[nu]m sub peccato. ut ex hoc o[mn]es homines illu[m] filiu[m] Abraae desiderarent de quo promissum erat: In semine tuo benedicent o[mn]es gentes .s[cilicet]. Chr[istum]. Tertiam quoq[ue] / introductionem hominum ad fidem Chr[ist]i. q[uo]nia nisi lex p[ro]cessisset / non habere[n]t noticia de Chr[ist]o venturo."

Petrus's third use comes from the end of Gal 3:22 and the end of 3:23 regarding the promise of Christ's appearing. In this way, Petrus carefully enumerated the uses directly from Gal 3.

This is the earliest example of an explicit threefold use yet known.[155] This passage consolidated the manner in which Peter Lombard and Thomas Aquinas described the usefulness of the Law. Petrus Aureoli presented the civil use, theological use, and lastly the prophetic use of the Law.

NICHOLAS OF LYRA

Nicholas of Lyra (c. 1270–1340), a Franciscan scholar who also taught at the University of Paris, wrote a substantially new postil[156] commentary based on the earlier medieval glosses. Like Petrus Aureoli, Nicholas sought to interpret the text literally rather than allegorically or mystically as in other medieval commentaries.[157] His notes on 1 Tm 1:8–9 described a twofold power of the Law: regulating and constraining.[158]

In answering Paul's question at Gal 3:19, Nicholas wrote, "Here he responds to the qu[esti]on and shows the threefold usefulness of the Law."[159] Nicholas then defined three distinct uses as follows:

> First is punishment of sin, because in the Law are determined certain grave punishments for specific sins. . . . Here is set forth the second use by which man is concluded under sin, because the Law was showing [what was] sin. . . . Here is set forth the third use by which man is introduced to faith of

---

[155] This text and others were brought to the attention of modern scholars by Heinrich Denifle in *Die abendländischen Schriftausleger bis Luther über Justitia Dei (Rom. 1,17) und Justificatio* (Mainz: Kirchheim & Co., 1905), 202.

[156] A *postil* is a sermon study. Much more will be said about postils in ch. 7 and especially in ch. 14.

[157] Nicholas de Lyre, *Postilla super totam Bibliam* (de Venetiis: impensis Octaviani Scoti, 1488). Nicholas's method is thought to have significantly influenced Luther. For example, Luther's 1515 *Lectures on Romans* exhibit clear dependence upon Nicholas of Lyra's *Postilla* (see LW 25).

[158] "Lex habet vim duplice[m]. s[cilicet]. regulatinam [et] coactina[m]."

[159] "Hic respondet ad q[uaesti]onem et ostendens triplicem legis utilitatem."

Christ for which the old law had become a certain argument.¹⁶⁰

Nicholas built on the work of Petrus Aureoli's threefold use of the Law and its application to people's lives by drawing on Scripture and on the insights of earlier commentaries.¹⁶¹ Nicholas likewise presented the civil, theological, and prophetic uses in the same order. Lyra's commentary became a standard tool for interpreters in the late medieval period, one that played an important role in forming literal or plain sense approaches to reading the Bible, used by Luther and other Reformers. In view of this Heinrich Denifle concluded,

> From Lyra, of course, the author [Luther] has taken the threefold *utilitas legis*. ... Lyra himself, however, was dependent in this on Petrus Aureoli.¹⁶²

CONCLUSION

The medieval theologians drew on the classical, biblical, and patristic traditions when writing about the use of human laws and the divine law. The patristic writers had made distinctions but did not settle on specific and consistent terminology. Nor had they provided systematic treatment of the topic. It appears that the careful enumeration of the usefulness of the Law of Moses began at the University of Paris in the thirteenth century, some two hundred years before Luther and Melanchthon. The medieval writers came to list three or four uses of the Law of Moses.

---

[160] "Prima est punitio peccatoru[m]. quia in lege determinantar certe [et] graves pene pro determinatis peccatis. . . . Hic ponitur secunda utilitas que est hominum conclusio sub peccato. quia lex peccatum ostendebat. . . . Hic ponit[ur] tertia utilitas que e[st] introductio ho[min]um ad fid[em] christi ad qua[m] lex vetus fuit queda[m] dispositio."

[161] According to Denifle, Johannes de Casali (1320–post 1375) also wrote about a threefold use of the Law in his *Lectura super epistolas S. Pauli*, which are not available to me. Denifle 202, n. 2.

[162] "Aus Lyra hat nämlich der Autor die dreifache utilitas legis genommen. . . . Lyra selbst war aber hierin abhängig von Pet. Aureoli" (p. 202). Denifle published his research in the era when Luther scholars such as Kawerau supported the idea that Luther taught a threefold use of the Law. The next generation of scholars, such as Elert and Ebeling, somehow missed this historical insight as they worked to establish the two uses consensus.

The medieval glosses supplied everything necessary for the Reformation era doctrine of the Law: (1) biblical basis, (2) distinction of uses, (3) introduction of technical terms, and (4) enumeration of uses. This is evidence that a mature doctrine of the use of the Law predated the Reformation.[163] In view of this, the Reformers did not create a new doctrinal category. They interacted with deep, carefully considered teachings of earlier theologians.

The medieval theologians also consistently presented a prophetic use of the Law, noting that the Law of Moses proclaimed the coming of Christ. For them there was no contradiction in speaking of "the Law of the Gospel" or of describing the New Testament as a new law. However, these ways of speaking contributed to confusion about the doctrines of repentance and justification, which sparked the Reformation.

Alongside the tradition of the biblical commentaries was the study of canon law, which introduced the term "office of the Law" as another way of speaking about the purpose, function, effect, or use of the Law. Given all that we have seen in the writings of patristic and medieval theologians, it is perhaps best to summarize the various terms they use:

---

[163] It seems that the medieval exegetical tradition preserved and defined the doctrine of the usefulness of the Law. The doctrine did not receive the same emphasis in the dogmatic tradition. If these observations prove true, they could explain why modern scholars did not recognize that Luther drew his views from earlier theologians since modern scholars have tended to focus on the dogmatic writings for creating histories of doctrine. Gabriel Biel (d. 1495) wrote about the Law in his commentary on Peter Lombard's *Sentences*. See *Collectorium circa quattuor libros Sententiarum*, Wilfridus Werbeck and Udo Hofmann, eds. (Tübingen: J. C. B. Mohr, 1979), Book III, Dists. 37 and 40. His comments do not clearly anticipate the Reformation doctrine of the use of the Law. Johann von Staupitz, Luther's mentor in the Augustinian Order, does not appear to have written on the doctrine of the use of the Law. A summary of von Staupitz's teaching is provided by Franz Posset, *The Front-Runner of the Catholic Reformation: The Life and Works of Johann von Staupitz* (Hants, England: Ashgate Publishing Limited, 2003), 303–304.

Table 7
Medieval Terms for the Usefulness of the Law

work of the Law	*opus legis*
usefulness of the Law	*utilitas legis*
office of the Law	*officium legis*
cause or purpose of the Law	*causa legis*
effect of the Law	*effectus legis*
power of the Law	*vis legis*

Most of these terms focus on what the Law does to the person who hears it, which typically describes curbing or accusing actions of the Law toward sinners. The expression "usefulness of the Law" seems unique in that it focuses on the benefit the hearer receives or derives from the Law. This term is best positioned for describing positively the role the Law served before the appearing of Christ and before the reception of the Gospel. It is a much more friendly term, which could even describe the believer's ongoing use of the Law. As the next chapter will show, Luther employs the medieval terms but two of them become favorites for him.

We also saw that Peter Lombard picked up the expression of Ambrosiaster and Augustine to write about the righteous man being a friend of the Law. Peter contributed interestingly to this expression by describing the righteous man's new relationship with the Law. Rather than fear the Law, the righteous man has a respect for the Law that keeps him from violating it, as he would not want to hurt the feelings of a friend.

PART TWO

THE REFORMATION

CHAPTER SEVEN

LUTHER'S EARLIEST TEACHING (1515–22)

We see threefold use of the Law, that is, mankind conducts itself in three ways with reference to it.

—Martin Luther

The Law plays a leading role in the life and teaching of Martin Luther. We do well to remember that Luther's father wanted him to study law as a career and sent him to the University of Erfurt for that purpose. So, from home as well as from school, friary, and ultimately from Scripture, Luther was made a companion of the Law, though it would seem, not a friend of the Law in those early days. Modern biographies of Luther pay special attention to Luther's fear and anxiety (Ger. *Anfechtung*) and rightly so. These were effects that the Law had on Luther and not simply features of his personality.[164] The Law, as we have seen, is not a friend of sinners and has no power to give life or righteousness (Gal 3:21). Even so, Luther would learn that the Law is very useful.

In 1509, 1510/11, and 1516, Luther had opportunity to learn about the usefulness of the Law in his studies of Augustine, Peter

---

[164] The tendency of modern biography to psychoanalyze historical figures who are removed from the biographer by hundreds of years seems problematic and itself worthy of analysis.

Lombard, medieval glosses on Paul's Letter to the Galatians,[165] and perhaps other theological writings. Wengert wrote that Luther's earliest expression for the use of the Law came in 1521.[166] However, now that we better understand the ancient and medieval teaching, we may see the matter differently.

THE USEFULNESS OF THE LAW

In Luther's *Scholia* on Romans (c. late 1515), he showed his debt to Paul and to the medieval theology of the use of the Law. In commenting on Rm 3:20, a classic passage for defining the theological use of the Law, Luther wrote:

> Through the Law comes the knowledge of sin. This knowledge through the Law comes in two ways, first, through contemplation, as we read below in chapter 7:7, "I should not have known what it is to covet if the Law had not said, 'You shall not covet.'" Second, through experience, that is, through the work of the Law, or through the Law that has been adopted together with the work. For in this way the Law becomes an occasion for sinning, since the will of man which is prone to evil is driven toward the good through the Law and thus becomes disinclined toward the good and tired of trying to do good, because it hates to give up what it loves, and it loves evil, as Scripture says. But yet, if it works and does what it is unwilling to do, compelled by the Law, then man understands how deeply sin and evil are rooted in him, which he would not have understood if he did not have the Law and had not attempted to work in accordance with it. . . . Here he is satisfied with briefly answering the objection that the Law is not of any use because the works of the Law do not justify. . . . The Law . . . prescribes good works and forbids evil. For if we were righteous and good, we would consent to the Law with ready will and delight in it, just as we now delight in our sins and evil desires. Hence: "Oh, how I love Thy Law!" (Ps. 119:97) and again: "But his delight is

---

[165] Kurt Aland, ed. *Hilfsbuch zum Lutherstudium* 4th ed. (Bielefeld: Luther-Verlag, 1996) lists collections of Luther's marginal notes on these texts during those years.
[166] See above, p. 8.

in the law of the Lord" (Ps. 1:2). Behold, thus it has come to pass that through the Law there is knowledge of the sin which is in us, that is, of our evil will which inclines toward the evil and abhors the good. How useful this knowledge is! For he who recognizes it, cries to God and in humility begs that this will may be lifted up and healed.[167]

In this passage Luther had the terms "work of the Law" (*opus legis*; Rm 2:15) and "useful" (*quod non inutilis sit*; also *utilis*). He was relating Paul's "work of the Law" to the medieval term "usefulness of the Law" (*utilitas legis*) in describing the theological use of the Law. The 1515/16 *Lectures on Romans* demonstrate Luther's theological maturation and how the doctrine of the Law stands with the doctrine of the Gospel.[168]

In the *Scholia* on Rm 5:20, Luther returned to consideration of the Law's purpose.

> Therefore he says *that sin might abound*. This expression is not causal but consecutive, because the conjunction "that" (ut) refers to what follows and not to the final cause of the Law.[169] For the Law did not come because of sin, although he also says this in Gal. 3:19: "Why then the Law? It was added because of transgressions, till the seed should come to whom He made the promise." ... Hence blessed Augustine in the above-mentioned book on the *Propositions*[170] of this letter says: "By this very word he has shown that the Jews did not understand the purpose for which the Law was given. For it was not given that it might give life—for grace alone through faith gives life—but it was given to show by how many tight bonds of sin they are held who presume to fulfill the Law by their own powers."[171]

Luther was following Augustine in his exposition and in emphasizing the theological use of the Law. He referred to the text of Augustine in

---

[167] LW 25:240; WA 56:253–54. See also my epilogue, p. 255.
[168] Robert Kolb, *Martin Luther: Confessor of the Faith* (Oxford: Oxford University Press, 2009), p. 51.
[169] "causam finalem legis." Cf. Thomas's term *causa* to describe uses of the Law.
[170] PL 35:2068.
[171] LW 25:306–307; WA 56:319.

which he described the four stages of man that, we will see, became important in shaping Luther's thought.

In Luther's *Scholia* on Rm 14:1, there are helpful comments on 1 Tm 1.[172] Luther linked the chapter to numerous other comments from Paul about the abrogation of Jewish laws and observances, including practices from the Law of Moses. Luther made it clear that Paul's opponents in 1 Tm 1 were Jewish teachers who insisted on the necessity of fulfilling legal requirements for salvation. (This scholion provides helpful background for understanding Luther's later exposition of 1 Tm, which will be treated in chapter nine.)

In this same scholion, Luther also mentioned the excesses of a medieval antinomian movement, the "Picards,"[173] who emphasized the abrogation of rules and practices. Luther wrote:

> The answer is that it is true on the basis of the new law that none of these things is necessary, but not in such a way that when one thing has been omitted it is permissible to do the opposite or something entirely different. . . . Therefore, as it was foolish at that time to give so much weight to these matters that they became matters of salvation, while both faith and love, which alone are sufficient, were neglected (this was completely in opposition to Christ, so that He said in Matt. 23:24: "You strain at a gnat and swallow a camel"), so also in our day and at all times it is both foolish and preposterous to make the Christian religion synonymous outwardly with these displays (as is the custom in our time) with distinctions of feast days, meats, dress, and holy places, while in the meantime the commandments of God are rejected along with faith and love.

> Hence although all of these things are now matters of the greatest liberty, yet out of love for God each is permitted to bind himself by oath to this or that goal. But he is thereby no longer bound to these matters by the new law but by his own oath, which he has taken upon himself by reason of his love for God. For who is so foolish as to deny that a person can

---

[172] LW 25:485–88.

[173] This is Luther's spelling for the *Beghards*, part of the lay religious group charged with Free Spirit teachings that are described as antinomian in modern scholarship. See pp. 62–66.

give up his liberty out of deference to another person and make himself a servant and bind himself to a certain place on such and such a day with such and such a work? But this must be done out of love and the faith that does not believe that he is doing these things as necessary for salvation but only of his own free will and out of a sense of freedom.[174]

In contrast to the Picards, Luther emphasized that Christian freedom led one in love to bind himself by oath in service to others. Christian faith, love, and status before God led to deference for others. The commandments did not disappear.

It is worth noting that very few Beguines and Beghards became involved in the Reformation.[175] Although some writers have charged that Antinomianism was an inherent consequence of Luther's theology,[176] the facts of history speak against this. Luther rejected Antinomian views from the start and did not attract the medieval mystical groups who had been involved in Antinomianism.

Luther still used the medieval expression "new law" (*nova lex*) to describe the New Testament though his understanding of the distinction between Law and Gospel was already at work. His well balanced comments about voluntary faith and love leading to good works fit well with the arguments he would provide in *On the Freedom of the Christian* (1520).

In the 1516/17 gloss of Luther's first *Lectures on Galatians*, he provided a heading for the third chapter as follows,

> The Galatians are rebuked and the apostle, showing the imperfection of the Law of Moses, says that righteousness is by faith, though having to be bound with the usefulness of the Law.[177]

---

[174] LW 25:488–90.
[175] See Simon 221, n. 11.
[176] See e.g., Frances Aveling's article on "Antinomianism" in *The Catholic Encyclopedia: An International work of Reference on the Constitution, Doctrine, Discipline, and History of the Catholic Church*, 15 vols., Herbermann, Charles G. et al. eds. (New York: The Encyclopedia Press, 1907), 564.
[177] WA 57 II:20. "Increpantur Galat<h>ae ac ostendens apostolus imperfectionem legis Mosaicae dicit iusticiam esse ex fide: annectendo legis utilitatem."

Here one sees again Luther's Law and Gospel distinction as well as the use of the Law within that distinction. At another point in the chapter, Luther provided a second reference to the use of the Law. Regarding Paul's question in Galatians 3:19 Luther wrote, "He himself abandons the motive of others. For the Law appears unnecessary, indeed unuseful, if it does not justify."[178]

Luther inherited his understanding of the use of the Law from the enduring influence of Paul in western theology and from ancient and medieval commentary on Paul's letters. Like earlier theologians, Luther cited 1 Tm 1:8–9 as a key to interpreting Galatians.[179] He also wrote about the abrogation of the Law of Moses in contrast to the enduring role of natural law.

Another early reference to the usefulness of the Law appeared in the 1519 *Lectures on Galatians* where Luther provided a detailed explanation for how the Law increases transgression. Luther asked, "Who would ever have expected such an answer, one that is certainly opposed to all who are wont to speak intelligently about the usefulness of the Law?"[180] He followed with a long argument from associating Gal 3:19 with Rm 5:20, interacting with the interpretation of Jerome, whose commentary on Galatians focused on the civil use of the Law when answering Paul's question of Gal 3:19.[181]

We find Luther working with three categories of Law from Scholasticism: natural law, the written law (Moses), and the law of the Gospel. He also commonly distinguished moral law and ceremonial law. He filled his work with the common medieval distinctions.

Also in the 1519 *Lectures on Galatians*, we find Luther drawing on the now familiar idea of a change in status with respect to the Law. We have seen the beginnings of this idea in the first century teachers: Jesus, Philo, and Paul. We have also seen the idea of friendship with the Law in Ambrosiaster, Augustine, and Peter Lombard. Luther, too, used this idea and expression. He wrote:

> We are not free from the Law (as I have said above) in a human way, by which the Law is destroyed and changed, but

---

[178] WA 57 II:26. "Obicit sibi ipsi aliorum motivum: videtur enim lex superflua, immo inutilis, si non iustificat."

[179] WA 57 II: 43, 72, 74, 105.

[180] LW 27:269; WA 2:522 has *de utilitate legum*.

[181] Cf. Peter Lombard's emphasis on Romans 5:20, p. 59 above.

in a divine and theological way, by which we are changed and from enemies of the Law are made friends of the Law.[182]

Luther fully embraced this idea that the Law endures for the righteous man but that his relationship to the Law is different by grace through faith in Christ. The Christian is free from the Law in a divine and theological way since Christ has redeemed him. The Law does not change, that is, the natural and moral law that are constant. Instead, God changes us with His good gifts and Spirit.

In 1521 Luther wrote about the "office of the Law,"[183] the expression that he would consistently use interchangeably with "use of the Law" in later writings. Melanchthon used the expression earlier in his 1521 *Loci Communes*.[184] As noted in the previous chapter, the same expression appeared in the first pages of Gratian's *Decretum*, which Luther and Melanchthon would have read early in their careers.[185] It appears that Luther or Melanchthon adapted this term from canon law for describing the uses and effects of the Law of Moses.

Luther's terms "usefulness of the Law" (*utilitas legis*) and "function of the Law" (*officium legis*) show the influence of medieval commentators and canon law on his theological development. They were foundational to his doctrine of the Law.

THREEFOLD USE OF THE LAW

In the *Christmas Postil* (*Weihnachtspostille*) of 1522,[186] Luther provided his most extensive early comments on the use of the Law. The elector commissioned these postils to guide evangelical preachers. WA 10/I.1:VIII–IX lists 26 printings of German editions (1522–1544) and two printings of Martin Bucer's Latin translation (1525 and 1526). In other words, these postils were among Luther's

---

[182] LW 27:347.
[183] *Judgment on Monastic Vows* (1521) LW 44:302.
[184] See pp. 191–92.
[185] See pp. 57–58. Luther purchased a copy of *corpus iuris canonici* in 1505 when he began study of canon law. Ironically, he burned volumes of canon law after Roman officials began burning his books. See E. G. Schwiebert, *Luther and His Times* (St. Louis: Concordia, 1950), 20.
[186] For an explanation of postils, see p. 164.

most widely distributed—and therefore influential—writings. They were in constant use throughout Lutheran regions.

Historians of doctrine have focused on a portion of Luther's 1522 postil that described a twofold use of the Law;[187] they have largely neglected or not understood a most significant passage where Luther wrote explicitly about a "threefold use of the Law":[188] Luther's sermon for New Year's Day on Gal 3:23–29.

> We see three attitudes toward the Law; that is, mankind conducts itself in three ways with reference to it. Some regard it utterly, and boldly oppose it by a dissolute life. To them it is practically no Law. Others because of the Law refrain from such a course and are preserved to an honorable life. But while outwardly they live within the Law's prohibitions, inwardly they are enemies of this their tutor. The motive of all their conduct is the fear of death and hell. They keep the Law only externally; rather, it keeps them externally. Inwardly they neither keep it nor are kept by it. The third class observe it both externally and with the heart. This class is the tables of Moses, written upon outwardly and inwardly by the finger of God himself.

The Lenker edition, cited here, obscured Luther's reference to the use of the Law. Luther began the passage with the expression "threefold use of the Law" (*dreyerley brauch des gesetzes*), which is the German equivalent to Nicholas of Lyra's *triplicem legis utilitatem*. Luther provided a much more extensive explanation of the insight as it

---

[187] See e.g., Ebeling, *Word and Faith* 64.

[188] *Church Postil*, Lenker 6:272–274; WA 10/I.1:457–58. Legal historian, John Witte, Jr., has written, "Luther also touched lightly on a third use of the law. This use, grounded in St. Paul's discussion of the law as 'our schoolmaster to bring us unto Christ' (Galatians 3:24), became known in the Protestant world as the "educational,' 'didactical,' or 'pedagogical' use of the law. Law, in this sense, serves to teach the faithful, those who have already been justified by faith, the good works that please God. Luther recognized this concept without explicitly expounding a doctrine of the third use of the law. He recognized that sermons, commentaries, and catechism lessons of the many Old Testament passages on law are directed, in no small part, to teaching the faithful the meaning of God's law." *Law and Protestantism: The Legal Teachings of the Lutheran Reformation* (Cambridge: Cambridge University Press, 2002), 103–104.

related to Gal 3 and broader Pauline theology. However, before considering more of the passage, a closer examination of the history of its interpretation is needed.

EBELING'S ASSESSMENT

Ebeling was well aware of WA 10/I.1:456, line 8–457, line 13 as a potential source for the Reformation doctrine of a third use of the Law. However, he dismissed a connection between Luther's teaching here and the dogmatic tradition about a third use. He wrote,

> The threefold use of the law which Luther speaks of here, bears solely on the question of fulfilling the law. . . . Luther expressly describes this third method in a way that excludes the *tertius usus legis* as Melanchthon understands it. . . . This distinction of a threefold use of the law is only inserted by Luther in the form of a parenthesis in a context where the real topic is as plainly as may be the *duplex usus legis*, in the sense that there are said to be "two things for which the law is necessary and good, and which God expects of it." . . . Our conclusion therefore is, that the formula "threefold use of the law" is indeed found in Luther for the first time, yet it only expresses a passing thought and is then dropped again, while at the same time the doctrine of a twofold use of the law is already established in essence and still awaits only its final conceptual formulation.[189]

Note well that Ebeling assessed the passage based on what came later—Melanchthon's understanding—rather than broader history in western Christian thought. Ebeling was not aware of the medieval tradition on teaching the use of the Law. It was inappropriate for him to dismiss the passage because it did not speak in the same manner as Melanchthon or later dogmatic theologians. Ebeling's focus on finding the mature dogmatic expression for the Reformation prevented him from focusing on how Luther taught the doctrine of the Law.

Ebeling also characterized Luther's threefold teaching as "the form of a parenthesis," which allowed him to dismiss its importance. Yet it is noteworthy that other historians have characterized 1521–22

---

[189] *Word and Faith* 64–65.

as especially important for Luther's development of the doctrine of the Law and the distinction between Law and Gospel.[190]

There is a further element missing from Ebeling's analysis. He focused the reader's attention on two of Luther's statements that, outside of their context, might cause the reader to conclude that the righteous man had nothing to do with the Law: "Here is no Moses . . . here are those unto whom there is no law."[191] With this focus, Ebeling made it sound as though the righteous man is lawless in Luther's thought. He gives the impression that Luther left the Law out of his third category of mankind. The analysis below will demonstrate that this is not at all the case.

Ebeling's assessment did provide helpful caveats. For example, earlier in the text Luther did indicate that he would write about two responses to the Law.[192] Ebeling was right to note that within the passage Luther distinguished what "God expects of [the Law]" and what mankind does with the Law. The following table summarizes Luther's teaching in the passage.

Table 8
Divine and Human Uses of the Law (1522)

Divine use one:	To preserve discipline among us
Divine use two:	To know yourself and be humbled
Human (mis)use one:	Bold opposition by a dissolute life
Human (mis)use two:	Outward keeping of the law, being kept by the Law
Human use three:	Keeping the Law both outwardly and inwardly

Modern scholarship, influenced by the dogmatic tradition has tended to describe only divine use of the Law: how the Holy Spirit uses the

---

[190] See e.g., Bernhard Lohse, *Martin Luther: An Introduction to His Life and Work* Robert C. Schultz, trans. (Philadelphia: Fortress Press, 1986), 52. Lohse explained that the conflict with Karlstadt in the winter of 1521–22 caused Luther to reflect deeply on the uses of the Law and the dialectical relationship between Law and Gospel. He saw Luther writing especially about the civil use of the Law at this time.

[191] Lenker 6:274; WA 10/I.1:458; Ebeling, *Word and Faith* 64.

[192] "Alszo sehen wyr disze tzwey stuck auch ynn allen menschen." WA 10/I.1:452. The Lenker translation added the heading, "The Office of the Law." Lenker 6:270.

Law in a person's life. However, in this passage Luther clearly had in mind how mankind uses and misuses the Law, which was a topic for earlier theologians as found in the *Glossa Ordinaria*[193] and even St. Paul in 1 Tm 1:8–9. As we shall see, Luther wrote about the divine and human uses of the Law alongside one another throughout his career.

Since Luther did not explicitly enumerate a third divine use in the passage, Ebeling rejected it as an example of teaching a third use. However, not all scholars agreed fully with Ebeling's assessment. In the critical edition of the Lutheran Confessions one finds reference to WA 10/I.1:457, line 2–458, line 18 followed by the word "triplex," meaning that this passage from the *Weihnachtspostille* taught a threefold use of the Law.[194] One must also bear in mind the earlier scholarly consensus of Kawerau, Seeberg, Loofs, and Aner,[195] who were doing their research and writing at about the same time Denifle published his research about the medieval "threefold usefulness of the Law" (*triplex legis utilitatas*).[196]

Readers should note the fact that Luther did provide three positive statements of the Law's use, with the third being use of the Law by the believer. There is also a divine action under this third category, "This class is the tables of Moses, written upon outwardly and inwardly by the finger of God himself."[197] Luther remarkably described the believer's outward life and inward heart as the "tables of Moses," making the righteous man an embodiment of the divine Law. He followed with extensive comment on mankind's use and abuse of the Law, which also requires careful assessment since Luther continued to comment on the use of the Law throughout the passage.

THE PATTERN OF LUTHER'S TEACHING

Luther's dialectical and rhetorical argument in the postil is to present a contrast between those who misuse God's Law and those who use it properly. He first described three classes of mankind that use or

---

[193] See p. 57.
[194] See *Die Bekenntnisschriften der evangelisch-lutherische Kirche*, 10th ed. (Göttingen: Vanderhoeck & Ruprecht, 1986), 962, n. 2.
[195] See p. VI.
[196] See p. 68.
[197] Lenker 6:273.

misuse the Law (WA 10/I.1:456, line 19–457, line 13). He then repeated the teaching by illustrating it with an extended analogy based on Israel's responses to the Law of Moses (WA 10/I.1:457, line 14–458, line 14). We shall consider these passages in order, beginning with the description of the three classes of mankind.

> The first class are righteous neither without nor within; the second are only outwardly pious and not in heart; but the third are thoroughly righteous. Upon this point Paul says (1 Tim 1, 8), "But we know that the Law is good, if a man use it lawfully." But in what way is it lawfully used? I answer, "Law is not made for a righteous man, but for the lawless" (verse 9). And what are we to understand by that? Simply that he who would preach the Law aright must be governed by these three classes. He must not by any means preach the Law to the third class as an instrument of righteousness;[198] this were perversion. But to the first class such preaching is in order. For them is the Law instituted. Its object is that they may forsake their dissolute life and yield themselves to the preserving power of their tutor. However, it is not enough for them to be guarded and kept by the Law; they must learn also to keep it. So, in addition to the Law and beyond it, the Gospel must be preached, through which is given the grace of Christ to keep the former. There is a considerable difference between observing the Law and being preserved by it; between keeping and being kept. The first class neither keep it nor are kept; the second are kept; and the third keep it.[199]

Luther emphasized the three classes as a guide to preachers. Knowing the audience(s) would help the preacher proclaim the Law appropriately. There is also some correspondence in his three categories with the first three categories of Augustine's stages of man: before the Law, under the Law, and under grace. However, we shall see next that Luther was not working in exactly the same way as Augustine.

Luther then followed with his biblical analogy. Here again, the Lenker translation hid Luther's theological term "use of the Law."

---

[198] Cf. warnings in *Glossa Ordinaria* and Peter's *Glossa Magnatura*.
[199] *Church Postil*, Lenker 6:273; WA 10/I.1:456–457.

Luther literally introduced the analogy as "three attitudes toward the use of the Law" (*drey weyse am brauch des gesetzs*). This refers to the three ways mankind uses the Law.

> These three attitudes of mankind toward the [use of the] Law are prefigured in certain acts of Moses. First, where he broke the tablets when the Jews worshiped the golden calf. Ex 32, 19. The breaking of the tables, and the people's consequent failure to receive them, suggest the first class, who do not receive the Law at all, but break it. Second, Moses brought other tables, which were received by the people and the skin of his face shone, but Aaron and the Israelites could not endure the shining of Moses' face, and he was compelled to cover it with a veil when he would speak to them. Ex 34, 30–33. Here is suggested the second class, who receive the Law but only for outward observance. With them it is too bright for inward obedience; they are afraid of it.
>
> Hypocrites make for themselves a veil, as Paul explains (2 Cor 3, 13–15)—the arrogance of their works, of their external righteousness. They will not look the Law squarely in the face and see how futile is their righteousness. As Paul says, to this very day the veil is upon their hearts.
>
> Then, too, Moses leads the people no farther than to the Jordan, slays only two kings—Sihon and Og—and gives only two and a half tribes of Israel their portion of the land. Here is illustrated half-hearted righteousness; insignificant, outward righteousness. Then, there in the wilderness of Moab, Moses dies; the Law can go no farther.
>
> Now, third: Joshua succeeds Moses and leads the whole multitude dry-shod through the Jordan, into all parts of the promised land. There is now no Moses, no Law; only Joshua, Christ, who leads by faith and fulfills all Moses' commandments. Thus is suggested the class to whom no Law is given, as Paul says,[200] and who becomes righteous, not through works, but through grace; that is, their good works are not performed through constraint of the Law. Moses is not

---

[200] 1 Tm 1:8–9.

in evidence with them. With all this explanation, Paul should, I think, be easily understood in this lesson.[201]

Luther's analogy portrayed a time when the Law is given (twice under Moses) and a time when the Law of Moses is not given, the time of Joshua when the Law is fulfilled by faith. Luther's understanding of the "time of the Law" is important for understanding how he wrote about the use of the Law of Moses, especially as he interpreted Gal 3.

As stated above, Luther's analogy here is somewhat different from Augustine's stages of mankind. First, Luther used a purely Old Testament analogy whereas Augustine's third category reached into the New Testament, though one should note that Luther has Joshua as a type of Christ and that the life associated with the third category is "through grace" (Augustine had "under grace").

Second, when Luther said that there is no Law for the third category, he meant that there is no Law of Moses given to them. That is, the ceremonial and civil laws given through Moses, which were intended to constrain the people. Luther did not say that in the third attitude toward the use of the Law people are suddenly lawless. On the contrary, he wrote of them now keeping the Law and of them receiving grace for that purpose. In other words, "Moses is not in evidence with them" because they are not constrained by the ceremonial and civil laws of Moses. Nevertheless, they now keep the natural, moral law[202] that is always with them.[203] They do this not from constraint but willingly and by grace, which distinguishes their lives, works, and status with respect to the Law. "Christ . . . fulfills all Moses' commandments." They are righteous through Christ and learn from Him, by grace, "also to keep it [the Law]. So in addition to the Law and beyond it, the Gospel must be preached, through which is given the grace of Christ to keep the former."

---

[201] *Church Postil*, Lenker 6:273–274; WA 10/I.1:457–458.
[202] Luther learned these distinctions from Scholasticism (Peter Lombard, PL 192:838; Gabriel Biel, Book III Dist. 37H and 40A). They are in use during the 1519 *Lectures on Galatians*.
[203] A look through Ebeling's articles reveals no mention of the natural law or a description of what Luther meant by "Moses" or the "Law of Moses." The references to Moses in the article are in the brief quotations from Luther on p. 64 of *Word and Faith*.

Distinguishing when Luther used "Law" to mean the constraint of the ceremonial and civil laws given by Moses and when he meant the enduring natural and moral Law of God is essential for correctly interpreting the passage. At times, "Moses" means "constraint." Otherwise, one lands in a contradiction where the righteous man is keeping the Law and hearing it preached to him though he does not really have the Law. An overly literal reading of "There is no Moses, no Law," which does not account for Luther's rhetoric and distinctions leads to misinterpretation and an only-two-uses theology.[204]

As noted above, Ebeling emphasized that all Luther's discussion of the threefold use of the Law occurs in the context of his teaching about two offices or uses of the Law. But Ebeling did not describe the larger dialectical and rhetorical pattern of Luther's teaching, which is summarized in Table 9 below.

Table 9
Luther's Pattern of Teaching on the Law (1522)
First divine use
Second divine use
    First human misuse
    Second human misuse
Third human use by grace in Christ
Analogy repeating earlier points

Because Luther described the use of the Law with a contrast, he naturally divided his teaching about the third use of the Law from the

---

[204] Luther's 1523 treatise on *Temporal Authority* makes this clear as well, where he wrote, "For [Christ] is a king over Christians and rules by his Holy Spirit alone, without law. Although he sanctions the sword, he did not make use of it, for it serves no purpose in his kingdom, in which there are none but the upright. . . . Christ, without constraint and force, without law and sword, was to have a people who would serve him willingly. . . . Those who do not believe are not Christians; they do not belong to Christ's kingdom, but to the worldly kingdom where they are constrained and governed by the sword and by outward rule. Christians do every good thing of their own accord and without constraint, and find God's word alone sufficient for them" (LW 45:93, 118). Luther's phrase "without constraint" is key for understanding the difference between the civil use of the Law and the righteous man's use of the Law.

first two uses. As we explore later passages from Luther in the following chapters, we shall watch for this contrast and pattern of teaching.[205]

THE TERM THIRD USE OF THE LAW

Ebeling supplied one more necessary point to make on Luther's postil sermon on Gal 3:23–29. He noted that Bucer translated the 1522 *Christmas Postil* with the expression "threefold use of the Law" (*triplex usus legis*). His Latin translation appeared in 1525.[206] Ebeling was right to point out that this was the earliest appearance of *usus legis* noted in his day. This was the term Luther would later use in his 1531 Galatians lectures and that Melanchthon would use in the 1535 *Loci Communes*.[207] In my research, I recently discovered an earlier appearance of "use of the Law." (See p. 255.)

Since Luther delivered his Galatians lectures in Latin and Melanchthon wrote the *Loci* in Latin, it is tempting to conclude that they consulted Bucer's Latin translation of Luther's postil on Galatians and so settled on the term "use of the Law" (*usus legis*) rather than the ancient and medieval "usefulness of the Law" (*utilitas legis*). Yet one must hold out the possibility that a medieval theologian coined the term *usus legis*. In chapter sixteen, at the end of the survey of Luther's writings, I will supply a survey showing that Luther used the medieval terms and "use of the Law" together and interchangeably.[208]

Advocates of the only-two-uses consensus have tended to see something only negative and threatening about the Law, which was how Luther and genuine Lutherans must think about the matter.

---

[205] Cf. also the progression in the *Glossa Ordinaria* for 1 Tm 1:8–9, where two purposes of the Law are plainly presented, followed by digression on human need for and use of the Law.

[206] *Word and Faith* 62–63. WA 10/I.1:456, Latin n. 3; 457, Latin n. 2.

[207] Desiderius Erasmus (c. 1469–1536) used the term *usus legis* in later commentaries but I have not determined when the expression first appeared in his writings since a limited number of editions are available to me. Erasmus's *In epistolam Pauli ad Galatas Paraphrasis* (Argentina, 1520), 49, included awareness of the medieval expression *utilitas legis*; see also the 1522 *Paraphrases in Novum Testamentum* (*Opera Omnia* [Lugduni: Petri Vander, 1706], 954).

[208] See pp. 176–77.

Certainly Luther taught about the threatening character of the Law but he also drew upon the longer tradition of seeing the "usefulness" or "benefit" God intended through the Law. When one appropriately uses the Law, benefit results. By grace through faith, the one declared righteous in Christ sees that God indeed intended the Law for our good.

As in earlier writers, one can also see here in Luther that the righteous man has a new status and attitude toward God's natural and moral law. Before grace, he is in violation of the Law or constrained by it with fear. After receiving grace, his attitude toward the Law is changed. He does not act from constraint but willingly. He is changed from an enemy of the Law into a friend of the Law.

CONCLUSION

Luther did not introduce the doctrine of the use of the Law to Christian theology nor was he the first theologian to enumerate three uses of the Law as historians of doctrine have asserted. Luther taught about the usefulness of the Law in substantial agreement with earlier commentators. His terminology and order of uses stem directly from his predecessors. However, unlike Petrus Aureoli and Nicholas of Lyra, Luther adjusted the third use of the Law from being a prophetic use, announcing the coming of Christ, to include the righteous man's use of the Law. He emphasized that justification changed the believer's attitude toward and use of the Law of Moses so that the believer no longer keeps the Law from compulsion. The Law, kept by Christ, could now be kept by those who were righteous through Christ, an insight noted in the *Glossa Ordinaria* on 1 Tm 1:8–9. The believer has a new status by grace through faith so that he may now look upon the natural, moral law as a friend. He becomes a living tables of Moses and keeps the Law both inwardly and outwardly without constraint.

Although Luther enhanced the prophetic use from the list of uses taught by Petrus, Nicholas, and others, he did not abandon the prophetic use. For the sake of clarity, Luther would eventually re-label the prophetic use as "promise" and ultimately as "Gospel." We may see in these changes the significance of the doctrine of the use of the Law to the refinement of the Law and Gospel distinction.[209] Whereas scholastic theologians had consistently written about "the Law of the Gospel" or the New Testament as "the new law," Luther would see the need to clearly distinguish and label the doctrines of Law and Gospel in order to distinguish the doctrines of justification and sanctification. Subsequent chapters will document Luther's growth in these teachings.

---

[209] The distinction, of course, has independent existence from the enumeration of uses of the Law, and deep roots in Pauline and western theology.

CHAPTER EIGHT

REGARD FOR MOSES (1522–25)

The third kind of pupils are those who see Moses clearly, without a veil.

—Martin Luther

Martin Luther and Andreas Karlstadt were colleagues for nearly ten years at Wittenberg. Karlstadt installed Luther as a professor of theology and Bible in 1512. As a Thomistic and Scotist theologian, Karlstadt at first opposed Luther's new approach to theology. However, Luther's great knowledge of Scripture deeply impressed him. Karlstadt devoted himself also to studying Scripture and Luther's views soon won him over. Karlstadt came to see himself as a founder and contributor to the reforms.

By the 1520's important differences between the colleagues began to appear. Among the most important differences was that Karlstadt tended to read the Law of Moses as though it literally applied to Christians in the present whereas Luther emphasized that God gave the Law of Moses especially for Israel. Both men regarded the New Testament in Christ as a fulfillment of the Law but Karlstadt chose aspects of the ceremonial and civil laws of Moses and sought to apply them in Wittenberg.

While Luther was in hiding at the Wartburg in 1522, Karlstadt enacted his vision for reform in Wittenberg. This included destruction of images and altars, which zealous followers carried out in a violent manner. The disturbance of the peace frightened many people at Wittenberg who believed that the Reformers were wrong or were moving too fast. When Luther received news of these drastic changes and the appeal from the Wittenberg church that he would return as their preacher, he slipped out of the Wartburg and set out to restore order. After confronting Karlstadt and his associates, Luther preached a series of Lenten sermons that focused on facing death, maintaining order, and love for weaker brothers who were not ready for change. His sermons about the place of the Law and patience in the Christian life calmed the people of Wittenberg and restored the peace.

The previous chapter demonstrated that Luther introduced the doctrine of a threefold use of the Law to the Reformation. A further matter to consider is how deeply Luther held this doctrine or whether he abandoned it in favor of only two uses of the Law. Ebeling argued for two uses when he wrote that Luther used the term first but in passing, dropping it from his theological vocabulary.[210] But as noted, Ebeling had not understood the ancient and medieval background for the doctrine of the use of the Law. In this chapter we will begin to test the depth of Luther's commitment to a threefold use.

THREEFOLD CATEGORIES

We have already seen in chapter five that Augustine drew from the Book of Romans four stages of man, the first three of which correspond somewhat to the typical three uses of the Law and the last of which describes the peace associated with everlasting life. The medieval teachers received Augustine's teaching and further disseminated it. As a student of Scholasticism, Luther learned to think about the Law in a threefold way. For example, he learned that there were three types of precepts in the Law of Moses: civil, ceremonial, and moral.[211] He also learned about three types of civil law: mosaic, imperial, and canonical. In the previous chapter, we noted Luther's familiarity with the popular distinction of natural law, written law of Moses, and the law of the Gospel as well as the threefold use of the Law. Luther's training was rich with threefold descriptions of the Law.

In the 1523 *Preface to the Old Testament*, Luther described the Law in a threefold way. Like the postil in chapter seven, this preface was one of the most widespread and influential texts of Luther. It

---

[210] *Word and Faith* 65.
[211] Peter Lombard, PL 192:838; Gabriel Biel, Book III Dist. 37H and 40A.

appeared in 1523 and reappeared constantly in editions of the Luther Bible beginning in 1535. In this passage, the titles he gave the Law characterized its purposes.

> The laws are of three kinds. Some speak only of temporal things, as do our imperial laws. These are established by God chiefly because of the wicked, that they may not do worse things. Such laws are for prevention rather than for instruction, . . . Over and above these two are the laws about faith and love. All other laws must and ought to be measured by faith and love.[212]

"Prevention" (Ger. *weer gesetz*) corresponds to what Luther later called the civil use of the Law. "Instruction" (Ger. *leer gesetz*) has some correspondence with what Luther later called the theological use of the Law, particularly the pedagogical role of the Law. Thirdly, Luther described a category of laws about faith and love. Note in the third category that the believer is active and evaluating these laws ("measured"), characteristic of the righteous man who would take up the Law and use it, as described in the medieval glosses.

In a second passage of the *Preface to the Old Testament*, Luther described three pupils of the Law. Again, the kinds of pupils correspond to the use/misuse of the Law and the time of the Law that Luther described in the 1522 postil.

> For the law has three kinds of pupils. The first are those who hear the law and despise it, and who lead an impious life without fear. To these the law does not come. They are represented by the calf worshipers in the wilderness, on whose account Moses broke the tables of the law [Exod. 32:19]. To them he did not bring the law.

> The second kind are those who attempt to fulfill the law by their own power, without grace. They are represented by the people who could not look at the face of Moses when he brought the tables of the law a second time [Exod. 34:34–35]. The law comes to them but they cannot endure it. They therefore put a veil over it and lead a life of hypocrisy, doing outward works of the law. Yet the law makes it all to be sin

---

[212] LW 35:240; WA DB 8:16.

> where the veil is taken off. For the law shows that our ability counts for nothing without Christ's grace.[213]

In this passage, Luther first presented two abuses of the Law: bold opposition and fearful, outward obedience. Although the people know of the Law, they do not receive it as they should but oppose it or veil it. Consequently, they cannot receive the benefits of the Law. One may readily see the similarity between Luther's teaching here and Luther's comments in the postil on Gal 3 (1522) where he described the two times Moses gave the Law to the people.[214]

Luther next introduced the third kind of pupils. In the 1522 postil on Gal 3, he drew the biblical analogy for this group from the story of Joshua. In this case he drew an analogy with the life of David.

> The third kind of pupils are those who see Moses clearly, without a veil. These are they who understand the intention of the law [*des gesetzs meynung*] and how it demands impossible things. There sin comes to power, there death is mighty, there Goliath's spear is like a weaver's beam and its point weighs six hundred shekels of brass, so that all the children of Israel flee before him unless the one and only David—Christ our Lord—saves us from all this [I Sam. 17:7, 24, 32]. For if Christ's glory did not come alongside this splendor of Moses, no one could bear the brightness of the law, the terror of sin and death. These pupils fall away from all works and presumption and learn from the law nothing else except to recognize sin and to yearn for Christ. This is the true office of Moses and the very nature of the law.[215]

Take note that the third kind of pupil learns two things from the Law: (1) to recognize sin, what Luther would later call the theological use of the Law, and (2) to yearn for Christ, which corresponds to the prophetic use of the Law taught by ancient and medieval theologians. In this passage, we see Luther reaching back to earlier views. As is so often the case, Luther has not settled on only one way of expressing himself. The following table illustrates Luther's pattern of argument.

---

[213] LW 35:245; WA DB 8:26.
[214] As with the Early Church Fathers, Luther was writing about the Law of Moses. He was not writing about an abrogation of the natural law.
[215] LW 35:245–46; WA DB 8:26.

Table 10
Luther's Pattern of Teaching in the *Preface to the Old Testament*
    First misuse
    Second misuse
    Theological use (i.e., second use)
    Prophetic use

Luther presented the first and second misuses together. He used the same biblical analogy for them that he presented in 1522. We see then a significant point of consistency in describing the first two misuses of the Law. We also see variety in Luther's thought as he interacted with the categories learned from the medieval tradition.

Knowing more about the medieval background is helpful for fully recognizing what Luther was teaching. It is also helpful to let Luther be Luther rather than narrowly compare him with Melanchthon or the Formula of Concord. In this case we see that Luther freely mixed his ideas about the divine use and human use/misuse of the Law rather than provide a strict enumeration of divine uses.

A MAGISTRATE'S USE OF THE LAW

In December of 1524 Luther published *Against the Heavenly Prophets* as a response to his former colleague, Andreas Karlstadt. Karlstadt grew increasingly radical over the course of the Reformation. A part of this radicalism was an effort to reintroduce his understanding of the ceremonial law of Moses, which included such things as iconoclastic opposition to the statuary that was common in medieval churches. In order to respond to Karlstadt, Luther had to explain more fully how he differed from Karlstadt's view of the Law of Moses.

One feature of Luther's teaching that comes clearer at this time is what I will call a *magistrate's use of the Law*, which I mentioned at the end of chapter one in the standard list of terms. In *Against the Heavenly Prophets*, Luther compared the civil laws of Moses to the *Saxon Mirror* (*Sachsenspiegel*), a thirteenth century German legal code.[216] Luther held that the civil Law of Moses was binding for Jews but was not specifically given to Christians, though it was a fine example of a legal code.

---

[216] See LW 40:98.

In the summer of 1525, Luther referred to this view of the Law again in a sermon on *How Christians Should Regard Moses*. He described "Three things to be noted in Moses."[217] Here is another example of Luther providing a threefold description of the Law of Moses. He addressed the question, "Why then do you preach Moses if he does not pertain to us [Gentiles]?" He expounded three reasons.

(1) The civil commandments of Moses are useful but not binding for people today.

(2) The Law of Moses includes the promises and pledges of God about Christ.

(3) The Law of Moses provides for beautiful examples of faith, of love, and of the cross.

After commenting on his first category, the civil aspects of the Law of Moses, Luther wrote:

> There are other extraordinarily fine rules in Moses which one should like to accept, use [*brauch*], and put into effect. Not that one should bind or be bound by them, but (as I said earlier) the emperor could here take an example for setting up a good government on the basis of Moses, just as the Romans conducted a good government, and just as the *Sachsenspiegel* by which affairs are ordered in this land of ours. The Gentiles are not obligated to obey Moses. Moses is the *Sachsenspiegel* for the Jews. But if an example of good government were to be taken from Moses, one could adhere to it without obligation as long as one pleased, etc.[218]

This magistrate's use of the Law corresponds in many ways with the civil use of the Law. However, it is not strictly the use provided by Moses since Christian rulers would take the code only as an example. Luther's second note above is essentially the prophetic use of the Law, which proclaims Christ. The third note is like the "laws of faith and love" described in the 1523 *Preface to the Old Testament* that corresponded to the righteous man's use of the Law.

In this threefold description, Luther provided a unique look at the usefulness of the Law, since it did not include a specific category for

---

[217] LW 35:166.
[218] LW 35:167.

the theological use of the Law. He wrote with considerable freedom rather than a strict enumeration, providing categories as he needed them for the topic at hand. At the end of *How Christians Should Regard Moses*, Luther summarized his thoughts by writing:

> We should not sweep Moses under the rug. Moreover the Old Testament is thus properly understood when we retain from the prophets the beautiful texts about Christ, when we take note of and thoroughly grasp the fine examples, and when we use the laws as we please to our advantage.... Thus where he gives commandment, we are not to follow him except so far as he agrees with the natural law.... We have our own master, Christ, and he has set before us what we are to know, observe, do, and leave undone.[219]

The Law of Moses is useful and one is guided in using it by noting its basis in the natural, moral law and by referring to the New Testament. Luther continued to hold the Law of Moses in high regard but described the freedom of Christian magistrates in using it and the benefit to the righteous man in using it.

CONCLUSION

Based on Luther's education in medieval scholastic categories, he commonly thought of the Law in a threefold way. In the 1523 *Preface to the Old Testament*, Luther referred to the various uses of the Law when describing the basic types of Law. (At times the Reformers write about manifold *use* of the Law, such as "threefold use." At other times they write about *uses* or *functions* separately. Either way seems acceptable so long as one views the Law of God as a unity with different applications for different types of hearers.) Luther's Old Testament preface stood as an example of his teaching throughout the sixteenth century and beyond. In the preface, Luther likewise referred to the prophetic use of the Law known from early western theologians and medieval commentators.

In 1524–25 Luther introduced another use of the Law, which I have termed the magistrate's use of the Law. This use differs from the other four uses described so far because it belongs to a Christian magistrate who uses the Law of Moses as an example for creating a

---

[219] LW 35:173.

civil legal code. It is not a binding use as under Moses and the "time of the Law." We see then at least five uses of the Law in early Luther, as well as a broad commendation that Christians "use the laws as we please to our advantage." We do not see a strict only-two-uses approach.

Chapter Nine

Luther's Early Interpretation of 1 Timothy (1525–28)

> It is the Law's function to show good and evil, because it shows what one must do and reveals sin, which one must not commit.
>
> —Martin Luther

Karlstadt's interpretations and applications of 1 Timothy likely ignited Luther's concern about his longstanding colleague. Already in 1521 Karlstadt interpreted 1 Tm 3:2 and 5:9 on the topics of celibacy and marriage in ways that encouraged the necessary end of all monastic vows and required monks to get married.[220] This legalistic interpretation of 1 Timothy may have been the first point at which Luther recognized a difference between himself and Karlstadt on the doctrine of the Law. They did not see Christian freedom, the Christian life in the same way.

In this chapter, we will look carefully at Luther's interpretation of 1 Tm 1:8–9. We have seen already that, like ancient and medieval theologians, Luther associated Gal 3 with 1 Tm 1:8–9. Although historians of doctrine have noticed this, few have offered careful assessment of Luther's use of 1 Timothy 1 for the doctrine of the Law. Martin Schloemann, however, provided a few pages on the

---

[220] Schwiebert 524.

development of Luther's interpretation.[221] We begin with Schloemann's assessment before turning to Luther's texts to read them in light of the broader history of the doctrine.

SCHLOEMANN'S ASSESSMENT

As noted in the introduction (pp. 5–6), researchers tend to approach the doctrine of the use of the Law with a simple evolutionary scheme. Schloemann's assessment provides an example of this. However, Schloemann actually noted that Luther wrote about a third use of the Law. He divided Luther's developing thought on 1 Tm 1:8–9 into four "arenas":

1. The Christian lives on the basis of the Law, which is positive and normative (1516/17 *Lectures on Galatians*).

2. Righteousness based on the Law is excluded; the Christian lives free in the Spirit (1525 sermon on 1 Tm 1).

3. The Christian life has no lawful use of the Law, which is only appointed for the unrighteous and for the Christian insofar as he is still fleshly (1528 *Lectures on 1 Timothy*). In other words, Luther has arrived at the first and second uses of the Law and explicitly rejected a third use based on faith and love.

4. Luther continued to affirm his conclusions from 1528. The spiritual use of the Law is now clearly the theological use of the Law (1531 *Lectures on Galatians*).

Schloemann's observations are helpful for identifying the enduring importance of 1 Tm 1:8–9 in Luther's thought on the use of the Law; he has gathered important texts.

In a footnote, Schloemann expressed surprise that historians of doctrine had not noticed the significance of 1 Timothy and Luther's comments for the debate on the use of the Law and the third use of the Law in particular. He wrote:

> On this point, as is clearly seen from the writing, an *express rejection of the third normative use of the Law* exists from the

---

[221] *Natürliches und Gepredigtes Gesetz bei Luther* (Berlin: Alfred Töpelmann, 1961), 22–31.

pages of Luther, which appears to be yet unnoticed in the debate over this question.[222]

Given that Luther expressly used the words ".3. officium,"[223] it is indeed remarkable that this passage has received virtually no attention even though the text is readily available in various editions of Luther's works.

If Schloemann's observations are correct, it would certainly settle the question about the third use of the Law. However, there are problems in Schloemann's observations that finally led him to a misreading of Luther's teaching. The following pages will provide comment on the texts and on Schloemann's assessment.

As noted in chapter 7, Luther was already working with the medieval doctrine of the use of the Law in 1515 during the *Lectures on Romans*. Schloemann assumed a slower, gradual development in Luther's views. He was not aware of the broader history of the doctrine when he wrote his assessment of Luther's interpretation of 1 Tm 1:8–9. He did not see that medieval interpreters defined multiple uses of the Law and that, indeed, this was already beginning in the patristic period.[224]

1516/17 LECTURES ON GALATIANS

Schloemann's goal was to investigate Luther's preaching about the Law. For his first "arena" in Luther's teaching, he focused on a passage in the *Scholia on Galatians* that did not expressly speak of the "usefulness of the Law" (*utilitas legis*), though it cited 1 Tm 1:

> Thus good preachers assail against riches, pleasures, indeed against women, not because these are evil, but because they serve an evil use, in this way also the whole Law [is used], 1 Timothy 1: "[the Law] is good, if someone uses it

---

[222] "Daß an dieser Stelle, wie aus der Nachschrift deutlich zu ersehen ist, eine *ausdrückliche Ablehnung des tertius usus normativus legis* von seiten Luthers vorliegt, scheint in der Debatte über diese Frage noch nicht bemerkt worden zu sein" (p. 26, n. 73).

[223] WA 26:17. The periods placed around the three indicate that it is used as an abbreviation for "third." See the English translation in LW 28:235, "third function." On the meaning of *officium*, see pp. 57–58.

[224] See p. 51.

lawfully." But they do not use it "lawfully," who trust [in it] proudly.[225]

Schloemann understood this passage to mean that Luther was basing the Christian life on keeping the Law and appropriate humility, which represented Luther's immature thought about the doctrine of the Law.[226] In fact, Luther was drawing on a passage from Augustine that spoke against having confidence in the works of the Law as a basis for justification.[227] For Luther, humility was often a consequence of the theological use of the Law as he would state in the 1531 commentary on Gal 3.

Schloemann did not comment on a second passage from Luther on 1 Tm 1 where Luther used careful analysis of the passage from Augustinian theology. He distinguished the letter of the Law, which kills, from the Spirit of the Law—faith/love that gives life and fulfills the Law (1 Tm 1:5).

> And so clearly it may be said: The Law of the Spirit and of the letter differ [from one another] as a sign and a thing signified or as a word and a thing; but a sign is not necessary for having something signified. So, "the Law is not appointed for the righteous man."[228]

Luther argued that God did not appoint the letter of the Law, which kills, for the righteous man. The righteous man does not need the written Law of Moses since he is like a good tree that naturally bears good fruit.[229] But this does not mean that the Law is unavailable to the

---

[225] "Sicut boni predicatores invehuntur in divicias, voluptates, immo in mulieres, non quod mala hec sint, sed quia malo serviunt usui, ita et universa lex, prima Timothei primo: 'Bona est, si quis ea legittime utatur.' Non utuntur autem 'legittime,' qui eam confidunt superbe." WA 57 II:72.

[226] Luther lived under the discipline of the Augustinian order at this time; the comment about preaching against women has to do with the vows of celibacy and not misogyny.

[227] "Beatus Augu[stinus hoc autem 'destructa' ipsa opera legis, immo 'superbiam gloriantem' et confidentem in operibus legis." WA 57 II:71.

[228] "Et ut clarissime dicatur: Lex spiritus et littere differunt sicut signum et signatum seu sicut vox et res; sed habito signato non est necessarium signum. Ita 'nec iusto lex est posita.' " WA 57 II:74.

[229] WA 57 II:73, line 19. He is righteous inside and out. In other words, he has both faith in the heart and love in his outward deeds. Cf. Ps 1:2–3. See also Jer 31:33.

righteous man. The Law itself—the Law of the Spirit—is there for the righteous man even though the word of the Law is not appointed to make him righteous. The righteous man has the Law naturally and uses it freely.

Unfortunately, Schloemann did not include Luther's references to 1 Tm 1 in the 1522 *Christmas Postil* (*Weihnachtspostille*) as part of his evaluation of Luther's development. Instead, Schloemann moved on to a later text.

1525 SERMONS ON 1 TIMOTHY 1

In the tempestuous year of 1525, while writing against Erasmus, the heavenly prophets, and the Peasants' Revolt, Luther prepared two sermons covering 1 Tm 1:3–11.[230] In these sermons Luther again described misuse of the Law and right use of the Law. He placed great importance on the teaching that Christians are at the same time sinners and saints (*simul justus et peccator*),[231] even noting that the right use of the Law depended on this theology that he had introduced in the 1515 *Lectures on Romans*.[232] Schloemann correctly identified these sermons as describing the civil and theological uses of the Law and noted Luther's strong emphasis on the role of the Holy Spirit.[233] However, Schloemann did not see the compatibility of these observations with what Luther had already written about the Law and the Spirit in 1516/17. Schloemann assumed a significant evolution in Luther's thought.

---

[230] WA 17 I:102–134.

[231] WA 17 I:114–15.

[232] WA 17 I:122. See Ernest B. Koenker's essay "Man *simul justus et peccator*" in *Accents in Luther's Theology*, Heino O. Kadai, ed. (St. Louis: Concordia, 1967), 98–123. Koenker illustrates how important the distinction was to Luther's thought. It helped Luther sort out the issues over the doctrine of the Law in Augustine and Scholasticism. According to Koenker, Luther wrote of the Christian as wholly sinner and wholly saint. He likely wrote this way when emphasizing the doctrine of original sin and justification. Koenker also pointed out that Luther could write about the Christian progressing in righteousness through the struggle of mortification and the cycle of daily repentance and faith. These different ways of writing are not due to inconsistency in Luther's thought so much as the complexity of the Christian as sinner and saint, still needing and using the Law under the grace and salvation bestowed by the Gospel.

[233] Schloemann 25.

Luther explained that, since the Law is eternal, Christ is our only refuge.[234] Therefore, Christians must remain unconfused by the Law, though the old nature must always have it.[235] In the *Lectures on Galatians*, Luther was applying 1 Tm 1:8–9 for students of theology. Here Luther was applying the passage for a different congregation. Luther introduced some colorful illustrations of his insights in order to show the purpose of the Law.

> Now the worldly sword and outward rule is not needed or used for the pious but only for the evil. Thus it is also with God's Law. The judge has nothing to do with a pious citizen, who harms no one, but only with thieves and murderers. So one would not set out a dog for a sheep, which bites no one. For it can frighten no one to do harm. However, one would set out a dog for the wolf. If [the wolf] were not there, there would be no guard or need to watch. So here is the Law put in place not for the pious but only for the evil.[236]

Notice how Luther spoke about the Law and its role in the lives of the evil. They require the "outward" use of the Law that barks and bites to frighten them away from evil deeds. Luther used "externally" to describe the terror of the Law (p. 79) also in the 1522 *Christmas Postil*. The righteous do not need this outward preaching of the Law, not because they are lawless, but because they reference the Law within—the natural, moral law that God has written on their hearts. Indeed, they are "the tables of Moses, written upon outwardly and inwardly by the finger of God himself" (p. 79).

Further in the passage Luther also emphasized a contrast between the work of the Spirit and the work of the Law.[237] He showed how their work stands together. For example, the Law warns the believer

---

[234] WA 17 I:117.

[235] WA 17 I:122–23.

[236] "Wie nu das weltliche schwerd und eusserliche regiment nicht not noch nütz ist den frommen, sondern allein fur die bösen, Also ist es auch mit Gottes gesetz. Mit einem frommen bürger, der niemand leid thuet, hat der richter nichts zu schaffen, sondern nur mit dieben und mördern, Also darff man einem schaff keine hunde legen, das es niemand beisse, denn es kan niemand schaden nach leid thuen, sondern dem wolff mus man sie legen, wenn der nicht were, were keiner hut odder wache not, Also ist hie das gesetz gestellet nicht den frommen, sondern nur den bösen." WA 17 I:124.

[237] WA 17 I:125–26.

so that the Spirit is not driven out. We should do good and keep the Law, though the desire to do good depends on Christ and the Spirit.[238] Finally, Luther returned to his emphasis on the Christian as both righteous and sinner at the same time (*simul justus et peccator*).[239]

Luther recognized that the complexity of a Christian complicated the theology of the Law and its use, since a Christian is both righteous and sinful at the same time. On the one hand, the Christian had the natural law written in his heart and the Spirit led him to keep it (cf. righteous man's use). On the other hand, the Christian continued to need the preaching of the Law for the sake of recognizing sin and repenting (cf. theological use). It is this complexity that requires a distinction between uses of the Law, as illustrated by the table below.

Table 11
The Stages of Man and the Use of the Law

BEFORE LAW	UNDER LAW	UNDER GRACE	IN PEACE (HEAVEN)
	peccator	*peccator et justus*	*justus*
	civil use	civil use	
	theological use	theological use	
		righteous man's use	righteous man's use

◄ ─────── natural law/moral law/*lex aeterna* with mankind at all times ─────── ►

The civil use outwardly restrains the unrepentant sinner before his conversion by threats and punishment. It is always in force in human society, whether the citizens are Christians or not. The theological use speaks to the sinner before conversion, driving him toward repentance and despair in his own righteousness. The theological use continues in the life of a Christian by addressing the sinful nature. So, the theological use applies both before and after conversion, which is why the Reformers would say that the Law always accuses—it always has this role for a person whether under the Law or under grace. However, for the righteous man, the Law takes on a still different role. In so far he is righteous by grace through faith, the Law no longer constrains him. This righteous man's use of the Law is different from the civil use because (A) the Holy Spirit is working through the righteous man to bring forth the fruit of the Spirit in

---

[238] WA 17 I:128.
[239] E.g., WA 17 I:133.

keeping with the Law, (B) the righteous man takes up the Law and uses it willingly, (C) the righteous man uses the Law "without constraint" in active obedience, and (D) keeping the Law by grace through faith actually pleases God whereas civil righteous or outward obedience does not please God.

The medieval texts we explored in chapter six did not fully address this complexity. For example, Rhabanus and the *Glossa Ordinaria* describe the believer withdrawing from the sinful life overtime[240] but they do not clearly teach that the righteous man remains a sinner saved by grace alone. This is Luther's observation, which seems to move him toward writing about a third use of the Law and transforming the medieval, prophetic use of the Law—the new law (*nova lex*), or the law of the Gospel—into the clearer and simpler Reformation category of *Gospel*.

REFORMATION ERA ANTINOMIANISM

Before considering Schloemann's comments on the *Lectures on 1 Timothy*, we need to recall an intervening event. Chapter six noted a medieval antinomian movement to which Luther responded in the *Lectures on Romans* in 1516. Luther's teaching on Christian freedom unfortunately led to confusion among some fellow Reformers. In 1527 while Melanchthon was drafting the *Visitation Articles*, John Agricola (1494–1566) aroused a dispute about the use of the Law in repentance. There was also a second Antinomian Controversy, which took place after Luther's death. That will be briefly described in chapter twenty.[241]

In October of 1527 the Latin *Visitation Articles* were published at the same time Agricola was completing his *One Hundred Thirty Common Questions*.[242] Questions 114–116 illustrated Agricola's views, which came to be known as Antinomianism:

---

[240] See pp. 54, 56.

[241] For more on these controversies, see F. Bente, "The Antinomian Controversy," in *Historical Introduction to the Symbolical Books of the Evangelical Lutheran Church* (St. Louis: Concordia, 1921), 161–72; Timothy J. Wengert, "Antinomianism," in *Oxford Encyclopedia of the Reformation* 1:51–53.

[242] Timothy Wengert, trans. in *Sources and Contexts of the Book of Concord*, Robert Kolb and James A. Nestingen, eds. (Minneapolis: Fortress Press, 2001), 13–30.

114. Should the Law of Moses also compel Christians?

Answer: Christians do out of desire and love everything that God demands of them.[243] For they are sealed by the spontaneous Spirit of Christ. Therefore, no law should compel them. For [1 Tm. 1:9] "to the righteous no law is given." In addition, as soon as the Gospel becomes a matter of compulsion and rules, then it is no longer the Gospel.

115. How then should we use it?

Answer: As Christians use all creatures over whom they are lords: without reservation of conscience, to God's glory and their use, when, where, and as often as they desire. As they might use Greek and Latin books and histories, so they use Moses and everything that he wrote, as long as he doesn't bother our conscience or compel us.

116. Why is Moses given to the Jews?

Answer: Moses is the Jewish common law. And just as the Romans and we Germans follow imperial law, so the Jews had to follow Moses, as an external order that has nothing to do with the gentiles, Acts 15[:10].

Agricola, like Luther, was wrestling with the application of 1 Tm 1:8–9. Also like Luther, Agricola described the believer taking up the Law of Moses and using it for his benefit in a manner very similar to the righteous man's use of the Law.[244] However, Agricola did not teach that the Law of Moses was useful for convicting the conscience (theological use) or for compelling the believer to do good works. He had misunderstood Luther's teaching about the place of the Law in the Christian life, raising the question of whether antinomianism was an inherent outcome of Lutheran theology.[245]

A brief comment on this issue is in order. I wonder whether it was really Luther's teaching that led Agricola to his Antinomian views. Agricola placed an emphasis on love as a bond between God and the

---

[243] Here is an interesting point in Agricola's argument where he acknowledges, perhaps unintentionally, an on-going voice for the Law, which makes demands of the righteous.
[244] See pp. 79, 83.
[245] See p. 77.

believer. This emphasis on love was likewise important to medieval mysticism, the environment in which medieval antinomian views arose. It is certainly possible that Luther's preaching of freedom confused Agricola. However, we see in other Reformation events that what Luther said or wrote merely introduced the opportunity for others to revisit or revive ideas already present in the medieval era (e.g., the Peasants' Revolt, which was preceded by many other such revolts). A closer look at Agricola's ideas about love may show medieval mysticism to be an equally or even more significant factor in Reformation era antinomianism. This requires further research.

In November 1527 Luther met with Melanchthon and Agricola at the Torgau Castle to help resolve the tensions between them. Luther maintained the necessity of preaching the Law; he agreed substantially with Melanchthon and was able to quiet the concerns of both his colleagues for the present.[246]

These emerging tensions over the use of the Law are important for understanding the context of Luther's *Lectures on 1 Timothy*, which he began at Wittenberg on January 13, 1528, only a month and a half after acting as a mediator between his colleagues disputing over the role of the Law in conversion and in the Christian life. Schloemann's assessment mentioned this important historical context only in passing.

1528 LECTURES ON 1 TIMOTHY

On January 15, 1528, Luther reflected on the use or office of the Law. His comments are complex and even contradictory at points. In this example, Luther was clearly wrestling with the opinions of

---

[246] See Ken R. Schurb, "Philip Melanchthon, the Formula of Concord, and the Third Use of the Law" (Unpublished Doctoral Dissertation, The Ohio State University, 2001), 18. See also Silcock 39–44. Schurb sees Luther and Melanchthon in substantial agreement. Silcock sees things differently. He writes, "It became clear in the course of the discussions that both Agricola and Melanchthon had diverged from Luther, but each in a different direction. Each represented one side of Luther's theology so that neither retained the antithesis between law and gospel, which is the distinguishing mark of his theology. Melanchthon thought that this position had been vindicated, and Agricola conceded that his advocacy of the younger Luther in favor of the older Luther found no support in the present phase of discussions" (*Law and Gospel* 42; see also p. 44).

opponents[247] and the question of how to describe the role of the Law in the life of a believer. His main point is made in commenting on 1 Tm 1:8.

> To sum up all of this: Use the Law as you wish. Read it. Only keep this use away from it, that you credit it with the remission of sins and righteousness. Beware of making me righteous by the Law. Rather use it to restrain. You must not give the Law the power and virtue to justify.[248]

Here Luther voiced his chief concern. He supported the use of the Law for both believers and unbelievers. He was chiefly concerned that no one ascribe to the law the power to justify.

> The Law is abused when I assign to the Law more than it can accomplish. Good works are necessary and the Law must be kept but the Law does not justify.[249]

In chapter six, we saw that medieval theologians were investigating the effect or power of the Law. Thomas Aquinas explored the question of whether the Law could make someone good.[250] Nicholas of Lyra's *Postilla* on 1 Tm 1 included discussion of the power of the Law.[251] In the *Lectures on 1 Timothy*, Luther did not explicitly describe an opponent. He never stated whether a contemporary resource or teacher was teaching explicitly that the Law justifies sinners who can keep it.

Luther next commented on 1 Tm 1:9, which stirred further reflection on the same matter.

> The Law frightens and causes trembling—these are the spiritual effects of the Law. It really has a double function: in an external way to repress violence and spiritually to reveal sins. It restrains the wicked to prevent their living according to their own flesh, and it shows the Pharisees their sins to keep them from pride. Satan, every wicked theologian, and even nature cannot bear to have their works condemned.

---

[247] See LW 28:231, n. 17.
[248] LW 28:231–232.
[249] LW 28:232.
[250] See p. 62.
[251] "Vim legis." See p. 67.

> Those who have the firstfruits of the Spirit have the battle to fight against confidence in our own works.[252]

The following table illustrates Luther's pattern of thought.

Table 12
Luther's Pattern of Teaching in the *Lectures on 1 Timothy* (1528)

First use (restrains)
Second use (reveals sin)
    Misuse by Satan and wicked theologians
Battle against confidence in works

Here, stated in brief, is a pattern of argument similar to the one in the 1522 postil. Luther paired up a description of the first and second uses of the Law, followed with a description of misuse of the Law, and then commented on the Christian life.

At the close of that day's lecture Luther stated:

> The Law is laid down *for the lawless*. This gives the Law both its civil and spiritual functions: that wicked man is restrained and is led to a knowledge of himself. Those are the two functions. By its civil function it restrains crass sinners who rush in before they reveal all things as free. This must be the Law with its own punishment. Many people are greedy, and yet they live with a beautiful and holy appearance. Paul in Rom. 1 assails the Gentiles for their crass and manifest sins. In chapter 2 he assails the very decent-appearing Jews who beneath their hypocrisy kept encouraging the worst sins so that these holy sinners are put to shame. Rom. 2. There we have the true use, and you should not assign more to the Law than to restrain and humble the proud saints that they may be led to understanding. When this occurs, there is no further function of the Law.[253]

In this lecture, Luther presented a new biblical analogy based on Paul's argument in the Book of Romans, which first condemned the Gentiles and then the Jews with the first and second uses of the Law. At this point Luther even concluded that there are no other uses. He

---

[252] LW 28:233.
[253] LW 28:234.

then attacked an unstated opponent for misusing the Law, typical of his pattern of argument (presenting use then misuse for contrast).

> Why, then, do you preach that one is justified thereby? The just man ought not have the Law except as a restraint and to reveal sin. But it does not take away sin. But in the case of manifest sinners, it restrains; in the case of secret sinners, it reveals. In the case of the just man, it cannot restrain, because there is nothing to restrain; it cannot reveal, because he has done nothing concealed. It is the good use of the Law to restrain and to reveal sin; but it is misuse thereof to say that it takes away sin.[254]

In this passage, Luther did not state who these false preachers were, whether the heavenly prophets and the scholastic theologians whom he mentioned in the previous lectures, the Jewish teachers described in 1 Tm, or someone else. Most likely, Luther had the Judaizers in mind, as he stated in the 1515–16 *Lectures on Romans*.[255] What is clear is that Luther was not rebuking his colleagues Agricola and Melanchthon, with whom he had recently dialogued on the use of the Law.

Yet, here is a confusing passage: Luther assigned the twofold use of the Law to "saints," believers addressed in the Book of Romans, and the "just man rather than the unjust." Then he contradicted this point by stating that the just man had nothing to restrain or conceal, remembering the wording of 1 Tm 1:9. His comments failed to include a clear statement of how the Christian as sinner and saint (*simul justus et peccator*) factored into the use of the Law. The day's lecture closed in a most confusing way, illustrating that Luther had not finally, clearly settled on one way to talk about the role of the Law in the life of a believer, though he knew what he did not want to say—the Law justifies sinners.

On January 20, Luther began the lecture again, expressing himself with greater clarity and confidence. This transition from one lecture to the next is most significant, yet Schloemann overlooked it.

> We have treated these two points: the Law is good, and it was not laid down for the just. I have also mentioned that we

---

[254] LW 28:234.
[255] See above, p. 76.

> understood those two points as characteristic for recognizing Christians. The wicked do not understand that the Law is not for the just man. Against this, Rom. 13:10 proclaims that love is the critical point of the Law, and beyond that it says (Rom. 7:16): "The Law is good." The two functions of the Law are to reveal sinners and restrain them.[256]

Luther defined the first two offices or functions of the Law as ways in which the Law acts upon those who hear it. In other words, he described the work of the Holy Spirit using the Law to restrain sin and to reveal sin, driving a person to despair of his own righteousness. Then Luther defined a third office of the Law passively and negatively. This point appears at the beginning of Luther's lecture after he had collected his thoughts and would then clarify his position.

> The third function, however, to remove sin and to justify, is limited to this: The Lamb of God, and not the Law, takes away sin. It is Christ who removes sin and justifies. Consequently, we must distinguish between the function of the Law and that of Christ. It is the Law's function to show good and evil, because it shows what one must do and reveals sin, which one must not commit. The Law therefore is good because it shows not only evil but also the good which one must do. But beyond that it does not go. It does not kill Og and King Sihon. It merely reveals good and bad; Joshua [does the rest].[257]

The Law does not justify a person or remove sin. In this third office, Christ removes sin and justifies the sinner. The comments about Christ take one back to the prophetic use of the Law taught by the ancient and medieval theologians. However, Luther also goes on to talk about the role of the Law in a non-prophetic way. He did not speak first of the Spirit using the Law, nor did he speak of the Law's effect on the person hearing it. Yet he emphasized that the Law still stands there showing good and evil—this use of the Law does not go away. In this explanation, Luther safeguarded the office of Christ to justify and the office of the Law to show right and wrong. Though the Law is fulfilled by the office of Christ, the Law still stands.

---

[256] LW 28:235.
[257] LW 28:235.

In this description of the third function of the Law, Luther also returned to the analogy he used in the 1522 postil when he wrote about the "threefold use of the Law."[258] There Luther used a three part biblical analogy of (1) the golden calf incident, (2) the veil incident, and (3) the conquest under Joshua. Here, he skipped over the first two parts of the analogy to focus directly on the third, "[The Law] does not kill Og and King Sihon. It merely reveals good and bad; Joshua [does the rest]." In this analogy, Luther linked his earlier thoughts about a threefold use/misuse by mankind with the three offices of the Law described in the 1 Timothy lectures. In other words, we see a connection and point of consistency in Luther's thinking about threefold use of the Law. This analogy is one that researchers should watch for in the future since we have seen it applied to the threefold use of the Law twice and other examples may shed further light on how Luther and other theologians were thinking about the doctrine of the Law.

These observations again call into question Ebeling's conclusion that the 1522 postil did not really have to do with Luther's teaching about use of the Law. In both passages Luther wrote about the human use/misuse and the divine use of the Law. In studying these two passages where Luther explicitly mentioned a threefold use of the Law and three offices of the Law, a broader picture of Luther's thinking about the Law emerges, which is portrayed in Table 13.

Table 13
Luther's Uses or Offices of the Law

Basic Use:	To reveal good and evil, show what one must do (WA 26:17; LW 28:235).
Divine Use 1:	Restrain (WA 10/I.1:454–55; 26:16; LW 28:234–35).
Misuse 1:	Bold opposition (WA 10/I.1:456, ln. 10–11; 26:16; Lenker 6:272; LW 28:234).
Rgt. Man's Use 1:	Live together in peace (WA 10/I.1:454, ln. 17; Lenker 6:271) or, forsake the dissolute life (WA 10/I.1:457, ln. 6; Lenker 6:273).
Divine Use 2:	Know our sin (WA 10/I.1:454–55; Lenker 6:270–71; WA 26:16; LW 28:234).
Misuse 2:	Mere outward obedience (WA 10/I.1:456, ln. 15; Lenker 6:273) or, self-justification and hypocrisy (WA 26:16; LW 28:234).

---

[258] See p. 84.

Rgt. Man's Use 2:	Know self for repentance (WA 10/I.1:455, ln. 5–6; Lenker 6:271–72; WA 26:16; LW 28:234).
Divine Use 3:	Luther has the prophetic use of the Law here: Christ removes sin and justifies (WA 26:17; LW 28:235). He also speaks of God's use of the Law in the lives of the righteous: He writes the tables of Moses outwardly and inwardly (WA 10/I.1:456, ln. 18; Lenker 6:273) or, the Law reveals good and evil (WA 26:17; LW 28:235).
Misuse 3:	Luther does not specifically enumerate this misuse, which would admonish against returning to justification by the Law (cf. Paul's warnings in Gal).
Rgt. Man's Use 3:	Observe and keep the Law both outwardly and inwardly (WA 10/I.1:256, ln. 17; 257, ln. 13; Lenker 6:273).

Theologians of the only-two-uses consensus have emphasized Melanchthon's helpful observation that the Law always accuses. In the case of the Christian, this power of the Law addresses itself to the sinful nature. It is perhaps equally important to emphasize that also the Law always reveals good and evil, the basic use that Luther described in the *Lectures on 1 Timothy*, a function of the Law that the righteous man may find useful as He lives out his calling before God. The righteous man, in so far as he is righteous by grace through faith, befriends the Law and works with it both outwardly and inwardly.

Table 13 shows that Luther wrote about the prophetic use of the Law under the third use label, where he was really including statements of the Gospel (e.g., "the Gospel must be preached" (Lenker 6:273); "only Joshua, who leads by faith" (Lenker 6:274); "Christ removes sin and justifies" (LW 28:235). Nevertheless, Luther included alongside these statements of Gospel a number of statements about the Law in the Christian life. In these statements, we see a use of the Law that differs from the civil and theological uses:

> The third class observe [the Law] both externally and with the heart. (Lenker 6:233)

> This class is the tables of Moses, written upon outwardly and inwardly by the finger of God himself. (Lenker 6:273)

> Their good works are not performed through constraint of the Law. (Lenker 6:274)

> It is the Law's function to show good and evil. (LW 28:235)

Those who are constrained by the Law or who live in fear of its threats do not observe the Law with their hearts. Only the righteous by faith could be described as living "tables of Moses." Under the third use, the Law still stands to show good and evil. In other words, in these instances while writing about the third use of the Law, Luther described the righteous freely observing the Law without constraint while seeing that the Law continues to show for them what is good and evil.

This is a matter different from Luther's descriptions of the civil and theological uses. He was describing the believer's new status under grace and the Gospel while showing how the believer continued to use the Law, though now without its constraint or condemnation. These statements are not the same as Melanchthon's third use in the *Loci* but are similar to the Formula of Concord VI 2, 7.[259] As we consider Luther's later teaching, we will see him continue to write about the righteous man's use of the Law for the Christian life.

LUTHER'S VERBS

Thus far, we have focused on Luther's phrases when describing the Law. This is where the research has focused in the past, especially fixed on the phrases about the number of uses. But the study of phrases can only treat a portion of the matter. This is because phrases omit one of the weightiest parts of speech: verbs.

When writing about the Law and the commandments in the Christian life, Luther regularly used some noteworthy verbs. Luther wrote of God "exercising" the believer or the believer "practicing" the Law. These expressions help us see how the believer's relationship to the Law has changed after conversion. In the 1527 *Lectures on Titus* Luther commented extensively on 1 Tm 4:7, "Train yourself, however, in godliness."[260]

> I have been thinking about our next series of lectures, so that we are not idle and do not eat our bread in vain, especially because Paul admonishes us (cf. 1 Tim. 4:7): If we have a talent from the Lord, let us train [Lat. *exerceamus*] ourselves

---

[259] See pp. 265, 273.
[260] In Luther's German translation, "Ube dich selbs aber an der Gottseligkeit." WA DB 7:267.

in godliness. The highest work of godliness is to meditate on the Word of God in order that we may teach and exhort one another.[261]

This thought harkened back to an emphasis in the medieval glosses and commentaries. The believer rightly uses the Law (1 Tm 1:8–9) for the sake of those around him. He fulfills it as an example to them.[262] He teaches it to bring them to repentance. In the following citation of the 1528 *Lectures on 1 Timothy*, the English terms "train," "exercise," and "practice" are used to render forms of Latin *exercere*.

Train yourself in godliness.[263] This passage also has been exposed to corruption. "I have taught you this sound doctrine. Now see to it that you practice it in your work. 'Train yourself.' Godliness is the worship of God. Train yourself to worship God." First, the level of exercising godliness is without doubt the teaching of others. "Avoid myths. Rather, train yourself by teaching." The largest part of εὐσέβεια ("godliness") is devoted to teaching. Whoever teaches the Word of God correctly should train himself for godliness. He does not lay the Word down in his napkin, as a lazy slave does (cf. Luke 19:20). He keeps it in use[264] so that it may not rust or rot away. Rather, let him declare it every day. We read in John 15:2: "He will prune." For the man to whom God entrusts this work God stirs up enemies—his own flesh and the devil. God gives him many people that that gift of the Spirit may not lie idle but that the man may walk in the training of the Spirit. "You have the gift. You have been nourished" (v. 6). Elsewhere he says: Be urgent in season, etc." (2 Tim. 4:2). Keep at it.[265] Don't become weary or lazy.

---

[261] LW 29:3; WA 25:6.

[262] See e.g., p. 56.

[263] LW 28:321–22; WA 26:76–77. The original text does not so fully quote the text of 1 Tm here. The editor for LW has provided fuller passages for the reader's convenience. The *Lectures on 1 Timothy* are macaronic, mostly Latin with occasional German phrases and expressions.

[264] The text has *conservat in usu* (WA 26:76, ln. 31). Cf. the expression *usus legis*.

[265] Ger. expression, "das getrieben sei."

> *For while bodily training is of some value.* He does not condemn this, but bodily training is far inferior to training in godliness. Isn't it godly to exercise one's body with farming and the work of his hands? Also, in all the other duties of magistrates there is physical exercise. Why does he make a distinction here with this training? He is speaking about physical exercise, first, so that he speaks about bodily training—fasting. ... It has, however, no comparison with the exercise of godliness, because such training involves inviting to and increasing the kingdom of Christ. You see, teaching, comforting, exhorting, praying, and writing are the exercising of godliness whose fruits stream over to other people. "In such practices train yourself that you may enrich many souls, etc." This is true godliness. ... Paul and Anthony had an excellent reputation; they lived in the desert, but they lived for themselves. Paul, Anthony, you were saints. But the Bishop Himself has cut you off. "The weightier matters of the Law[266] ... These you ought to have done without neglecting the others," says Christ (Matt. 23:23).

Note the reference to Mt 23:23, which makes clear that Luther was writing and commenting on the use of the Law and not general use of the Word. He did not describe the Law in its typical role of condemning. Instead, he described the believer exercising with it, as an athlete might exercise or as an artisan might ply his trade. This exercise should take place daily, in reciting the Word of God and teaching it, but also in doing what it says.

Wengert recognized this teaching about the Law in Melanchthon, recording an example from the 1528 *Scholia on Colossians* and connecting the teaching explicitly with Melanchthon's earliest reference to the third use of the Law in the 1534 *Scholia on Colossians*.[267] However, Wengert did not see that the teaching was readily available in Luther in 1528.

In the expression "Keep at it" above, we see another one of Luther's weighty verbs: Ger. *treiben*. In a most basic sense, this verb means "to drive." The modern reader may quickly envision the

---

[266] Lat. *graviora legis*.
[267] Wengert 194, 196, n. 87. On Melanchthon's teaching, see chapter sixteen below.

operation of a vehicle. This is not the usual sense in Luther's day. The imagery is that of driving or herding animals.[268] The Law chases us down; though in repentance, it drives us to Christ. But *treiben* is also used in the sense of "teaching" or "exercising," which is what Luther had in mind here.[269] In other words, the verb had connections to what Luther called the second and third offices of the Law.

CONCLUSION

Luther's teaching on 1 Timothy helps us fill an important gap in the research on how Luther understood the use or office of the Law. As Schloemann noted, researchers on the use of the Law have largely neglected this teaching, even though it sparked the one undisputed context where Luther spoke explicitly of a *third office* of the Law.

Luther's early reflections on 1 Tm 1:8–9 show him writing about the usefulnesss of the Law and the "Law of the Spirit" available to the righteous man in contrast to the "letter" of the Law that reveals sin and brings death. Luther was still at this early stage working out the uses of Law and Gospel. His sermons of 1525 show him struggling over how the uses of the Law and the Gospel fit together with his observation that the Christian is righteous and sinner at the same time.

Luther's 1 Timothy lecture on January 20, 1528 was something of a breakthrough for these issues over theological terms. It also demonstrated strong agreement with his 1522 postil where he described threefold use of the Law. Together, the passages confirm that Luther taught not only about divine uses of the Law but also about the righteous man's use of the Law and that he definitely taught about a third use.

Luther described the Law revealing good and evil, also for the Christian life. At the same time, he described the office of the Gospel or the ancient and medieval prophetic use of the Law. These two teachings appear side by side under the third office. Perhaps this complexity led Luther to distinguish more simply between Law and

---

[268] E.g., the German term *Schaftreib*, one who moves the sheep to pasture. Luther commonly used "lead" (*führen*) for the role of a shepherd, an image he explicitly linked with the Gospel (see his *Commentary on Psalm 23* [1535–36] LW 12).

[269] Cf. usage in the preface to James. See the introduction to James in *The Lutheran Study Bible* (St. Louis: Concordia, 2009), 2131, which illustrates how Luther used *treiben* with both Law and Gospel.

Gospel and the first two offices of the Law as a means of amplifying the Gospel while letting go of medieval prophetic use of the Law.

In these same years, we have also seen that Luther clearly continued to speak of the use of the Law in the Christian life through his dialectical and rhetorical patterns of use, misuse, and Christian life. Further, we see in the teaching on 1 Tm 4:7 that Luther provided detailed reflection on the use of the Law for the righteous man through his verbs (*exercere, üben, treiben*). He described the believer exercising, training, teaching, and practicing with the Law not for the sake of justification but for service, goodness, and worship.

These observations illustrate the complexity of describing the dialectical uses of Law and Gospel as well as the Christian life as sinner and saint. We see him working thoughtfully with the ancient and medieval categories, while trying to address what they had not addressed. This is such a different picture of Luther from the romantic, heroic Reformer who creates new categories of theology whole cloth while abandoning and burning his bridges to scholasticism. This research offers a more conservative view of Luther as a late medieval theologian working with late medieval tools that he saw in a new way because of his careful study of Holy Scripture. I do not write this to undermine the freshness of Luther's thought and the brilliance that shows forth from his observations, which I treasure personally and professionally. On the contrary, I write this to show how Luther valued and worked with the heritage of ancient and medieval Christian teaching and how he stood in continuity with that teaching.

Chapter eleven will again address the question: since Luther in 1522 and 1528 wrote and spoke about a threefold use of the Law and a third office of the Law, why did he not write or speak in this threefold manner more often? But first, we continue to follow Luther's teaching chronologically with the 1529 catechisms.

CHAPTER TEN

THE CATECHISMS (1529–30)

There will be a spontaneous impulse and a desire gladly to do the will of God.

—Martin Luther

Although Luther had created a number of catechetical resources early in the Reformation, he realized that the reform needed a catechism for children.[270] He entrusted this task to his friends, Justus Jonas and John Agricola. Agricola was more diligent for the work. He prepared his *One Hundred Thirty Common Questions*, which gives us the first indication that Agricola had developed a different doctrine of the Law from Luther and Melanchthon. His new views would lead to the first antinomian controversy.

Luther himself determined to write a catechism for children in 1525. The Law was, of course, a major feature of Luther's catechisms. In fact, nearly half of the Large Catechism is devoted to expounding the Ten Commandments. In the catechisms, Luther repeated themes about the Law and the Christian life that we saw in the 1527 *Lectures on Titus* and the 1528 *Lectures on 1 Timothy*. This chapter will present a few examples of those themes, noting especially Luther's verbs.

---

[270] Charles P. Arand writes about the variety of resources Luther had created in *That I May Be His Own: An Overview of Luther's Catechisms* (St. Louis: Concordia, 2000). See his chapter on "The Versatile Catechism."

The Preface to the Large Catechism

The foreword to the 1530 *Deudsch Catechismus* includes a number of Luther's favorite verbs for describing use of God's Word.[271] He emphasized the verbs for exercise (*exercere, üben, treiben*) and related terms in the preface to the Large Catechism and his comments on the Close of the Commandments.

> A Christian, Profitable, and Necessary Preface, and Faithful, Earnest Exhortation of Dr. Martin Luther to All Christians, but Especially to All Pastors and Preachers, that They should Daily Exercise[272] Themselves in the Catechism, which is a Short Summary and Epitome of the Entire Holy Scriptures, and that They May Always Teach[273] the Same.

> We have no slight reasons for treating[274] the Catechism so constantly and for both desiring and beseeching others to teach[275] it.

After Luther encountered Antinomianism in late 1527, he began to emphasize the role of the Law more strongly. For example, one must remember that nearly half of the Large Catechism is devoted to teaching the Ten Commandments. This shows a sharply different attitude toward the Law from what we saw in Agricola's *One Hundred Thirty Common Questions*.[276]

As noted from Luther's lectures, he was fond of verbs that described the continuing use of God's Word in the believer's life. Luther used these verbs not just for teaching God's Word generally but also for using the Ten Commandments—God's Law. For example, he wrote:

---

[271] Longer preface, title/foreword and para. 1. The Kolb-Wengert edition does not include this foreword so I have cited it from the *Concordia Triglotta*.

[272] Luther's German is *üben*; the Latin translation has *exerceant*. Vincent Obsopoeus, rector of the school at Ansbach, prepared the 1529 translation. It is not clear to me who translated the 1530 forward.

[273] Ger. *treiben*; Lat. *proponant*.

[274] Ger. *treiben*; Lat. *urgemus*.

[275] Ger. *treiben*; Lat. *faciant*.

[276] See pp.106–108.

Moreover, what is the whole Psalter but meditation and exercises[277] based on the First Commandment?

CONCLUSION OF THE TEN COMMANDMENTS

For Luther, the giving of the Law was not simply a stop on the way to the New Testament. It continued to apply and even benefit the believer. In the Conclusion of the Ten Commandments, para. 319, we read:

> We must repeat the text that we have already treated above in connection with the First Commandment in order to show how much effort God desires us to devote to learning how to teach[278] and practice[279] the Ten Commandments.

Luther envisioned preaching the Law consistently to believers.

> It is useful and necessary, I say, always to teach, admonish, and remind young people of all this so that they may be brought up, not only with blows and compulsion, like cattle, but in the fear and reverence of God. These are not human trifles but the commandments of the most high Majesty, who watches over them with great earnestness, who is angry and punishes those who despise them, and, on the contrary, abundantly rewards those who keep them. Where people consider this and take it to heart, there will arise a spontaneous impulse[280] and desire gladly to do the will of God.[281]

Luther clearly has in mind the life of the believer who is changed by the call to repentance and faith and so has a different relationship to the Law. The believers are no longer driven "cattle." Instead, after learning the punishments and rewards of the Law there follows "a spontaneous impulse." In this case, the spontaneity is a consequence not only of the Gospel but also of the teaching of the Law. Christians respond to the Law very differently from those who are living under

---

[277] Ger. *übungen*; Lat. *exercitiaque*. The text is from the Longer preface, para. 18.
[278] Ger. *treiben*; Lat. *inculcandis*.
[279] Ger. *üben*; Lat. *exercendis*.
[280] Ger. *reizen und treiben*; Lat. *sponsa . . . propensi*.
[281] Close of the Ten Commandments, para. 330.

the condemnation of the Law. Luther here captures the attitude of the great psalm of the Word, Ps 119.

Luther's teaching about spontaneous fulfilling of the Law does not exclude the teaching of the Ten Commandments. It excludes a Law-based motivation for keeping the commandments: people fulfill the Law because they know what is right and genuinely want to do what God's Law says. They gladly take up the Law and put it into practice. Believers—those who genuinely fear God, an Old Testament expression for trust in God—respond positively to the hearing of God's Law because the Gospel has changed their hearts and made them glad to fulfill the Law by the Spirit. We must remember that in Luther's view the Law is always with us because God wrote it onto our hearts (Jer 31:33; Rm 2:15). Mankind is at all times under the influence of the natural law, whether one is an unbeliever or a believer declared righteous by grace through faith. So the believer never spontaneously keeps the Law without the presence and use of the Law. The believer takes up the Law willingly and uses it.[282] Christian freedom does not describe a lawless state of life.

THE SMALL CATECHISM

The Morning Prayer in the Small Catechism likewise assumed the constant use of the commandments.

> In the morning, as soon as you get out of bed, you are to make the sign of the holy cross and say: . . . After singing a hymn perhaps (for example, one on the Ten Commandments) or whatever else may serve your devotion, you are to go to your work joyfully.

The Table of Duties included just this sort of practice or use of the Law where Luther drew together:

---

[282] Paul Althaus well documented this aspect of Luther's teaching with extensive examples from WA 39 I, WA 7, and other sources in *The Theology of Martin Luther* Robert C. Schultz, trans. (Philadelphia: Fortress Press, 1966), 266–72. However, Althaus then unhelpfully asserted, "Luther does not use the expression 'the third function of the law [tertius usus legis]' " failing to note Luther's expressions in WA 10/I.1 and WA 26. Althaus did conclude, "In substance . . . [the third function] also occurs in Luther" (p. 273). Cf. Kolb and Arand 158.

The House Chart of Some Bible Passages for all kinds of holy orders and walks of life, through which they may be admonished, as through lessons particularly pertinent to their office and duty.

Here Luther shows from the Bible what God expects believers to do in their walk of life. Could there be a clearer example of teaching believers how to do good works? Just as the Law has its office to show what is right and what is wrong, the believers have their offices in which they keep God's Law through willing service.

Conclusion

Elert and other theologians have rightly emphasized the importance and centrality of Luther's teaching of the theological use of the Law and that the Law always accuses (*Lex semper accusat* in Ap IV 38). However, in the 1528 *Lectures on 1 Timothy*, Luther also clearly taught that the Law always reveals. In so far as the believer is free from the Law's condemnation, the Spirit leads him to take it up gladly and use it. The Christian responds in a very different way and is able to see the Law as a friend with whom one may spend the day with good conscience and even joy.

From the 1522 *Christmas Postil* to the 1529 catechisms we see significant consistency in Luther's teaching about the Law. Luther taught about the time under the Law, the giving of the Law to restrain (civil use) and to know one's self as a sinner (theological use). Yet he also wrote about the Law as an enduring revelation that the believer gladly keeps during the time of grace (the righteous man's use). The doctrine of the threefold use of the Law entered Reformation theology through Luther's teaching—not Melanchthon's, though Luther did not regularize or systematize the threefold use of the Law as we shall see in the next chapter.

CHAPTER ELEVEN

ENUMERATION IN THE *LECTURES ON GALATIANS* (1531, 1535)

> Give no more to the Law than it has coming, and say to it: "Law, you want to ascend into the realm of conscience and rule there. . . . Stay within your limits and exercise your dominion over the flesh."
>
> — Martin Luther

Investigations of Luther's doctrine of the Law have naturally focused on chapter three of his Galatians lectures and commentary. And rightly so, for it is surely one of the important texts for understanding Luther's teaching. In fact, the title for this book is drawn from Luther's 1519 *Lectures on Galatians*.

However, in this chapter we will see that over emphasis on the published 1535 *Lectures on Galatians* has misled researchers about Luther's doctrine of the Law. For those who believe Luther taught only two uses of the Law, the following passage is a proof text.[283]

> Here one must know that there is a double use of the Law. One is the civic use. God has ordained civic laws, indeed all laws, to restrain transgressions. Therefore every law was given to hinder sins. . . . The other use of the Law is the theological or spiritual one, which serves to increase

---

[283] E.g., William H. Lazareth's introduction to the translation of Paul Althaus's *The Divine Command* (Philadelphia: Fortress Press, 1966), vi.

transgressions. This is the primary purpose of the Law of Moses, that through it sin might grow and be multiplied, especially in the conscience. Paul discusses this magnificently in Rom. 7. Therefore the true function and the chief and proper use of the Law is to reveal to man his sin, blindness, misery, wickedness, ignorance, hate and contempt of God, death, hell, judgment, and the well-deserved wrath of God. Yet this use of the Law is completely unknown to the hypocrites, the sophists in the universities, and to all men who go along in the presumption of the righteousness of the Law or of their own righteousness. To curb and crush this monster and raging beast, that is, the presumption of religion, God is obliged, on Mt. Sinai, to give a new Law with such pomp and with such an awesome spectacle that the entire people is crushed with fear. For since the reason becomes haughty with this human presumption of righteousness and imagines that on account of this it is pleasing to God, therefore God has to send some Hercules, namely, the Law, to attack, subdue, and destroy this monster with full force. Therefore the Law is intent only on this beast, not on any other.[284]

In the 1535 *Lectures on Galatians*, Luther spoke so consistently of a twofold use of the Law, one wonders how he earlier had written of a threefold use in 1522 and 1528. Did this enumeration mean that Luther changed his doctrine about the use of the Law?

To merely count up uses leaves one in a quandary. The historian must consider more than the number of uses and express doctrinal statements. He must also consider the historical setting of Luther's teaching as well as his dialectical and rhetorical presentation of the teaching.

THE CONTEXT OF THE LECTURES

Chapter nine established that Luther's 1528 comment on the third office of the Law came shortly after the time Agricola introduced the issue of antinomianism, forms of which had appeared in both the ancient and medieval eras. The Galatians lectures of 1531 also

---

[284] LW 26:308–309.

followed significant historical and doctrinal events: the publication of John Eck's *Four Hundred Articles for the Imperial Diet of Augsburg* (May 1530), the presentation of the Augsburg Confession (June 1530), and the Confutation of the Augsburg Confession by Eck and other imperially appointed theologians.[285] In other words, Luther's lectures responded to this new series of confrontations with Roman theologians, which represented an intensity not felt since the early 1520s.

On July 3rd, 1531, in Luther's opening statement about the *Lectures on Galatians*, he acknowledged that the circumstances weighed on his mind.

> There is a clear and present danger that the devil may take away from us the pure doctrine of faith and may substitute for it the doctrines of works and human traditions.[286]

Again, toward the end of his opening argument he wrote:

> When [one] has lost Christ, he must fall into a trust in his own works. We see this today in the fanatical spirits and sectarians, who neither teach nor can teach anything correctly about righteousness of grace. They have taken the words out of our mouth and out of our writings, and these only they speak and write. But the substance itself they cannot discuss, deal with, and urge, because they neither understand it nor can understand it. They cling only to the righteousness of the Law. Therefore they are and remain disciplinarians of works; nor can they rise beyond the active righteousness. They remain exactly what they were under the pope.[287]

In comments on chapter five, Luther explained that he was providing a different type of commentary than he had prepared in 1519. "Our chief purpose this time," he noted, "has been to set forth the doctrine of justification as clearly as possible as we were expounding the Epistle to the Galatians."[288] In view of this setting, students of Luther's 1531/1535 *Lectures on Galatians* must not read Luther's

---

[285] See Robert Rosin's introduction in *Sources and Contexts of the Book of Concord* 31–33.
[286] LW 26:3.
[287] LW 26:9.
[288] LW 27:87.

lack of comment on the Christian life or sanctification as evidence that Luther was disinterested in these theological topics. They were simply not the chief focus as he joined battle once again with the views of the Roman theologians on the doctrine of justification, which remained his greatest concern.

LUTHER'S ENUMERATION

A second observation that needs to be made for the 1531/1535 *Lectures on Galatians* is that Luther was very flexible in his enumeration of doctrinal points. In this respect he differed from the Scholastics and other more systematic theologians who had a fondness for enumeration. For example, in the opening paragraphs of the argument for the Galatians lectures, Luther described four kinds of righteousness: (1) political, (2) ceremonial, (3) legal, and (4) the righteousness of faith (LW 26:4). He then subsumed the first two categories under the third and proceeded to focus on a distinction between: active righteousness and passive righteousness (LW 26:7, 11). Had he suddenly rejected the other two kinds of righteousness? No. His initial distinction fell outside of his focus and so did not continue to receive express comment.

One can readily see a similar situation prevailing with distinctions between the uses of the Law. By writing about a twofold use, Luther did not inherently deny a threefold use or even more uses if one were to stop and count them all out.[289] Although Luther persisted in describing a twofold use of the Law, one must note that he also described the ongoing role of the Law in the life of a believer. Again, from his opening argument,

> Let us learn diligently this art of distinguishing between these two kinds of righteousness, in order that we may know how far we should obey the Law. We have said above that in a Christian the Law must not exceed its limits but should have its dominion only over the flesh, which is subjected to it and remains under it. When this is the case, the Law remains within its limits. But if it wants to ascend into the conscience and exert its rule there, see to it that you are a good dialectician and that you make the correct distinction. Give

---

[289] Cf. his command, "Use the Law any way you wish" (LW 28:231) in the *Lectures on 1 Timothy*.

no more to the Law than it has coming, and say to it: "Law, you want to ascend into the realm of conscience and rule there. You want to denounce its sin and take away the joy of my heart, which I have through faith in Christ. You want to plunge me into despair, in order that I may perish. You are exceeding your jurisdiction. Stay within your limits, and exercise your dominion over the flesh. You shall not touch my conscience. For I am baptized; and through the Gospel I have been called to a fellowship of righteousness and eternal life, to the kingdom of Christ, in which my conscience is at peace, where there is no Law but only the forgiveness of sins, peace, quiet, happiness, salvation, and eternal life. Do not disturb me in these matters. In my conscience not the Law will reign, that hard tyrant and cruel disciplinarian, but Christ, the Son of God, the King of peace and righteousness, the sweet Savior and Mediator. He will preserve my conscience happy and peaceful in the sound and pure doctrine of the Gospel and in the knowledge of this passive righteousness.[290]

Here Luther described the believer taking account of the Law and using it, applying a limit to guard his conscience. Note how Luther's description of the Christian as both sinner and saint at the same time is in full force as we observed in earlier examples of his teaching. Luther soon followed with this statement:

> Whoever knows for sure that Christ is his righteousness not only cheerfully and gladly works in his calling but also submits himself for the sake of love to magistrates, also to their wicked laws, and to everything else in this present life— even, if need be, to burden and danger. For he knows that God wants this and that this obedience pleases Him.[291]

The believer submits to the Law and suffering for the sake of love and from his desire to please God. Such statements about the believer using the Law come even in Luther's comments on Gal 3[292] where he most vigorously wrote of a twofold use. In the *Lectures on Galatians*, Luther was clearly teaching that the Law's accusations are abrogated

---

[290] LW 26:11.
[291] LW 26:12.
[292] LW 26:340–341; 343–345.

from the believer's conscience and cannot be used for self-justification. Nonetheless, the believer has the Law and uses it. The earlier approaches continued to appear.

A MATHEMATICAL TRAP

Theologians who read the Galatians lectures and come away insisting on only two uses of the Law have snared themselves in a mathematical trap. Indeed, Luther warned:

> Nothing is more closely joined together than fear and trust, Law and Gospel, sin and grace; they are so joined together that each is swallowed up by the other. Therefore there cannot be any mathematical conjunction that is similar to this.[293]

In this way Luther admonished his hearers to exercise special care in handling the distinctions and the relationship between Law and Gospel lest they be severed from one another. In the 1535 *Lectures on Galatians*, chapter three, we find five places where Luther wrote about two uses of the Law. However, when we compare these published comments to Rörer's notes on the 1531 lectures, we see that in three cases Luther did not explicitly speak of two uses. Ebeling recognized a similar phenomenon in the published commentary. He described an example of how the commentary edited by Rörer chose the term *politicus* to replace the term *civilis*. According to Ebeling, Luther did not participate in the publication of the commentary but left it to others who gave it a polished form.[294]

Table 14 below presents five passages from the lectures on Galatians 3. It provides the English translation followed by the 1535 commentary and the 1531 Rörer's notes from which the commentary was derived.

---

[293] LW 26:343.
[294] *Word and Faith* 69–70.

Table 14
Luther's Enumeration

1531:	"Therefore I have said: this passage distinguishes the powers either civil or theological, because first the Law was needed broadly for restraining the ignorant."[295]
1535:	"That is why I have said that this passage from Moses is to be understood in two ways, politically and theologically. For the Law was given for two uses. The first is to restrain [etc.]." (LW 26:274)[296]

1531:	"One can explain [it] morally, because God ordained also civil laws, in a civil sense. There they are needed to restrain transgressions."[297]
1535:	"Here one must know that there is a double use of the Law. One is the civic use. God has ordained civic laws, indeed all laws, to restrain transgressions." (LW 26:308)[298]

1531:	"Therefore, diligently note and discern, what the function of the Law is, what is its use. We do not reject works of the Law and Law, on the contrary we require [it], but in its own use, namely to restrain transgressions civilly and to reveal or show [transgressions] spiritually."[299]
1535:	"We say that the Law is good and useful, but in its proper use, namely, first, as we have said earlier, to retrain transgressions; and secondly, to reveal spiritual transgressions." (LW 26:313)[300]

1531:	"Further: first, civilly. Second, it terrifies, it increases sin and induces it."[301]

---

[295] "Ideo dixi: hunc locum potestis intelligere sive Civiliter sive Theologice, quia 1. lata lex ad cohercendos rudes." WA 40 I:429.
[296] "Itaque dixi hunc locum Mosi intelligi dupliciter, Civiliter et Theologice. Est enim lex lata ad duplicem usum: Primum ad cohercendos rudes et malos." WA 40 I:429.
[297] "Man kans exponere moraliter, quia deus ordinavit etiam Civiles, in Civili sensu. Ibi sunt ad cohercendas transgressiones." WA 40 I:479.
[298] "Hic sciendum est duplicem esse legis usum. Alter civilis est. Deus ordinavit civiles, imo omnes leges ad cohercendas transgressiones." WA 40 I:479.
[299] "Ideo diligenter notate et discernite, quid officium legis, quis eius usus. Non reiicimus opera legis et legem, imo exigimus, sed in suo usu, scilicet cohibere civiles transgressiones et revelare et ostendere spirituales." WA 40 I:485.
[300] "Exigimus dicimusque legem bonam et utilem, sed in suo usu, scilicet Primum ad cohercendas, ut diximus supra, civiles transgressiones, Deinde ad revelandas spirituales transgressiones." (WA 40 I:485)
[301] "Ultra modum: 1. Civiliter. 2. terrefacit, auget peccatum et facit reum." (WA 40 I:487–88)

1535: "In the first place, it acts as a civic restraint upon those who are unspiritual and uncivilized. In the second place, it produces in a man the knowledge of himself as a sinner." (LW 26:314)[302]

1531: "The use: but [use it] to prevent, in order that it prevents not only civilly—which is the lowest use—but [use it] also theologically, . . ."[303]

1535: "What I have stated earlier so often about both uses of the Law, the political or Gentile use and the theological use, indicates clearly [etc.]." (LW 26:343)[304]

As these examples illustrate, Luther did not enumerate uses of the Law as often as the 1535 commentary would indicate. To illustrate the difference mathematically, Luther explicitly enumerated the number of the uses of the Law in only 40% of these examples. The editing provided the other 60% of the examples found in the published commentary. In other words, Rörer's editing helped regularize the doctrinal terminology of the use of the Law. This does not mean that Rörer improperly handled his responsibility or corrupted Luther's teaching. Editing typically brings greater regularity to a text; Luther expressed gratitude for the results. However, it does mean that scholars must be aware of the effects of editing.

To count up the number of uses in the Galatians commentaries and conclude that Luther taught only two uses of the Law is to read something into the passages that was not intended.[305] In other words, there is no evidence that Luther was trying to develop a specific and consistent numeration system as is often attributed to him. Luther's comments about numeration are never governed by the later, common distinctions and ordering of three uses of the Law as appeared in

---

[302] "Primum civiliter cohercet carnalis et rudes. Deinde aperit homini cognitionem sui, quod sit peccator." (WA 40 I:487–88)

[303] "Usus: Sed sic arcere, ut non tantum civiliter arceat,—que est infimus usus,—sed etiam theologicae, . . ." (WA 40 I:530)

[304] "Quae supra toties inculcavi de ustroque legis usu, Politico seu gentili et Theologico, satis indicant legem non esse positam iustis, sed, ut alibi Paulus docet, iniustis." (WA 40 I:528)

[305] This point is illustrated by other passages, as when Luther wrote, "This now is the first work of God, that we know ourselves, how condemned, miserable, weak and sickly we are" (*Church Postil*, Lenker 2:368). Here Luther called the traditional second use of the Law the "first" to emphasize its priority in repentance. His discussion of the uses was typically sequential or chronological.

Melanchthon and FC VI where the doctrine was given more dogmatic treatment. One should note that not even these later dogmatic writings argue that there are *only* three uses of the Law. Modern theologians who insert the term *only* into the doctrinal discussion are making a historical and logical mistake with far-reaching consequences.[306]

Modern readers must also consider Luther's point that Paul's comments in Gal 3:1–24 focused on the topic of conversion. Such a focus would naturally exclude or diminish consideration of the Christian life and sanctification.[307]

THE PATTERN OF LUTHER'S TEACHING

Earlier we noted that Luther taught on the third use of the Law after presenting the twofold use of the Law and misunderstanding of those uses. A similar phenomenon appeared in Luther's lectures on Galatians 3.

After teaching extensively about the twofold use of the Law and misunderstandings of the Law (*Lectures on Galatians* [1535] LW 26:304–340), Luther eventually turned to a brief description of the place of the Law in the life of a believer as sinner and saint (LW 26:340–343). Then Luther turned again to describe the twofold use of the Law and misunderstandings of it (LW 26:343–348) followed by comment on the role of the Spirit in the believer's life (LW 26:349–353).

The 1531/1535 *Lectures on Galatians* did not follow Luther's earlier pattern of argument absolutely. They provided a much longer presentation. But the earlier pattern of (1) understanding, (2) misunderstanding, (3) understanding in the life of the believer, is there.

---

[306] Late medieval and Reformation era logic was very sensitive to the use of all-inclusive and exclusive terms in ways that modern thinkers are not (cf. e.g., the Reformation's use of the *particularis exclusivae*). To argue that Luther had only two uses of the Law requires supporting passages from Luther in which he explicitly makes such an exclusive argument. The context of such statements would also need to be explored to determine whether Luther wrote the passage with rhetorical flourish or hyperbole, which he often liked to do. See "Luther's Use of All-Inclusive and Exclusive Terms" in *One True God* (St. Louis: Concordia, 2007), 52–53.
[307] LW 26:248.

THE TEXT EFFECT

A general observation from the history of biblical interpretation may help explain some of the phenomena in Luther's teaching. An interpreter's description of doctrine is closely guided by the passage he is interpreting. So, for example, a Church Father interpreting a passage from Paul may sound like an advocate of justification by grace alone and faith alone (e.g., John Chrysostom in his sermons on the Pauline Epistles). However, the same interpreter expounding a different passage may sound like a synergist. The passage before him colors his wording/teaching.

Luther was also subject to this effect. When teaching on Gal 3, he focused on the particular issue of that passage, which was the doctrine of justification as Luther himself stated. When writing about a different text under different circumstances, Luther would bring out a different emphasis. For example, one sees a strong emphasis on the doctrine of the Law and its application to the believer in Luther's exposition of the Ten Commandments (see chapter ten). This emphasis did not mean that Luther had suddenly de-emphasized the Gospel. It simply meant that as a focused interpreter, he concentrated on the text before him and it affected his statements of doctrine.

CONCLUSION

For several reasons, Luther's 1535 *Lectures on Galatians* chapter three cannot rightly be defended as evidence that Luther taught only two uses of the Law as Ebeling argued in his influential article of 1950. First, the editorial process regularized the 1535 *Lectures on Galatians*. Second, although it is certainly true that Luther wrote about two uses of the law explicitly on a number of occasions, we have also noted that he wrote elsewhere about a threefold use or third use of the Law. Third, Luther often focused his comments on the topic at hand without trying to write comprehensively or to enumerate all possibilities.[308] In the Galatians lectures Luther was focused especially on the doctrine of justification, which naturally placed his emphasis on the theological use of the Law. To read Luther's

---

[308] Timothy F. Lull writes with exclamation that Luther was not a systematic theologian but wrote to address specific concerns and situations. See *Martin Luther's Basic Theological Writings*, 2nd ed. (Minneapolis, MN: Augsburg Fortress, 2005), xix.

comments in the 1535 commentary as normative for all his teaching violates basic principles of contextual reading. Ebeling's article pulled together much helpful data on Luther's doctrine of the use of the Law—more than anyone had gathered before. But Ebeling also overlooked many aspects of the history that could have better guided his conclusions and the conclusions of future researchers.

Most of the passages we have examined thus far are exegetical. In the next chapter we will examine a dogmatic text from Luther that Werner Elert and others handled as a proof text for enumerating two uses of the Law in Luther's theology.

CHAPTER TWELVE

THE SMALCALD ARTICLES (1536–38)

> The Holy Spirit does not allow sin to rule and gain the upper hand so that it is brought to completion, but the Spirit controls and resists so that sin is not able to do whatever it wants.
>
> —Martin Luther

In the Smalcald Articles, Luther did something puzzling. He described the doctrine of justification as "the first and chief article" (SA II) right after introducing the doctrines of the Trinity and Christology as the first article of the treatise (SA I). In view of this, one wonders how justification is first. Is this an example of Luther's hyperbole or is there something definitely first and chief about the article of justification?

At other times, Lutheran theologians have described the distinction between Law and Gospel as the highest art in Christendom and as an especially brilliant light. Later, we will also see that Melanchthon stated that Christian theology must begin with the function of the Law. As a twentieth century Lutheran theologian, Gerhard Ebeling described the distinction between Law and Gospel as the central issue of theology.[309] All of these observations raise the question: how do justification, Law, and Gospel fit together in the priorities of Lutheran theology?

---

[309] *Luther: An Introduction to His Thought*, R. A. Wilson, trans. (London: Collins, 1970), 118.

In this chapter, we will look especially at Luther's teaching about the uses of the Law in the Smalcald Articles. But we do so with these larger questions about priorities in mind, in part because the Articles greatly influenced the development of the only-two-uses consensus, which has reshaped discussion of Law and Gospel as the central issue in theology.[310] Before looking at the Smalcald Articles themselves, it will be helpful to learn more about why twentieth century scholars read Luther as they did and why they emphasized Law and Gospel.

THE THUNDERBOLT OF GOD

Twentieth century Luther scholars emphasized the theological use of the Law in large measure because Luther himself emphasized it, calling the theological use "The foremost office or power of the Law." It reveals mankind's corrupt nature and terrifies with God's wrath against sin (SA III II 4–III 2). Perhaps no better description of this emphasis in Luther scholarship can be found than Werner Elert's chapter "Under the Wrath of God" in *The Structure of Lutheranism*.[311]

In the sections on "Primal Experience," "Sin," and "The Law and the Wrath of God," Elert argued that the Law confirms for us the primal experience that the righteous God opposes our sin with wrath so that, monstrously, even the very best and noblest things about mankind are subject to condemnation and death. References to "enmity," "enemy," and "hostile" govern the passages of Elert's text. Rm 8:7 stands behind these terms: "For the mind that is set on the flesh is hostile to God, for it does not submit to God's law; indeed, it cannot." Elert provided numerous references to Luther's writings that substantiate the point.

When reading Elert's comments one cannot help but remember the fact that he wrote this in the wake of two World Wars during which he witnessed the decimation of Germany's youth. He is writing, as it were, in a graveyard for his family and students, which perhaps contributed to his dark and brooding descriptions of the Law. Nonetheless, twentieth century Luther scholars emphasized the theological use of the Law in Luther because Luther himself emphasized it. This fact provided them with a clear warning against the idea that the Law could be a teacher, a guide, a friend—even to

---

[310] See, e.g., Murray 9.
[311] Vol. 1 (St. Louis: Concordia, 1962).

the righteous. They amplified important warnings: we cannot simply set aside the "foremost office and power of the Law"; Melanchthon's saying that the "Law always accuses" should return quickly to mind if preachers and teachers are to take the use of the Law seriously.

A historical question is whether these important points for Luther and Luther scholarship excluded a third use of the Law from an appropriate home in Luther's theology. Since we have seen Luther at times speaking of a third use and indeed of a friendship with the Law, the Smalcald Articles offer an important test for whether Luther's doctrine would truly allow for a third use of the Law. With these observations, we may take a closer look at the Articles' teaching on the Law.

Luther's Argument

Theologians who contend for an only-two-uses consensus often point to the Smalcald Articles to support their case. They rightly point out that Luther mentioned only two offices of the Law in the article "Of the Law" (SA III II).[312] However, in chs. 7–11 we have seen that Luther typically presented his teaching on the use of the Law with a contrast between right use and misuses before turning to the topic of how the Law serves in the righteous man's life.

In this section we will apply what we have learned about Luther's dialectic and rhetoric in our investigation of SA III II–III. Luther's articles in this portion of the Smalcald Articles do not have firm boundaries. For example, his teaching "On the Law" continued into the next article, as the opening line for "Of Repentance" shows. It states, "The New Testament retains this office of the law and teaches it" and follows with various biblical texts. Luther's argument about the Law spilled over into the article on repentance.[313]

Luther's concerns for teaching Law and Gospel also gave the article on repentance its shape. He described the effects the Law has on various hearers, harkening back to his comments in the 1522 postil. He likewise added warnings about misuse of the Law and false

---

[312] See Lazareth, para. 7, who associates this view with "The twentieth-century Luther renaissance.
[313] SA III III begins with, "Solch Amt [* des Gesetzes] behält das Neue Testament und treibet's auch."

repentance. Below is an outline that shows the progression of Luther's argument across articles two and three.

Table 15
Luther's Pattern of Teaching in the Smalcald Articles (1537)
First office of the Law (II 1–3)
Second office of the Law (II 4–5)
True repentance (III 1–3)
Gospel/conversion (III 4–6)
    Warning against only Law (III 7–9)
    Warning against false repentance (III 10–29)
True repentance (III 30–40)
    Warning against false repentance (III 41–42)[314]
True repentance (III 43–45)

From II 1–III 6, we see Luther teaching God's use of Law and Gospel leading to conversion. He then introduced warnings about misuse of the Law. The theological use of the Law continues to have a role in the life of a believer, revealing his sin on a day-to-day basis and driving him toward repentance. These warnings addressed problems raised by Luther's colleague, John Agricola.

In III 40, where Luther first turned back to the topic of true repentance, he began to describe the Christian life as one of true, on-going repentance that contended against the flesh. He cited the example of the apostle Paul who "wars" not by his own powers but by the "gift of the Holy Ghost."[315]

In III 44 he again returned to the matter of true repentance and the struggles of the Christian life. He ended with the work of the Spirit in the Christian while reaching back to one of the first words he used when describing the office of the Law. The Spirit is now the subject of this verb. He "represses and restrains"[316] the sinful nature in the believer.[317]

---

[314] Paras. 42–45 were added by Luther in 1538 before the Smalcald Articles were published. Hence the repetition in the pattern of warning about misuse before teaching about true repentance in the Christian life.

[315] Cf. "war" passages in the *Antinomian Disputations*. See p. 141.

[316] The terms are *steuert und wehrt*; cf. SA III III 1.

[317] Cf. the Spirit's work in Jn 16:8–11.

The Law—applied by the Holy Spirit—has an ongoing role in the believer's life, "restraining" the sinful nature. Though this role is similar to the civil office of the Law Luther described in SA III II 1–2, it is also different. God has changed the believer's relationship to the Law. The Spirit enables the believer to resist temptation and keep the Law. As Luther stated in 1522, "The third class observe it [the Law] both externally and with the heart. This class is the tables of Moses, written upon outwardly and inwardly by the finger of God himself."[318] We should also remember Luther's observation that the righteous keep the Law without constraint, which is clearly a different matter from the first use of the Law.[319]

JUSTIFICATION AS FIRST, CHIEF, AND CENTRAL

Having viewed Luther's pattern of teaching about the use of Law and Gospel for conversion and the Christian life, we may return to some of the questions raised at the beginning of the chapter. Luther's statement that justification is "first and chief" is more than an example of his hyperbole. Also, the emphases of earlier Lutheran theologians on Law, Gospel, and justification were not misplaced. Some further observations will help us make sense of these priorities in doctrine.

The distinction between Law and Gospel is simply reading the Holy Scriptures for what they are: the proclamation of the righteousness of God and His power to judge and to justify sinners. To illustrate the point, "righteousness" is the persistent theme of the Holy Scriptures.[320] English does us a bad turn that obscures this point by dividing the Scriptures' great emphasis under two widely occurring word stems: "right-" and "just-." The alert student of Scripture, however, notices the connection and traces this emphasis that Luther himself discovered at the beginning of his career: the righteousness of God is His power to save.[321]

---

[318] *Church Postil*, Lenker 6:273.
[319] See pp. 104–105 for a description of differences between the civil use and the righteous man's use of the Law.
[320] See *The Lutheran Study Bible* xxvii; see also "justify," p. 1903.
[321] LW 25:9.

Ebeling made an excellent observation[322] that helps us understand why Luther then called this theme of Scripture and theology "first and chief." Through Law and Gospel, the doctrine of justification manifests itself continually in the teaching of the Church each time proclamation takes place. The day-in, day-out practice of the Church draws justification forward among all doctrines because we handle it every time we turn the pages of the Scripture. We speak of it every time we open our mouths to teach or preach. Since the Scripture is all about righteousness or justification that God brings about through the proclamation of Law and Gospel, and since God Himself is only known through this proclamation, the doctrine of justification rises in stature. The distinction between Law and Gospel rises with it. As this happens, justification does not leave all other doctrines behind. It properly leads us into them, including an appropriate understanding of the role of the Spirit and of the Law in the Christian life.

Conclusion

The Law of God falls upon sinners like a devastating thunderbolt of God's wrath. Elert and other twentieth century Luther scholars elevated this important feature of Luther's teaching, which is an essential point of balance to any discussion of the role of the Law in repentance and the life of a believer.

Yet, in the Smalcald Articles, we see that Luther's earlier dialectical and rhetorical pattern on the use of the Law also found a home in his mature thought. Luther presented warnings about false repentance followed by comments about the role of the Spirit and the Law in the Christian's life.

We see in the example of the Smalcald Articles how insufficient it is to read Luther's teaching about the civil and theological uses of the Law and then close the book as though Luther had nothing more to say. He persistently followed his teaching on the civil and theological uses with warnings about misuses—stepping away from his main argument—before commenting on the role of the Law in the Christian life, which he had enumerated as a third use in 1522 and 1528.

The importance of distinguishing the uses of the Law, and of distinguishing Law and Gospel, stem from their importance to the

---

[322] *Luther: An Introduction to His Thought* 116–18.

doctrine of justification, which is "first and chief." Without the proclamation of Law and Gospel, salvation is impossible and the sinner remains an enemy of God. Through the proclamation of the Law God breaks the sinner's trust in self and in works. In the Gospel, God declares the sinner righteous, creates faith in him, and grants His Holy Spirit so the sinner can see that God is not simply a God of wrath but indeed a loving heavenly Father. The Christian life becomes a pattern of daily repentance that wars against the sinful nature. "The Holy Spirit does not allow sin to rule and gain the upper hand so that it is brought to completion, but the Spirit controls and resists so that sin is not able to do whatever it wants" (SA III III 43).

CHAPTER THIRTEEN

THE *ANTINOMIAN DISPUTATIONS* (1537–39)

> The gospel . . . uses the office of the law to go after and expose the vices and to prepare for life, how the new people, saints, ought to walk in the new life.
>
> —Martin Luther

Luther's 1528 meeting with his friends John Agricola and Philip Melanchthon sadly did not put an end to misunderstanding and conflict. Charges that Melanchthon taught an incorrect doctrine of the Law reemerged in 1536, which led to a renewed conflict between Luther and Agricola. As so often happens, friends overreact to one another and weary one another. The lingering issues between Agricola and Melanchthon became new issues for their students and ultimately for Luther again, who realized he needed to address the problems directly. Seventeen years earlier, these men had gathered at the outer wall of Wittenberg to set fire to canon law. Melanchthon made the invitation. Agricola likely arranged the wood and set the fire. Now Agricola found it too difficult to sit down with Luther and Melanchthon to rehearse the role of the Law in repentance and how preachers should teach about the Law from their pulpits. Wengert sums up the matter this way:

> Luther, whose moderate temperament was always inclined to defend his friends, now took the lead in defining the work of the law within the life of the Christian. Differences between

his and Melanchthon's solutions to this dilemma would cause their theological heirs a host of divisions over justification, good works, and uses of the law. At this time, however, they were still united in opposition to the Roman legalism and evangelical antinomianism.[323]

Luther's theses and disputations against the Antinomians (1537–1539) offer a great example of Luther's mature theological reflection on the use of the Law. Jeffrey Silcock, in his doctoral dissertation,[324] translated the theses and disputations into English, which I will cite throughout this chapter. Silcock is preparing a revised translation for the extension volume of *Luther's Works*, LW 61.

Because Luther presented this material at different times and for different occasions, take note of the following table, which shows the relationship between the theses, the disputations based on them, and Luther's treatises against the Antinomians after his repeated attempts to reconcile Agricola to the biblical doctrine of the Law.

---

[323] Wengert, *Law and Gospel* 210.
[324] "Law and Gospel in Luther's *Antinomian Disputations*, with Special Reference to Faith's Use of the Law," (Concordia Seminary, St. Louis, 1995).

Table 16
Theses and Disputations against the Antinomians (1537–39)

First Theses:	After December 7, 1537 (WA 39:342–347)
First Disputation:	December 18, 1537 (WA 39:360–417). Included 37 arguments.
Second Theses:	December 1537 (WA 39:347–350)
Second Disputation:	January 12, 1538 (WA 39:419–485). Included 30 arguments.
Third Theses:	Before January 7, 1538 (WA 39:352–354).
Fourth Theses:	Before January 7, 1538 (WA 39:352–354).
Fifth Theses:	Aug. or Early Sept. 1538 (WA 39:354–357).
Third Disputation:	September 6, 1538 (WA 39:489–584). Included 46 Arguments. Promotion Disputation of Cyriacus Gerichius
Sixth Theses:	c. September 5, 1540 (WA 39:358).

Treatise *Against the Antinomians*. First half of 1539 (WA 50:461–477; LW 47:99–119). Addressed to Caspar Güttel. Intended for Agricola's recantation.

Against the Eislebener. 1540 (WA 51:429–44).

Franklin Sherman, the editor for LW 47, characterized Luther's work in the first two disputations as follows:

> Luther, in his remarks prepared for these two disputations [against the Antinomians], holds firmly to the necessity for humbling the sinner through the preaching of the law before the greatness of the redemption accomplished in Christ can be realized. The law is not superseded by the gospel; rather it serves continually as God's instrument in bringing men to the gospel. Even the Christian, Luther points out, constantly needs the law's rebuke.[325]

---

[325] LW 47:103–104. In a footnote Sherman explained one of the peculiarities of the second disputation, which garnered much scholarly attention and helped establish the *only* two uses consensus. "The text of the third [second] disputation has been shown by modern scholars to have suffered emendation, probably by insertion of Melanchthonian material. See Elert, *Law and Gospel*, pp. 38 ff., and, in addition to the other works there referred to, Gerhard Ebeling's further comments on the textual question in his essay, "On the Doctrine of the *Triplex Usus Legis* in the Theology of the

Sherman's comments give a general overview of the disputations, but they do not fully describe what Luther taught about the believer's relationship to the Law.

EBELING'S ADMONITION

Advocates of the only-two-uses consensus have neglected to explain Luther's doctrine of the Law in the *Antinomian Disputations*. Ebeling acknowledged the problem. He wrote that Luther did not regularly write and speak with the term *usus* as one finds in the *Lectures on Galatians*. His *Antinomian Disputations*, which took place at about the same time as the publications of the lectures, hardly resort to the term *usus*. This gives further proof that preference for this term in Luther's writings was likely the result of editing and not an emphasis in Luther himself. Indeed, the expression twofold use of the Law only appears once in the disputations! Luther did not express himself in formulas or with regularity.[326]

Ebeling added in a footnote, "It is noteworthy that in the six lists of theses against the Antinomians (WA 39/I, pp. 345–58) *usus legis* never occurs, nor indeed the words *usus* and *uti* at all" (p. 72). These observations again emphasize how free Luther was in his use of terminology. This being the case, we should acknowledge that Luther did not always speak of two uses of the Law or three uses of the Law. He did not affix his thoughts in one way. He expressed himself as he needed.[327]

This chapter will concentrate on the passages that describe the continuing role of the Law in the life of the believer. It will relate Luther's mature teaching against Antinomianism to his earlier teaching about a threefold use of the Law and a third office of the Law.

Reformation," *Word and Faith* 62–78, especially p. 62, n. 2." (*Against the Antinomians* [1539] LW 47:103–104, n. 8). See also note 7 in the introduction above.

[326] *Word and Faith* 71–72.

[327] Silcock helpfully titled Luther's description of the Law in a Christian's life as faith's use of the Law. He hesitated to call Luther's teaching a third use of the Law.

First Disputation

In the disputations, Luther emphasized that God desired to restore His people to the delight of the Law and obedience that Adam had in paradise. This delight is not something Christians generate of themselves; it comes through the Spirit.

> When Adam was first created, not only was the law possible for him, but it was also delightful. He performed this obedience, which the law required, with a perfect will and a cheerful heart, and indeed perfectly. ... Because Christ willingly submitted himself to his own law and endured all its curses, through it he obtained the Spirit for all who believe in him. Impelled by him, they begin to fulfill the law also in this life, and in the future life their obedience of the law will be supremely delightful and perfect, that is, they will do it with body and soul, as the angels do now.[328]

The Christian has a changed will because of the redemption in Christ and the gift of the Holy Spirit. As a consequence, the believer has a new relationship to the Law. Before this redemption and gift there was at best an outward fulfilling of the Law. Now, in Christ and through the Spirit, the believer truly begins to fulfill the Law.

In the passage above, Luther used the term "obedience," which he used occasionally before.[329] In the disputations, it appeared more often, as the next citation shows.

> The law indeed demands and shows what is to be done, but where is that will which obeys and does what the law requires? Who will give it? Christ, who came to fulfill the law, he gives the will to do the law, imperfectly, of course, in this life, on account of the remnants of sin that cling to the flesh, but perfectly in the life to come.[330]

The gift of Christ is perfect, but the remnants of sin in us continue to impede the Christian's longing to do good and to fulfill what is good. The new understanding and use of the Law depends on an

---

[328] Disp. 1, Arg. 1; Silcock 128. Note that in this case Luther assumed the eternality of the Law. See p. 264.
[329] E.g., see p. 131.
[330] Disp. 1, Arg. 5; Silcock 149.

understanding that we are both saint and sinner at the same time (*simul justus et peccator*).

> He gives the Holy Spirit to those who believe in him that they may take pleasure in the law of the Lord, according to Psalm 1[:2], and that thus their hearts may be restored through it, and this Spirit gives them the will to do it. . . . Therefore, to the extent that the Spirit is in us, we too delight in the law. However, to the extent that we are of the flesh, the law also remains, yet in such a way that it cannot drive us to despair.[331]

When Luther wrote, "their hearts may be restored through [the Law]" he had the cycle of daily repentance in view. In repentance, where the Law drives the believer back to Christ rather than to despair, the believer sees clearly the benefit, use, and goodness of the Law. The believer begins to hear the Law with pleasure and delight.

Christians continue to need the Law for the purpose of daily repentance and mortification of the flesh.

> For those outside Christ, the exaction of the law is sorrowful, odious, and impossible. On the other hand, for those under Christ, it begins to become delightful, and possible in part, but not as a whole. Therefore, it should be taught among Christians, yet not on account of faith, which has the spirit subject to the law, but on account of the flesh, which resists the spirit of the saints (Gal. 5[:17]). Insofar as the flesh lives, the law has not been abrogated, yet it does not rule but is compelled to be subject to the spirit and serve it.[332]

Luther saw that the theological use of the Law was an ongoing benefit to the believer, what traditionally is known as the second use of the Law. However, Luther also noted how this use of the Law is different with the believer. The Law is not a lord who rules over the Christian. It is subject to the spirit of the saints. It serves them in their ongoing need for daily repentance (mortification). In other words, the saints now *use* the Law—it is useful and beneficial to them (cf. Luther's earlier comments about a threefold use and a third office of the Law).

---

[331] Disp. 1, Arg. 6; Silcock 150.
[332] Disp. 1, Arg. 7; Silcock 154.

Luther continued to speak about the use of the Law with two steps. But note that He also described Christ's "office" that begins even in this life: to restore the lost innocence and joyful obedience to the Law.

> The law therefore is necessary, first, on account of the stubborn and untaught, that they may be coerced, secondly, on account of the faithful, who still have remnants of sin. For just as sin and death never rest but repeatedly perturb and sadden the godly for as long as they live here, so the law repeatedly returns and terrifies the consciences of the godly. But when we are raised, it will simply be abolished; it will not teach us nor will it demand anything from us. Thus it is Christ's office to restore the human race, also in this life, to that lost innocence and joyful obedience to the law, which in paradise was in the positive [degree].[333]

The "innocence" and "joyful obedience" Luther described are surely not the theological use of the Law, which involves fear and terrors. They are also not the civil use of the Law, which involves restraint and not a positive, joyful obedience. Where does that leave us? Luther here described the righteous man's use of the Law, the inward and outward keeping of the Law he described earlier in the 1522 *Christmas Postil*.

In later passages of the disputation, Luther described the preaching of the Law to the godly as "admonition."

> Let us not give ear to those who desire to see the law banished from the church. For its office is continually necessary and useful, not only because the hardened are to be frightened, but also because the godly are to be admonished to continue in the repentance that they have begun until the end of their life.[334]

He also described the use of the Law in mortification as different from the theological use of the Law in conversion. The Law puts the hearer to death (mortifies) in conversion. However, in the Christian life, the Holy Spirit focuses this mortification on the flesh, to keep it in check.

---

[333] Disp. 1, Arg. 7; Silcock 154.
[334] Disp. 1, Arg. 21; Silcock 204.

> Mortification in the justified however is not contrition, if indeed I have been liberated from the law [Rom. 7:6; 8:2], as Paul says: he [Christ] redeemed us from the curse of the law [Gal. 3:13]. But the law remains as well as mortification because our flesh is always rebellious. Therefore, the Holy Spirit or faith always impresses the law on his flesh that it may give over, lest sin be allowed to rule [Rom. 6:12] or do as it pleases. But this mortification is bearable and is a mark of the justified.[335]

In the first disputation, Luther did not explicitly mention a third use or office of the Law. Yet it is clear that Luther distinguished the use of the Law in the life of the believer from the use of the Law in society and in conversion. The theological use of the Law becomes noticeably different for those who have received redemption and the Spirit. For them, the Law is not a ruler but a servant. Think here of St. Paul's analogy of the pedagogue (Gal 3) whose relationship to the son is changed when the son becomes mature: the pedagogue no longer rules over the son but is properly recognized as a servant.[336] As we described in chapter seven, Luther saw a change in status for the believer, not only before God but also in relationship to His Law.

SECOND DISPUTATION

Early in the second disputation Luther characteristically wrote of a twofold use of the Law, "You know that the use of the law is twofold, first for restraining sins and then for exposing sins" (Disp. 2, Arg. 6; Silcock 303). He later distinguished a twofold keeping of the Law and the role of Christ and the Spirit in the believer, which he also described in the first disputation (p. 149).

> Indeed, not a part, but the whole law is needed. But the dispute is about keeping it: whether, that is, we keep the law by our human powers? No, we do not. Then who does? Christ. He keeps it all and then afterwards we keep it in part, though not by our own powers but by the power of the Holy

---

[335] Disp. 1, Arg. 32; Silcock 237.
[336] Cf. also Lombard's idea of the Law as a friend (p. 60 above and Luther's use of the same expression p. 78).

Spirit who has been given in our hearts in whom we cry, Abba Father [Rom. 8:15].[337]

In these points, nothing is really new. The believer begins to keep the Law both inwardly and outwardly as described in the 1522 postil. However, in the twenty first argument, Luther introduced a different way of speaking about the use of the Law.

> The law has already been considerably softened through justification, which we have on account of Christ, so that it ought not terrify the justified. . . . The law is not to be taught to the godly in such a way that it convicts and condemns, but that it may spur them on to do good. . . . The law is to be softened for them and is to be taught as in the exhortation: Once you were heathen but now you have been sprinkled and washed with the blood of Christ [1 Cor. 6:11; 1 Peter 1:2]. Now, therefore, offer your bodies for obedience to righteousness put off the desires of the flesh, and do not be fashioned after yourself [cf. Rom. 6:12–19; 12:1–2].[338]

Luther used the term "exhortation" to describe a different preaching of the Law to the justified. The preacher would use the Law in a softened way—not to drive to repentance but to move believers to do good works. This way of speaking comes very close to what some regard as Law motivation. But notice that Luther rooted the admonition in the promise: because the righteous man is redeemed, therefore, he offers himself to obedient service.

Here again one sees that Luther taught a different use of the Law for believers. In this case the emphasis is on the preacher using the Law in this new way. Elsewhere it is the Spirit or the believer who uses the Law. The result (or fruit, to use Pauline language) is obedience. We see then a theme broadening in Luther's teaching about the use of the Law in the life of the believer. He can speak of the Spirit using the Law in the life of the righteous man. The righteous man taking up the Law and using it, and the preacher exhorting or admonishing the righteous man to service through a softened preaching of the Law that speaks in view of the believer's justification. Here, as elsewhere, we see a remarkable variety of ideas

---

[337] Disp. 2, Arg. 16; Silcock 359.
[338] Disp. 2, Arg. 21; Silcock 371–72.

and expressions in Luther, this time centering on the role of the Law in the life of the righteous.

MELANCHTHONIAN FORGERY?

Werner Elert noted that the Second Antinomian Disputation ends with a problematic passage that describes three uses of the Law. It states, "Thirdly, the law is to be retained so that the saints may know which works God requires."[339] The earlier generation of Luther scholars took this passage as clear evidence that Luther taught a third use. They did not grapple with the complex textual history of the passage.

In 1948 Elert described the textual problems. He also argued that the earlier generation of scholars viewed the passage incompetently since the questionable text described the civil use of the Law as the pedagogical use, whereas Luther described the theological use as the pedagogical use.[340] Ebeling's 1950 article on threefold use of the Law provided some correction to Elert's observations about the various manuscripts but essentially confirmed his finding that someone likely added the passage on the three uses of the Law later; it was not part of Luther's Antinomian Disputation.[341] Elert characterized the passage as a forgery drawn from the second period of Melanchthon's *Loci Communes*. Ebeling wrote that the circumstances of the passage would require further, time-consuming investigation by resorting to the original manuscripts. Even so, he did not hold out hope that scholars could solve the mystery.[342] Elert's discoveries and Ebeling's confirmation essentially launched the only-two-uses consensus. From that point forward, scholars joined the consensus with little dissent.

However, in 1978 Eugene Klug criticized Elert's conclusions about Luther's doctrine of the Law. He wrote:

> Werner Elert argued that not only is the term "third use of the Law" foreign to Luther, but the concept itself. His argument is largely built on the contention that the words, "Thirdly, the law is to be retained so that the saints may know which works God requires," appended at the end of Luther's Second Disputation Against the Antinomians, are a forgery and that

---

[339] *Law and Gospel* 38.
[340] *Law and Gospel* 39.
[341] *Word and Faith* 62–63, n. 2.
[342] *Word and Faith* 63, n. 2.

they were interpolated from Melanchthon's *Loci Communes*. It is possible that such an interpolation may have occurred. But to dismiss out of hand the fact that Luther nonetheless used the *concept* of the third use of the Law, if not the exact term, is without substantiation.[343]

Klug raised a valid point, though like other twentieth century scholars, he was unaware that Luther had in fact twice earlier written about a third use. Unfortunately, his critique was not followed by a more thorough investigation.

Elert's and Ebeling's warnings about the textual issues and theological deviations in the passage in the Second Antinomian Disputation seem appropriate. However, we have also seen repeatedly how varied Luther's terminology can be on the use of the Law. In view of this, it seems unwise to render certain judgment without further investigation and documentation of the theological and textual issues. As will be shown in chapter sixteen, Luther could write about the believer using the commandments to inform himself about which deeds to do. Elert went too far in asserting that Luther would not write about a third use as we have established. In the end, Klug's point about Luther's theology and terminology were appropriate.

The controversial ending to the second disputation is not needed to show that Luther taught a threefold use of the Law or a third office of the Law. The passage remains a mystery, though in view of this research one can understand how the writer of the passage believed it had some compatibility with Luther's broader teaching. It is perhaps an example of a disciple wishing to regularize Luther's teaching as one sees happening in Rörer's editing of Luther's *Lectures on Galatians* (see chapter eleven). One can be empathetic with this zeal to tame the wild diversity in Luther's self-expression.

THIRD DISPUTATION

The third disputation is considerably longer than the others since it served as a doctoral disputation for Cyriacus Gerichius and as an evaluation of Antinomian doctrine. It is divided into a morning and an evening session, with the afternoon session devoted to refutation of Antinomianism. We begin analysis with the following passage:

---

[343] *A Contemporary Look at the Formula of Concord* (St. Louis: Concordia, 1978), 200.

> The church needs the law in order that not only might the ungodly be restrained by it as with chains, but also that the godly, who still have a remnant of sin in the flesh, can be admonished and convicted lest they become secure and begin snoring. Furthermore, the church needs the law that the godly may be aroused, as it were, to battle and warfare against the remnants of sin and temptations, which will be great and many at any age. It has been laid down also for the holy and righteous Paul, not insofar as he is holy and righteous, but insofar as he is flesh and must be convicted by the law.[344]

Luther described the benefits of the civil and theological uses of the Law, then added a "furthermore" regarding the Christian life, which described mortification and ongoing repentance. The passage is similar to Luther's earlier comment about lazy saints who continually need the Law.[345] The end of the passage shows how Luther interpreted and applied 1 Tm 1:8–9 through describing Christians as righteous yet sinners at the same time (cf. *Lectures on 1 Timothy*, p. 110).[346] Luther later wrote:

> But since in the present life we are not perfect and commit sin, the law must be taught and inculcated in order that we might be summoned to the battle, lest we become lazy and sluggish, and we perish.[347]

Due to the sinful nature, the Christian continually needs the teaching of the Law, a point that Luther emphasized in the Large Catechism (p. 122).

In Luther's answer to the fifth argument, he responded with analogies of light (cf. Jn 3:19–21), battle (2 Tm 2:3–4), and walking (Mi 6:8). Luther used both the terms "admonish" and "encourage" to describe the use of the Law in teaching the saints.

> The ungodly must be battered by the light of the law in order that in their terror they finally learn to seek Christ, and the

---

[344] Disp. 3, Arg. 2; Silcock 430–32.

[345] See p. 116.

[346] Note also, "The law is laid down and is not laid down for the righteous, that is, insofar as they are righteous" [1 Timothy 1:9] (Disp. 3, Arg. 26; Silcock 563).

[347] Disp. 3, Arg. 4; Silcock 453.

law is also to be taught to the godly in order to admonish and encourage them to stay in the fight and contest, so that they do not allow themselves to be conquered however much their flesh may afflict and scoff at them. Thus Micah 6[:8]: Walk attentively with your God. Therefore, the law is indeed taught to Christians, but with some privilege, because they triumph over these things, and do not yield, either to sins, if ever they are put before them, or to the law.[348]

This passage presented an optimism about the triumph of the saints over sin. The teaching of the Law "with privilege" appears similar to the comments about softening the Law in the second disputation. The preacher teaches with a confidence that the saints will do good and triumph. "In Christ we burst forth finally and thus begin to become saints, Christians, and lords of the law and of death [Rom. 7:25–8:2]" (Disp. 3, Arg. 10; Silcock 479). As at Disp. 1, Arg. 7,[349] Luther described the believer ruling over the Law. The mature Christian has a new relationship to the pedagogue.

Christ has fulfilled the law. But it has been added: Afterwards, see to it that you live a life that is holy, godly and pure, as is becoming of Christians. The thing is this, that up to this point you have heard: You are forgiven, but, lest you complain of having been abandoned altogether, I will give you my Holy Spirit, who will make you a soldier; he also utters great and indescribably groans in your heart against sin that in the end you become what you desire.[350]

The believer, by the gift of the Spirit, longs for good and battles against sin. He is never alone in the conflict. As in the first disputation, Luther again taught about mortification. Note that the righteous are active in the effort to mortify the remnants of sin. In a later passage, Luther spoke of the Gospel using the Law.

Insofar as they are righteous, they are not under the law, and [yet] they are to be convicted until they have mortified the remnants of their sins. That is how Paul clearly addresses the Corinthians, the Ephesians, the Philippians and the Hebrews

---

[348] Disp. 3, Arg. 5; Silcock 462.
[349] See p. 152 above.
[350] Disp. 3, Arg. 13; Silcock 490.

> as saints [1 Cor. 1:2; 2 Cor. 1:1; Eph. 1:1; Phil. 1:1]. . . . The Gospel . . . uses the office of the law to go after and expose the vices and to prepare for life, how the new people, saints, ought to walk in the new life.[351]

So a consequence of the Gospel is that the saints live as new people. The Gospel uses the office of the Law to show the saints how they "ought to walk." Although the saints have the Law written on their hearts (natural law) they continue to benefit from the teaching of the Law of Moses.

> The law of God is not so well known that there is no need for it to be taught or urged, for otherwise there would have been no need to give the law and to send Moses, nor do we know as much about the law as God would wish. . . . Here therefore it is necessary to be constantly admonished lest we forget God's commandment, especially since the law of God is the highest wisdom and so as the source, origin, and wellspring of all virtues and disciplines toward God and human beings, it is infinite because sin is infinite.[352]

Again Luther spoke with optimism about the beneficial use of the Law in the life of the believer, both as admonition and as a wellspring of virtues. The Law is infinite or unending in its use because sin is an ongoing problem.

Toward the end of the disputation, Luther addressed a comment specifically to Melanchthon in which he chided him for using a concessive argument in debate about the Antinomians.

> We cannot and ought not concede, nor do we wish to support what they say for they regard the law as some kind of external discipline, by which the godly may be admonished to lead a godly life. As far as I am concerned, Master Philipp, you concede too much to these antinomians, who openly say: Moses belongs to the gallows! You should be helping me to proceed against them, and regard them as our enemies.[353]

---

[351] Disp. 3, Arg. 21; Silcock 532.
[352] Disp. 3, Arg. 24; Silcock 554.
[353] Disp. 3, Arg. 40; Silcock 604.

The passage illustrates how the debate is over for Luther. He had moved from discussion with the Antinomians as colleagues to arguing against them as false teachers. In view of their false doctrine, Luther brought forth more clearly his own doctrine about the use of the Law in the life of the believer. The believer needs the admonition of the Law as a sinner and he benefits from the teaching of the Law as a saint. It is an office of Christ and of the Gospel that the Law remains useful to the saints. It is not merely an external discipline (cf. the civil use, which Agricola allowed) but is a delight to the saints who walk in it and regard it as the highest wisdom.

CONCLUSION

The *Antinomian Disputations* again show us how Luther never fully regularized his terminology on the use of the Law. He typically mentioned the civil and theological uses but here in an extended set of documents on the topic, Luther hardly mentioned the terminology at all. Ebeling even noted a lack of the most basic term *use* itself! Given these circumstances, we need to take Luther's teaching as a whole into account. It is difficult across his career to identify a particular evolution of this doctrine, in part because much of what Luther wrote about comes already from ancient and medieval tradition. We do see his thinking and comments working more and more with the Law and Gospel distinction, emphasis on the theological use of the Law, and that Christians are both sinners and saints at the same time.

Luther's mature thought does not exclude either explicitly or implicitly a threefold use. The *Antinomian Disputations* add more examples of Luther presenting his thoughts in the dialectical and rhetorical sequence of use, abuse, and use in the Christian life. Luther also placed greater emphasis on mortification, which the Holy Spirit works in the Christian life by using the Law. He could even write of the Gospel using the Law for this good purpose in a Christian's life.

The textual history and theological expression of the infamous addition to the second disputation requires further attention from scholarship, as Ebeling called for in 1950. Given the remarkable variety in Luther's comment on use of the Law, one could rightly hesitate in asserting that the passage must be a Melanchthonian forgery. One can readily imagine a scribe adding a note in a manuscript of the disputation in order to supply himself with a stable point of reference—Melanchthon's *Loci*—as he viewed and reviewed

Luther's variety. The addition might then seek an appropriate home in the manuscript tradition without implying anything sinister. I offer this merely as a theory with the hope that scholars will review the matter more closely as Ebeling also hoped.

CHAPTER FOURTEEN

LATER EDITIONS OF THE *CHURCH POSTIL* (1540, 1543)

> The best book I ever wrote [is] the *Postil*, which even pleases the papists.
>
> —Martin Luther

As noted in chapter seven, Ebeling regarded Luther's mention of the threefold use of the Law as a "parenthesis," a "passing" thought that Luther "dropped" from his theology in favor of an only-two-uses theology.[354] In essence, Ebeling offered an argument from silence: since Luther wrote no further about a threefold use of the Law, he must have abandoned the idea. However, in chapter nine we saw that Luther revisited the idea of a threefold use of the Law in his *Lectures on 1 Timothy*, something Ebeling did not note. We saw also in chapter eleven that Luther's expressions about the uses of the Law are quite varied and that the pattern of his dialectic and rhetoric as well as the need of the day—to clarify the doctrine of justification—emphasized the theological use of the Law. The chief issue of the day focused Luther on justification. This naturally left less time and emphasis for the doctrine of sanctification, where one would expect comments on a righteous man's use of the Law.

Yet Luther's persistent reference to what theologians call the first and second uses of the Law raises the question of whether Luther explicitly rejected a third use of the Law. This chapter will address

---

[354] *Word and Faith* 64.

that question while reviewing Luther's later publications of the *Church Postil*.

A BRIEF HISTORY OF POSTIL PUBLICATION

Luther began to write postil sermons in 1520. A postil (Latin *post illa*; "after those" words of the Bible text) is basically a sermon study, a tool for helping pastors preach well on the texts of the appointed readings. The medieval church had supplied such tools for preachers, though the quality of the works varied greatly. In chapter six, we looked at the much-valued postil of Nicholas of Lyra. Other medieval preaching resources were not so highly valued.[355] The churches of the Reformation had great need for a practical means of sharing evangelical doctrine at the local level so that the Reformation would get beyond Wittenberg and theologians and into the ears and hearts of all. The postils served this most important role. The preparation and publication of Luther's postils was requested by Elector Frederick the Wise.

The *Church Postil* includes material on the appointed Gospel and Epistle readings. It developed in stages of publication. Luther first released his *Christmas Postil (Weihnachtspostille)*[356] while hidden in the Wartburg Castle, translating the New Testament into German. He published the first edition in 1522. He soon completed the *Advent Postil (Adventspostille)* and a few years later the *Lenten Postil (Fastenpostille)*. The Advent and Christmas postils were rolled together in the *Winter Postil (Winterpostille)*. Numerous editions of the sermons followed, prepared by various publishers, editors, and translators. They eventually grew into the *Church Postil (Kirchenpostille)*, which treated the Bible readings of the Gospels and Epistles for an entire year, including feast days. Historians divide the editions into different periods based on Luther's involvement with them.

---

[355] See Preface to the Large Catechism, para. 2.
[356] The *Weihnachtspostille* is the Christmas portion of what became a broader collection of postils, known as the *Kirchenpostille*. Luther's colleagues also prepared a *Haus Postil* from sermons Luther preached in the years 1532–34.

Table 17
Development of the *Church Postil*

1520–27	Luther worked on postil sermons and prepared them for publication.
1527–35	Luther entrusted publication of the postil sermons to Stephan Rodt, who served as editor and substantially changed the content of some portions of the work. Luther was ultimately not satisfied with the results of Rodt's editing.
1535	Luther mentioned his desire to have Kaspar Creuziger oversee future editions of the postil.
1540–44	Luther and Creuziger prepared editions of the postil. E.g., Luther himself improved the Luft edition of 1540 and the Wolrab edition of 1544 (WA 10/I.1:x).
1544	*Church Postil: The Exposition of the Epistles and Gospels for the Whole Year* (See Lenker 1:4).

Oddly, even though the *Church Postil* was the most widely published and used of Luther's exegetical works, it tends to receive less attention than some of his other writings. (E.g., Bernhard Lohse's helpful survey of Luther's writings does not cover the postils; English anthologies of Luther's writings do not include citations of the postils.) E. G. Schwiebert devoted several pages to the history and significance of Luther's postils in *Luther and His Times*. Schwiebert described the postils as one of Luther's most influential works, alongside his translation of the Bible and editions of the catechisms.

> Luther's own personal dynamic concept of religion became available to a much wider following, for in the *Postillen* he expounded the dynamic of Christian ethics in Christ's redeemed, the inner relationship between Law and Gospel. It may be said that no single source was more effective in planting the seeds of Lutheranism so widely throughout German lands in the early [fifteen] twenties than were the enlarged editions of the *Winterpostille*.[357]

Editions of the *Church Postil* were so numerous and widely available that early collections of Luther's works did not include them. Martin Brecht noted that the postils deserved further attention as examples of Luther's theology since Luther worked out his views while writing such popular sermons and his ideas shaped by preaching flowed into his other writings.[358]

---

[357] Schwiebert 636. The *Winterpostille* included the sermons from the *Weihnachtspostille*.
[358] *Martin Luther* 2:16.

Neglect of Luther's postils may be an example of scholars looking past the obvious and everyday sources of Reformation theology in pursuit of more academic and unique topics of study. While the common man in a sixteenth century Reformation congregation was hearing his pastor preach at Christmas time about threefold use of the Law, a student at Wittenberg was hearing Luther's lectures on Galatians where he was emphasizing the theological use of the Law in response to the new challenges from Roman theologians to the doctrine of justification. One can see from these circumstances how persons might draw different conclusions about what Luther taught, a matter to be addressed below. However, before leaving the history of the postils, it is important to note a second set of postils prepared by Luther's colleagues from notes they took based on his sermons in 1532–34. The *House Postils* (*Hauspostille*) were sermons Luther preached at his home.

LUTHER'S MATURE THOUGHT

As noted above, editions of the *Church Postil* provide a helpful perspective on Luther's view of the "threefold use of the Law," which he described in 1522, and on later descriptions of a third use of the Law. Luther's comments on the use of the Law in these practical texts give a different look at the character of his theology. In earlier chapters we have looked at Luther's threefold use of the Law from 1522. Below are a few quotations from later postils (a broader collection appears in chapter sixteen).

> Christ, the truth, has come, not to destroy the Law, but to establish it, not only in himself, which was done long ago but in me and in all Christians.[359]

> Wherever these two doctrines—Law and Gospel—remain clear and bright, there shines the sun, that is, the Gospel, [and] the moon, that is, the Law. The moon looks like a copper-red kettle when it does not have the sun. Then the Law is terrifying, when the Gospel is not with it. However, when the sun shines on it, then the moon has a radiant light. So the sun gives eternal life. While the two lights are shining,

---

[359] *Church Postil*, Lenker 5:190.

one can know day and night distinctly. When they are taken away, it is sheer blindness and darkness.[360]

It is not the design of this doctrine [Gal 5:16–24] to forbid good works or to tolerate and refrain from censuring bad ones, or to prevent the preaching of the Law. On the contrary it shows clearly that God earnestly wills that Christians should flee and avoid the lusts of the flesh, if they would remain in the Spirit. . . . Thus their hearts become filled with love and a desire to obey God and to shun sin.[361]

In these passages Luther strongly urged the use of the Law for the Christian life. Christ would establish the Law in all Christians. It gives light and helps the believer see the Gospel for what it truly is. Though they both give light and are distinct, the Christian life needs both to shine upon it. Luther's mature thought here seems most compatible with a third use of the Law where the righteous man gladly takes up the Law and uses it for himself and for others.

Advocates of the only-two-uses consensus point to Melanchthon as the originator of a third use. Melanchthon first wrote expressly about the "third use" in his 1535 *Loci Communes*, well after Luther raised the idea. According to a Table Talk saying, Luther praised Melanchthon's *Loci* in c. 1542–43, after Melanchthon had been writing about the third use for about seven years.

---

[360] "Ideo Euangelium dicit: Sehet euch fur, lernet Gottes gebot, illa enim docent, qui veri status sint, qui ordinati sunt a deo et ei placeant, Meum Euangelium docet, das ir solt selig sein, dem tod entlauffen. An den 2 werdet ir genug zu lernen haben, Nemo wird gnugsam lernen kunnen, Ergo wo die zwo lere bleiben klar und hell, Lex und Euangelium, das leuchtet Son i.e. Euangelium, Mond i.e. lex. Der Mond sihet wie ein rotter kessel, quando non habet solem. Tunc lex est horribilis, cum Euangelium non adest. Wenn aber die Sonn drein scheinet, tum luna habet candidum lumen. Sic dat sol aeternam vitam, weyl die zwey liechter leuchten, kan man tag und nacht unterschiedlich erkennen, iis ablatis so ists lauter blindheit und finsternis." *Hauspostille* for the 18th Sunday after Trinity, WA 37:174. A translation for this postil exists in *Sermons of Martin Luther: The House Postils*, vol. 3, Eugene F. A. Klug, ed. (Grand Rapids, MI: Baker Books, 1996), 68–69. However, this English edition is based on the second Erlangen edition of Luther's Works (6:99) where the text is modernized and fleshed out so that the English translation ends up with such things as "the Law guides us through this temporal life," which is not found in the original notes.
[361] *Church Postil*, Lenker 8:255–56.

> If anybody wishes to become a theologian, he has a great advantage, first of all, in having the Bible. This is now so clear that he can read it without any trouble. Afterward he should read Philip's *Loci Communes*. This he should read diligently and well, until he has its contents fixed in his head. If he has these two he is a theologian, and neither the devil nor a heretic can shake him. The whole of theology is open to him, and afterward he can read whatever he wishes for edification. . . . There's no book under the sun in which the whole of theology is so compactly presented as in the *Loci Communes*. If you read all the fathers and sententiaries you have nothing. No better book has been written after the Holy Scriptures than Philip's.[362]

It is, of course, possible that Luther was unaware of what Melanchthon had written and taught about the use of the Law. Yet at the very least, Luther's writings raised no protests against his colleague's doctrine of the use of the Law—indeed we saw earlier that Luther sided with Melanchthon during the Antinomian Controversy.

Further, one must examine how Luther handled his own comments about a threefold use of the Law in later editions of the *Church Postil*. Available editions and notes on the text of the postil for Galatians 3:23–29 indicate that Luther did not change his text about a threefold use of the Law either by deleting statements from it or by adding cautions against it in the edits of 1540 and 1543.[363] This is a point of great significance when considering Luther's mature thought and the continuity of that thought with his earlier writings. Luther and Cruciger certainly reviewed the passage on threefold use of the Law since there were changes in spelling. However, Luther and his editor (a fellow Wittenberg professor alongside Luther and

---

[362] LW 54:439–40. Number 5511, recorded by Caspar Heydenreich. In the course of this Table Talk Luther also commended his work on Galatians and Deuteronomy, dismissing everything else he had written. Such hyperbole is common in Luther's rhetoric and must not be taken absolutely.

[363] See the preface and text of *Dr. Martin Luther's sämtliche Werke*, vol. 7 (Erlangen: Carl Heyder, 1827); the 2nd edition (Frankfurt am Main: Heyder & Zimmer, 1866); see also WA 10/I.1, which references variants from numerous editions.

Melanchthon) found no cause for alarm or conflict with Luther's doctrine in his earlier statements about the threefold use of the Law.

Conclusion

The postils, which seem overlooked in twentieth century Luther studies, were anything but overlooked in the sixteenth century. They were a primary means of spreading Reformation doctrine alongside Luther's Bible translation with introductions and catechisms. These most popular Luther texts help us see Luther's emphasis on the enduring use of the Law in the Christian life.

Ebeling asserted that Luther "dropped" the threefold use of the Law. The evidence of the 1540 and the 1543 *Church Postil* shows that Luther actually retained his earlier thought and comments for his "best book," which was so widely received in the sixteenth century. Ebeling's observation that Luther most often wrote about two uses of the Law is certainly a point well taken. But one cannot conclude from this point—or from any evidence—that Luther rejected a threefold use of the Law. On the contrary, one may see a different body of evidence emerging in the following:

- The 1522 postil
- Luther's dialectic and rhetoric of presenting two uses, abuses, and the Law in the life of a believer
- The 1528 *Lectures on 1 Timothy*
- The 1540 and 1543 edits of the *Church Postil*

These passages tell a different story. They show a consistency in Luther's thought whereby he retained his observation that a believer uses God's Law for his benefit in a way that is different from the civil and theological uses of the Law.

CHAPTER FIFTEEN

THE *LECTURES ON GENESIS* (1535–44)

> The Law must not be cast aside because of the promise of grace; but it must be taught in order that discipline and doctrine concerning good works may be retained, and in order that we may be instructed to know and humble ourselves after we have sinned.
>
> —Martin Luther

In 1535 Luther stated his intention to spend the last years of his life expounding—of all things—the Books of Moses. Luther had preached series of sermons on Genesis and Deuteronomy in 1523, Exodus in 1524, Leviticus and Numbers in 1527, and Deuteronomy again in 1529. Throughout the years, he continually preached on the Ten Commandments that Moses heard from God and carried down from Mount Sinai. At times, Luther wrote forcefully against "Moses" and his accusations that afflict the conscience. Yet, it is also clear that Luther valued Moses' counsel, turned to it repeatedly, and determined to share it with his hearers and readers. Luther was not adverse to Moses but saw the need to explain his place in the canon of the Church and his use in pulpit, society, and Christian life.

The last great embodiment of Luther's mature teaching is the *Lectures on Genesis*. The use of the Law is not a major theme in the lectures since Luther largely focused his comments on the particular texts before him (cf. "The Text Effect" in chapter eleven). However, Luther wrote about the use of the Law in his comments on the life of

Joseph, especially the portion that described Joseph testing his brothers (Gn 42–43). Here Luther emphasized the need for repentance, as one would expect.

> In this way Joseph practices the true, proper, and perfect use of the Law on his brothers. For this means leading them down to hell, mortifying and confounding them, not with a view to their destruction but rather for their life and salvation. For the Law was not given to the end that it should kill, although it really does kill when it works wrath and reveals sin. But it does not kill in such a way that one must remain and perish in death, as Judas and Saul perished, but only that it may perform its function. To this the promise must be added, lest despair follow, just as these brothers will finally come almost to the point of despair. Had they not heard the statement (Gen. 45:4) "I am Joseph," it would have been a trial unto death. But Christ does not seek this. No, He seeks humiliation, contrition, and condemnation unto life. Accordingly, true repentance is not contrition alone; it is also faith, which takes hold of the promise, lest the penitent perish. But these brothers have not yet arrived at perfect knowledge of sin. Therefore Joseph will continue to plague them. They must be put through the mill even more.[364]

Luther characterized the story of Joseph as a comedy, with the work of the Law as God playing with His children to bring about their correction. Joseph, like the Lord, used the Law for the good of his brothers.

The Norm of the Law

In the story of Jacob blessing Ephraim and Manasseh, Luther brought in the matter of the use of the Law again while writing about Joseph's concern that his firstborn son was losing his inheritance.

> But these matters must be referred to the two kinds of doctrine that are handed down in Christian theology and law, namely, to the grace of the promise and to the Law. The doctrine of the Law should be retained because it is necessary for the preservation of discipline. Therefore the Law should

---

[364] LW 7:257.

be kept very rigidly, just as Abraham upholds Ishmael, Joseph upholds Manasseh, etc. For the Law must not be cast aside because of the promise of grace; but it must be taught in order that discipline and the doctrine concerning good works may be retained, and in order that we may be instructed to know and humble ourselves after we have sinned. This is the true and necessary use of the Law.[365]

As in the *Antinomian Disputations*, Luther emphasized the ongoing need for the Law. He commented on the Law as discipline (cf. civil use) but noted that the Law was needed for teaching about good works. He placed last the theological use of the Law "to know and humble ourselves" as the true and necessary use (cf. this expression in the commentary on Gal 3). Luther continued:

For in this life we need government and parents, who uphold discipline by means of rewards and punishments and who keep the Law and govern and direct their conduct in a godly and prudent manner according to the norm of the Law. . . . The Law checks sin, shows the rod, and announces the wrath of God and punishment to those who sin. This is the proper office of the Law. It serves to restrain evil, stubborn, and smug sinners. But the kingdom of grace is a kingdom of mercy, of pardon, of redemption, and of liberation from sins and the punishments for sins.[366]

---

[365] LW 8:170.

[366] LW 8:170–71. Luther even hailed the wisdom of Aristotle, whose influence he had denounced as a younger man. "And among jurists there is an outstanding doctrine concerning ἐπιείκεια, and this doctrine should be carefully observed in all civil and domestic government. In the domestic sphere the head of a household needs both law and ἐπιείκεια. Aristotle also has a very fine passage about ἐπιείκεια in the fifth and most brilliant book of his Ethics. The government has been established to govern according to the rigor of the law, which it should by all means observe and uphold. Because there are innumerable occasions and countless dealings which, because of various circumstances, cannot all be included in a document and in laws, and few men see clearly where the law should be properly and prudently mitigated, for this reason Aristotle has pointed out the best way. Thus he also adapts a definition of virtue to it when he says: 'Virtue is a selective quality, consisting, so far as we are concerned, in a middle course based on some reason, as a wise man judges, as strength is the mean between wrath or

Notice the use of "we" in the passage, by which Luther associated himself with those who continue to need and benefit from the use of the Law. Here, at the end of his days, Luther expressed firm interest in an enduring use of the Law, a norm and a proper office to stand and serve God's great purpose in the kingdom of grace.

Typically Luther used the expression "proper office" to describe the theological use of the Law. But in this case he nearly merged the restraining power of the Law (civil use) with the revealing power of the Law (theological use). He again showed flexibility in expressing himself about the use of the Law.

In the midst of this firm emphasis on the enduring use of the Law, Luther noted:

> But from this Law God is exempt. Nor should He be subjected to it in order that He may act according to the Law. For He is its Lord and can manage and act otherwise than the Law commands. The kingdom of grace is one thing, and the kingdom of the Law is another thing.[367]

The believer continues to need the Law. God, indeed, maintains it or uses it alongside and in service to His kingdom of grace.[368]

CONCLUSION

Although the *Lectures on Genesis* do not provide many explicit examples of the use of the Law, they do illustrate Luther's continuing use of the doctrine, the flexibility of his expression, and his firm commitment to the role of the Law as a norm also for believers. The themes we have seen from the beginning continue to the end of his life.

---

boldness and cowardice.' But that middle course, or moderation, is subject to passions. For this reason Aristotle adds the words 'as a wise man judges,' or determines. This judgment could not be expressed in laws, but there must be a living law, namely, the government, which is the soul of the law and should note carefully where and how the law can be kept and how to moderate it if some impossible case should present itself." Aristotle, *Nicomachean Ethics*, Book 5, ch. 10. Cited at LW 8:171–72.

[367] LW 8:171.

[368] In the passage, Jacob "does not abolish the Law but carries out the business of the promise" (LW 8:175).

CHAPTER SIXTEEN

CONSISTENCY IN LUTHER'S TEACHING

> The Old Testament is thus properly understood when . . . we use the laws as we please to our advantage.
>
> —Martin Luther

The preceding chapters have shown that Luther used a consistent pattern of argument when teaching about the use and misuse of the Law. He typically divided his teaching about the divine use of the Law from the human use of the Law. We have also seen a significant shift in emphasis on the enduring role of the Law in the life of a believer. Before the Antinomian Controversy with Agricola (pre-1528), Luther wrote with greater focus on the role of the Law before justification, with less attention to the role of the Law after justification. From 1528–46, in view of Antinomianism, he wrote more often about the role of the Law in the life of the believer, without diminishing the role of the Law prior to justification, as a pedagogue leading to Christ.[369]

A researcher might conclude that Luther's doctrine of the use of the Law underwent a significant shift over the course of his career. However, one might also argue that Luther's doctrine did not change substantially. The changes in emphasis and terminology seem to be responses to the changing needs of the Church and Luther's maturation of the medieval categories, especially when one considers

---

[369] An exception to this observation is the *Lectures on Galatians*, ch. 3, the circumstances of which are described in chapter 11.

the significant continuity in the doctrine of the use of the Law from the Scholastics, to Luther, and to the Reformation generally.

Luther's uniqueness emerges in five ways: (1) intense emphasis on the theological use of the Law as needed in repentance; (2) complete removal of the Law from justification, due to his understanding of original sin and the power of the Gospel; (3) emphasis on the Holy Spirit and spontaneity for good works; (4) turning the ancient and medieval usefulness of the Law into a dialectically distinct message of Law and Gospel; and (5) describing the Christian as both righteous and sinner at the same time as a way to manage the complexity of the Christian life and its responses to the use of the Law and of the Gospel. The righteous man does good works without the constraint of the Law, keeping it by grace through faith in Christ Jesus. The theological use of the Law continues to reveal a Christian's sins, which leads to daily repentance and mortification of the sinful nature. We have noted that Luther, like other interpreters, wrestled with the meaning of 1 Tm 1:8–9. Yet, various passages throughout Luther's writings also present the idea that the Law has an ongoing role in the believer's life.

USEFULNESS AND USE

The question naturally arises whether Luther meant the same thing when he used the ancient and medieval term "usefulness of the Law" and the Reformation era term "use of the Law." The charted information in Appendix B helps to answer this question.

We see that the term "usefulness of the Law" appears in Luther's writings from c. 1516–35, nearly twenty years deep into his career as a theologian. "Use of the Law" runs from 1531–45, not quite as long but certainly well established. The appearance of the terms overlap from 1531–35 during the Lectures on Galatians and its publication. Overlapping both of these periods for "usefulness" and "use" appears "function of the Law" from 1521–37. Translators used the German term *Brauch* for both "usefulness" and "use" even as they used *Ampt* to translate *officium*. These observations do not absolutely rule out subtle differences in choice of terms but they do confirm that the terms overlap in Luther's teaching even as scholars generally see the

Reformers writing "office of the Law" and "use of the Law" interchangeably, not to mention other expressions.[370]

THE CHRISTIAN LIFE

The following is a sampling of passages from Luther presented in chronological order (year; citation). The passages were not drawn together by systematic research but simply came to hand while researching this book. Together with the many passages cited in chapters seven through fourteen, they help to illustrate the consistency in Luther's teaching over nearly 30 years.

> 1515–16: The apostle argues against their empty faith in the Law and their knowledge of it when he says that it was impossible for the Law to accomplish that which they presumptuously thought, namely, the abolition of sin and the acquisition of righteousness. In this the Law is not at fault, but their opinion of and confidence in the Law is vain and stupid. To be sure, the Law in itself is very good. It is as with a sick man who wants to drink some wine because he foolishly thinks that his health will return if he does so. Now if the doctor, without any criticism of the wine, should say to him: "It is impossible for the wine to cure you, it will only make you sicker," the doctor is not condemning the wine but only the foolish trust of the sick man in it. For he needs other medicine to get well, so that he then can drink his wine. Thus also our corrupt nature needs another kind of medicine than

---

[370] Cf. "power of the Law" in Appendix B. Wengert, a proponent of the only-two-uses consensus, acknowledged that Luther's expression "office of the Law" and Melanchthon's *causa* are equivalents of "use of the Law." See *Law and Gospel* 196. This correctly acknowledges the dynamic character of human language and personal expression. One must also account for the change of terminology that takes place over time. Both "usefulness of the Law" (Augustine to early Luther) and "use of the Law" (Luther and Melanchthon) are rooted in the Pauline teaching from 1 Tm 1:8–9, "Now we know that the law is good, if one uses it lawfully" (Vulgate: *Scimus autem quia bona est lex si quis ea legitime utatur*). By tracing the use of this passage, one traces much of the history of the dogmatic terminology.

the Law, by which it can arrive at good health so that it can fulfill the Law.[371]

1519. We are not free from the Law (as I have said above) in a human way, by which the Law is destroyed and changed, but in a divine and theological way, by which we are changed and from enemies of the Law are made friends of the Law.[372]

1521: Thus is can be said in the matter of a vow and its works that the works are still necessary, even after the vow has been set aside, for these works are still commandments, just as the fruits of righteousness, even though they are not necessary for the attainment of the righteousness, which is of faith alone, are still righteousness. Nor can the freedom of the gospel dispense with the commandments of God.[373]

1522: If you do not give forth such proofs of faith, it is certain that your faith is not right. Not that good works are commanded us by this Word [John 20:19–31]; for where faith in the heart is right, there is no need of much commanding good works to be done; they follow of themselves.[374]

1525: Moreover the Old Testament is thus properly understood when we retain from the prophets the beautiful texts about Christ, when we take note of and thoroughly grasp the fine examples, and when we use the laws as we please to our advantage.[375]

---

[371] *Lectures on Romans*, LW 25:350.
[372] *Lectures on Galatians* (1519) LW 27:347. Cf. Peter Lombard, PL 192:330.
[373] *Judgment on Monastic Vows* (1521) LW 44:298. The translation produces an awkward English sentence since "fruits of righteousness" are divided from "are still righteousness."
[374] *Church Postil* (Roths Sommerpostille, 1526), Lenker 2:374–75. Take careful note of the wording—Luther left room for preaching good works to believers but noted that they do not need "*much* commanding" (emphasis added) because faith naturally leads to good works. So, Luther left a place for the Law and works in the believer's life, even describing works here as signs of faith. Cf. his comments on softening the preaching of the Law in the *Antinomian Disputations* (p. 153), which refers to exhortation.
[375] *Prefaces to the Old Testament*, LW 35:173. See also p. 108 above.

1532: The doctrine of the Law, or the first light, is the moon. It teaches our obligation to bear fruits, as a good tree should. The other light is the sun. It speaks of the new man, of a different tree, telling us that we receive the Gospel from Christ. There we hear whence and how a man becomes good, namely, through faith. Thus the Gospel deals, not with our works but with grace and gifts, with the good that God does for us and presents to us through Christ. The Ten Commandments tell us about our duties toward God. Now, to be sure, the moon shines at night, but still it does not turn night into day. Christ, however, is the true Sun. He ushers in the morning and the day. He teaches us how to be saved and how to be delivered from death and sin. Therefore He says: "I am the Light which illumines the whole world"; for He alone liberates from sin, death, the devil, and hell.[376]

1532: True it is that the Law or the Ten Commandments have not been annulled so that we are exempt from them and not allowed to have them. For Christ set us free from the curse, not from the obedience of the law. No, that is not what God wants. He wants us to keep the commandments with total commitment and diligence; but not to put our trust in it when we have done so or despair if we have not. See to it, then, that you distinguish the two words rightly, not giving more to the Law than its due, otherwise you lose the Gospel.[377]

1533: Therefore, the Gospel says: Watch yourselves, learn the commandment[s] of God. For they teach what things should truly stand, what things are ordained by God and pleasing to Him. My Gospel teaches that you should be saved, to flee from death. With these two [doctrines], you will have enough to learn. No one can learn them well enough. Therefore, wherever these two doctrines—Law and Gospel— remain clear and bright, there shines the sun, that is, the Gospel, [and] the moon, that is, the Law. The moon looks like a copper-red kettle when it does not have the sun. Then the

---

[376] *Sermons on John*, LW 23:324.
[377] "The Distinction between the Law and Gospel: A Sermon by Luther, January 1, 1532," Willard L. Burce, trans., *Concordia Journal* 18 (April, 1992): 160.

Law is terrifying, when the Gospel is not with it. However, when the sun shines on it, then the moon has a radiant light. So the sun gives eternal life. While the two lights are shining, one can know day and night distinctly. When they are taken away, it is sheer blindness and darkness.[378]

1537: Thus there is first given us through Christ the sense that we do not fulfill the Law and that sin is fully and completely forgiven: however, this is not bestowed in a way or to the end, that we in the future need not keep the Law, and may forever continue to sin, or that we should teach, if we have faith then we need no longer to love God and our neighbor. But there is bestowed upon us the sense that the fulfilling of the Law may now for the first time be successfully attempted and perfectly realized, and this is the eternal, fixed and unchangeable will of God. To this end it is necessary to preach grace, that man may find counsel and help to come to a perfect life.[379]

1537: Christ, the truth, has come, not to destroy the Law, but to establish it, not only in himself, which was done long ago but in me and in all Christians.[380]

---

[378] "Ideo Euangelium dicit: Sehet euch fur, lernet Gottes gebot, illa enim docent, qui veri status sint, qui ordinati sunt a deo et ei placeant, Meum Euangelium docet, das ir solt selig sein, dem tod entlauffen. An den 2 werdet ir genug zu lernen haben, Nemo wird gnugsam lernen kunnen, Ergo wo die zwo lere bleiben klar und hell, Lex und Euangelium, das leuchtet Son i.e. Euangelium, Mond i.e. lex. Der Mond sihet wie ein rotter kessel, quando non habet solem. Tunc lex est horribilis, cum Euangelium non adest. Wenn aber die Sonn drein scheinet, tum luna habet candidum lumen. Sic dat sol aeternam vitam, weyl die zwey liechter leuchten, kan man tag und nacht unterschiedlich erkennen, iis ablatis so ists lauter blindheit und finsternis." *Hauspostille* for the 18th Sunday after Trinity, WA 37:174. A translation for this postil exists in *Sermons of Martin Luther: The House Postils* 3:68–69. However, the Klug edition is based on the second Erlangen edition of Luther's Works (6:99) where the text is modernized and fleshed out so that the English translation ends up with such things as "the Law guides us through this temporal life," which is not found in the original notes.
[379] *Church Postil*, Lenker 5:188. Luther is not teaching perfectionism. The "perfect life" refers to the life believers will enjoy in eternity (Lenker 5:193).
[380] *Church Postil*, Lenker 5:190.

1537: Therefore another thing is necessary, Christ will say, for you to know, namely, that you know and possess the man called Christ, who helps us to the end that this doctrine of the Law may be established and perfected in you.[381]

1537: The Ten Commandments, which deal with holy life and conduct toward God and man, cease too, in the sense that they cannot damn us believers in Christ. He became subject to the Law in order to redeem us who were under the Law (Gal. 4:5); yes, He became a curse for us to save us from the curse of the Law (Gal. 3:13). However, the Ten Commandments are still in force and do concern us Christians so far as obedience to them is concerned. For the righteousness demanded by the Law is fulfilled in the believers through the grace and the assistance of the Holy Spirit, whom they receive.[382]

1537: Although it is true that we have become friends solely through His blood, it is still necessary for Christians to manifest their real friendship toward one another; otherwise this friendship will be false and will amount to nothing. For you cannot call people friends if they show one another hatred, envy, or malice rather than love. "If you are really My friends," says Christ, "you will do what I command you."

It is surely kind and pleasing that Christ calls them His friends. For He would like to encourage and rouse us to pay heed to His love, to consider how He made the Father our Friend and how He proved Himself our Friend above all friends. But all of us who are His friends must also live in friendship with one another. This is a fine and an easy commandment; furthermore, it is given to us in the simplest and friendliest manner. For later (v. 15) Christ tells His disciples that He is not ordering them as slaves who must be held and forced to obedience with threats, but is exhorting them as friends to do this for His sake as their Friend. This is the lightest and sweetest of tasks, one which we should do willingly and without any bidding, just as Christ was not

---

[381] *Church Postil*, Lenker 5:193.
[382] *Sermons on John 1–4*, LW 22:38–39.

forced to die for us but died willingly and gladly. Therefore He wants to say: "I am not imposing a heavy burden and load on you, many sacrifices and manifold service of God, or anything that entails great expense or labor. I have imposed the Gospel, Baptism, and the Sacrament on you. And this is no commandment; it is your treasure, which I have given you gratis. I force no one to accept this, as Moses imposed the Law by force and under threat of punishment; but I let everyone who would like to accept it have the privilege of choosing it. You are not ordered to do this as a service to God; you are to accept it for your own benefit, to find your salvation there if you want to be saved. But now, since you have all received the treasure that you should have, do just this one thing: be joined together in the bonds of love. For just as Adam in Paradise was charged with one commandment, not to eat of one tree, and had free access to all the other trees, so I give you but one commandment and release you from many onerous commandments and many kinds of peculiar works imposed by Moses or by others. Still I do require this of you, that you love one another. This is your obligation even apart from My commandment, since you are My disciples as well as recipients of the same benefits from Me."[383]

1539: We need the Decalogue not only to apprise us of our lawful obligations, but we also need it to discern how far the Holy Spirit has advanced us in his work of sanctification and by how much we still fall short of the goal, lest we become secure and imagine that we have now done all that is required.[384]

1544: It is not the design of this doctrine [Gal 5:16–24] to forbid good works or to tolerate and refrain from censuring bad ones, or to prevent the preaching of the Law. On the contrary it shows clearly that God earnestly wills that Christians should flee and avoid the lusts of the flesh, if they

---

[383] *Sermons on John 14–16*, LW 24:252–53.
[384] *On the Councils and the Church*, LW 41:166.

would remain in the Spirit. ... Thus their hearts become filled with love and a desire to obey God and to shun sin.[385]

These passages, like those cited and considered in chapters seven through fifteen, show the shift to emphasize the enduring use of the Law for Christians after Luther experienced the problem of Antinomianism (1528). But one must note that the Law never really lost its place in Luther's thinking about the Christian life. A balanced reading of Luther, taking into account his rhetoric and hyperbole, shows a most steady doctrine of the use of the Law for the Christian life.

ADMONITIONS

Christopher Brown's introduction to a new translation of Luther's sermons provides yet another insight to Luther's thought about the use of the Law. Brown writes:

> Luther's activity in the pulpit was marked by controversy, not only the larger conflicts addressed in his published treatises but also local tensions. Luther sought to defend his own role within the church and to deal concretely with the issues raised in the Antinomian Controversy by preaching both the Law and the Gospel to a congregation whose corporate life often seemed to fall short in both good works and faithful devotion. ... These rebukes were often conveyed in admonitions or exhortations delivered from the pulpit after the sermon proper—a long-standing practice of Luther's, though not all the scribes who recorded his sermons took notes on the admonitions as well. These topical admonitions were unconnected to the texts for the day or to the rest of the sermon, though on occasion, perhaps with increasing frequency during these last years, the material of the admonition and the textual preaching might be combined.[386]

In a footnote Brown listed eighteen examples of these admonitions, explaining that most were "preserved from the years 1528–1532 in the anonymous hand of the Nürnberg Codex Solger 13." These admonitions show no shyness about preaching the Law to Christians

---

[385] *Church Postil*, Lenker 8:255–56.
[386] LW 58:xix–xx; see also n. 25.

and demonstrate Luther's expectation that Christians should put the teachings of God's moral Law into practice.[387] This practice connects well with themes of admonition and exhortation that Luther described in the *Antinomian Disputations*.

CONCLUSION

The Christian as a sinner never outgrows the use of the Law. In fact, as a righteous man, he takes up the Law and uses it for his benefit and the benefit of his neighbor. He delights in the goodness of the Law and may even regard it as a friend (*Lectures on Galatians* [1519] LW 27:347). This is not works righteousness nor is it legalism—this attitude and these works are the fruit of justification.

For Luther the Law and the Gospel are eternal doctrines revealed in both testaments.[388] They stem from the nature of God[389] and are ever needful to mankind. Yet their use and application vary depending on a person's need. What Luther wrote varied over the following circumstances:

Adam before the fall.

Mankind after the fall.

The saints struggling against the flesh.

The saints in eternity.

These categories of humanity found in Luther's writings correspond with Augustine's Stages of Man, which he drew from Paul's Letter to the Romans. This shows yet another aspect of consistency as Luther worked with the time honored categories of the Fathers.

---

[387] Although Luther was dealing with problems in practice, one can also see in the admonitions a certain optimism about the work of God's Word and the work of the Holy Spirit in the lives of believers, a confidence that they will have their proper effect. See Close of the Commandments, para. 330 on p. 121 above.

[388] Cf. the everlasting covenant described throughout the Old Testament (Lv 24:8; 2Sm 23:5; 1Ch 16:17; Ps 105:10; Is 55:3; 61:8; Jer 32:40; Ezk 16:60; 37:26) that included the Law and the promise. See also Mt 5:17–18; Rv 14:6. See also WA 17 I:117; WA 39 I:413.

[389] See LC I:15; Mt 19:17. See God's great confession of Himself in Exodus 34:6–7, which epitomizes this biblical insight. Luther interpreted the passage as the proclamation of Christ (WA DB 8:309).

The Law is variously used with and by people from start to finish. Luther wrote about the role of the Law in each of the circumstances of human life. Because Luther sought to overthrow the opinion that the Law was able to justify sinners, he focused most often on the use of the Law with fallen mankind, the theological use of the Law. With the rise of Antinomianism among some Reformers, he increased his emphasis on the use of the Law in other circumstances of human existence.

CHAPTER SEVENTEEN

MELANCHTHON ON THE USE OF THE LAW

Christian doctrine must begin with the function of the Law.

—Philip Melanchthon

On August 25, 1518, Philip Melanchthon passed through the Elster gate on the way to his new calling as a professor at Wittenberg University. He was only twenty-one years old, though already well recognized for his academic abilities and achievements. Universities at Ingolstadt and Leipzig had sought him for their faculties before he settled on Wittenberg, with life changing results.

Not quite two and a half years after arriving at Wittenberg, Melanchthon would invite his new friends and students to join him outside the Elster gate for the burning of canon law. Faculty members at Ingolstadt and Leipzig attacked the reforms that Melanchthon supported. Those professors, who might have wished for Melanchthon as a colleague just a few years earlier, now condemned him along with Luther, his closest friend on the Wittenberg faculty. Melanchthon and Luther would serve side by side at Wittenberg for twenty-eight years, constantly influencing one another's work. In the end, Melanchthon would write a biography for Luther based on notes from interviews with him not long before Luther's death.[390]

---

[390] See "Melanchthon's Memoirs" in Franz Posset's *The Real Luther: A Friar at Erfurt and Wittenberg* (St. Louis: Concordia, 2011), 149–69.

I begin the chapter on Melanchthon this way to emphasize the close bond between these two brothers in Christ. Historians and theologians at times seek to drive wedges between Luther and his younger colleague. That they differed on some points of theology and church practice is unquestionably true. Yet it is also true that their differences may be exaggerated.

As noted in the introduction, some scholars have attributed to Melanchthon the doctrine that there are three uses of the Law. They may praise him for placing greater emphasis on the Law or vilify him for reintroducing the doctrine of works righteousness and making theology subservient to the Law. Our earlier observations from medieval theologians and from Luther's writings call into question the idea that Melanchthon is the originator of the third use. One must ask anew, what did Melanchthon teach about the use of the Law and when did he teach it?

EARLY DOGMATIC WORKS

Melanchthon had some studies in law before coming to Wittenberg in 1518. Lowell Green writes that history records very little about Melanchthon's early interest in biblical studies. There is, however, a story about Melanchthon getting in trouble for reading the Bible during Mass at Tübingen.[391] The biblical doctrine of the Law engaged Melanchthon in 1519. When he was 22 years old, he received his bachelor's degree in theology and began to lecture on St. Paul's Epistle to the Romans. From the start, Melanchthon studied and taught theology in Luther's shadow. According to Fred Kramer, "It is possible that Melanchthon even used Luther's notes [from the Romans lectures of 1515–16] as a basis for his own work."[392]

In 1520 Melanchthon's students published *Lamplight Work of Theological Matters* from Melanchthon's lectures. These notes show Melanchthon's debt to training in scholastic theology and his love for organization and enumeration of points. They also show that Melanchthon readily appreciated Luther's emphases on the abrogation of the Law of Moses through Christ and on Christian

---

[391] *How Melanchthon Helped Luther Discover the Gospel* (Fallbrook, CA: Verdict Publications, 1980), 118.
[392] Philip Melanchthon, *Commentary on Romans*, Fred Kramer, trans. (St. Louis: Concordia, 1992), 8.

freedom. He devoted little space to the distinction between Law and Gospel; there are no references to the use of the Law at this early date, though as shown above, Luther was writing about the usefulness of the Law as early as 1515.

The *Lamplight Work of Theological Matters* became the basis of Melanchthon's 1521 *Common Topics of Theology* (*Loci Communes Theologici*). The following table gives an overview of Melanchthon's early study of Scripture and his life-long development of the *Loci*.

Table 18
Development of Melanchthon and His *Loci Communes*

1497	Melanchthon born in Bretten, February 16.
1509–11	Study at Heidelberg. Housed with theologian Pallas Spangel. Bachelor of liberal arts.
1511–14	Masters at Tübingen. Study of Scholastic theology, Latin Bible. Focused on classics, philosophy, and law.
1518	Called to Wittenberg. Work on Greek edition of Paul's Epistle to Titus.
1519	Finished Bachelors in theology at Wittenberg. Lectured on Psalms, Matthew, and Romans; edited Luther's 1519 *Labors on the Psalms* and *Lectures on Galatians*.
c. 1519/20	Development of 1520 *Lamplight Work of Theological Matters* (*Lucubratiuncula . . . Rerum Theologicarum*) published by students; *Theological Introduction of Philip Melanchthon to the Epistle of Paul to the Romans*.
1521	First edition of *Loci Communes* published. The first period of *Loci* publication ran from 1521–28.
c. 1522	First German translation of the *Loci Communes* by George Spalatin, based on 1521/22 eds. (*Die haubt artickel und furnemesten punct der gantzen hayligen schrift*).
1532	June 22 letter to Veit Dietrich expressed Melanchthon's desire to understand the consent of the will in the doctrine of predestination. Deviation from Luther began.
1535	Substantial new edition of the *Loci Communes*. Second period of *Loci* publication runs from 1535–41. Melanchthon included phrase, "Good works are necessary for salvation," which led to misunderstanding and controversy.
1536	Justus Jonas translated the 1535 ed. of the *Loci* into German.
1538	May 24 letter to Veit Dietrich expressed Melanchthon's personal, private struggles over the doctrine of the Lord's Supper. In public confessions, he maintained his earlier teaching in agreement with Luther.
1543	Substantial new edition of the *Loci Communes*. Third period of *Loci* publication ran from 1543–59. Justus Jonas translated 1543 *Loci* into German.
1548	Augsburg Interim, a church constitution restoring many Roman doctrines and ceremonies, is imposed by Emperor Charles V after his victory in the Smalcaldic War. It was not fully enforced. As a replacement for the Augsburg Interim, Melanchthon participated in the Leipzig Interim, which gave his prince, Maurice of Saxony, temporary alliance with the Roman Emperor, Charles V. The Interim included a compromising theological introduction and reinstituted some medieval, Roman ceremonies.

1559   *Chief Theological Topics* (*Loci Praecipui Theologici*); last edition edited by Melanchthon.

1560   Melanchthon died, April 19, having served diligently as a reformer and Wittenberg professor for 42 years.

THE FIRST PERIOD OF THE *LOCI COMMUNES*

In the 1521 *Loci* Melanchthon made numerous observations about the Law, including the following on natural law:

> The law is said to be the knowledge of sin. . . . Law is a judgment whereby the good is commanded and the bad is forbidden. . . . Some laws are natural laws, other divine, and others human. . . . Moreover, Paul teaches in Rom. 2:15 in a remarkably fine and clear argument that there is a law of nature. He comes to the conclusion that there is in the Gentiles a conscience which either defends or accuses their acts, and therefore it is law. For what is conscience but a judgment of our deeds which is derived from some law or common rule? The law of nature, therefore, is a common judgment to which all men give the same consent. This law which God has engraved on the mind of each is suitable for the shaping of morals."[393]

Melanchthon clearly drew upon his experience with the *Lectures on Romans*, following the observations of St. Paul, earlier theologians, and Luther without significant deviation. He emphasized what would be called the civil and theological uses of the Law.

Later Melanchthon contrasted scriptural teaching with human opinion about the Law.

> Scripture differs from human reason in its view of the power of the law. Scripture calls law "the power of anger," "the power of sin," "the scepter of the avenger," "lightening," "thunder." Human reason calls it "a corrector of crimes" and

---

[393] Philip Melanchthon, *Loci Communes Theologici*, Lowell J. Satre, trans. in *The Library of Christian Classics: Melanchthon and Bucer* vol. 19, Wilhelm Pauck, ed. (Philadelphia: The Westminster Press, 1969), 49–50. This translation of the 1521 Loci is based on the edition of Hans Engelland in *Melanchthons Werke in Auswahl*, vol. II, edited by Robert Stupperich (Gütersloh, 1952). I have also consulted the Latin in CR 21.

> "an instructor in living." For Cicero employs such language when he speaks of laws.[394]

Melanchthon enumerated two classes of mankind: (1) hypocrites who think they can keep the law; (2) those afflicted by the law. Calling the Law "an instructor in living" could have been a starting point for discussing the role of the Law in the life of a believer. But Melanchthon did not develop the idea in the locus and may have been speaking guardedly against it, contrasting human and divine wisdom.

Melanchthon turned to the topic of the use or function of the Law in comments on Galatians and Colossians.[395]

> In Gal., ch. 3, after the apostle in a long discussion has taught that righteousness is not attained by the help of only the law, he adds the question which seems justifiable: "Why then the law" (v. 19). That is, if it was of no help in attaining righteousness, I ask what use it was.[396] . . . To sum up, the proper work of the law is the revealing of sin, or, to put it more clearly, the bringing about of a conscience of sin; Paul calls it the "bond which stood against us with its legal demands" (Col. 2:14. . . . And in the justification of sinners the first work of God is to reveal our sin. . . . For the putting to death, the judgment, and the confounding of the sinner, wrought by the Spirit of God through the law, begin the justification and moreover the genuine baptism of man. And for this reason, just as the Christian life must certainly begin with the knowledge of sin, so Christian doctrine must begin with the function of the law.[397]

Melanchthon followed Luther's emphasis on the theological use of the Law and saw it as foundational to Christian doctrine. However, whereas Luther's earliest writing used the medieval theological term *usefulness of the Law*, Melanchthon began to express the doctrine differently. He persistently used *work of the Law*, St. Paul's term from Rm 2:15. He also used the legal term *function of the Law* before

---

[394] LCC 19:77.
[395] LCC 19:81–83.
[396] "quaeso quis eius fait usus" (CR 21:151).
[397] "ita a legis officio Christiana doctrina auspicanda est" (CR 21:154).

Luther, who published it later that year.[398] Melanchthon included the noun *use* in the article but did not have the specific phrase *use of the Law*.

In "The Power of the Law," Melanchthon explained that it was necessary to distinguish two classes of mankind: those who understand the Law carnally and those who understand it spiritually (LCC 19:77–83). The first class tries to fulfill the Law and become self-righteous hypocrites. The second experience the real work of the Law and recognize their sin. The difference between the two classes also shows the difference between true and false repentance (LCC 19:83).

WITTE'S ASSESSMENT

In *Law and Protestantism: The Legal Teachings of the Lutheran Reformation*, John Witte, Jr. provided a thorough, running comparison of Melanchthon's doctrine of the Law with Luther's doctrine of the Law.[399] Witte mentioned twenty-five points of comparison. In all but six points he emphasized that Melanchthon's doctrine was like Luther's or that Melanchthon was following Luther or medieval teachers. In other words, Melanchthon largely agreed with and taught Luther's doctrine of the Law. The six points of difference are as follows:

1. Melanchthon more explicitly described the content or doctrines of natural law (Witte 123).

2. He surpassed Luther in describing the philosophical basis of natural law (Witte 123).

3. He surpassed Luther in emphasizing that Christians need the instruction of the Law (Witte 128).

4. He held that the educational use of the Law was of greatest importance, whereas Luther emphasized the theological use of the Law (Witte 128).

5. He surpassed Luther in teaching that God wanted rulers to create and enforce laws regarding religious beliefs and practices (Witte 129, 131).

---

[398] Melanchthon published the *Loci* in April. Luther published *Judgment on Monastic Vows* in December, where he included *officium legis*.
[399] Pp. 122–40.

6. He surpassed Luther in teaching that the state, rather than the church, should hold and exercise legal authority (Witte 133).

One should note that these points of difference are examples of degree, emphasis, or amount of teaching on a topic. In other words, also in these examples one may see Melanchthon following Luther's teaching.

The fourth point above is of special interest for the present study on the use of the Law. In a following section, we shall test Witte's point against Melanchthon's 1535 and 1559 editions of the *Loci*.

WENGERT'S ASSESSMENTS

During the controversy with Agricola in 1527/28, Melanchthon and Luther more or less stood together on the role of the Law in repentance and the continuing need to preach the Law to believers.[400] Melanchthon's 1527 *Visitation Articles* sparked the dispute with Agricola, though they did not explicitly describe uses of the Law.[401]

Timothy Wengert discovered that Melanchthon first distinguished three uses of the Law in his 1534 *Scholia on Colossians*, prior to his explicit mention of the third function of the Law in the 1535 *Loci Communes*.[402]

> As much as the law may have carved out for Moses things that had to be interpreted, it would be just as useful to teach that God gave the law for these three reasons: to coerce the flesh and to terrify or humble. The third reason pertains to the righteous, that they may practice obedience.[403]

---

[400] *Law and Gospel* 131–38. See also Schurb 18. Silcock questions whether Luther agreed with Melanchthon fully. See n. 246.

[401] Melanchthon began the articles by emphasizing the preaching of the Law for repentance (CR XXVI:9). The last article, "Concerning the Law," described two effects of the Law: (1) to coerce the flesh and (2) to terrify the conscience (CR XXVI:28). It also emphasized the need to diligently teach the Law in the churches.

[402] *Law and Gospel*, 177–210. See also *Word and Faith* 62, 74–75.

[403] "Quoties autem aliqua Moisi lex inciderit tractanda, profuerit docere, quod Deus dederit legem propter has tres caussas: ad cohercendam carnem, & ad terrendum seu humiliandum. Tertia ad iustos pertinet, ut excerceant obedientiam." On Luther's use of *exercere*, see p. 116.

Wengert saw Melanchthon's strong emphasis on forensic justification, his loci method of assigning definitions, and his interest in ecumenical relations as factors in developing a third use of the Law. In *A Formula for Parish Practice*,[404] Wengert described another cause for the development of a third use of the Law. He noted that also c. 1534 Melanchthon had dialogued with moderate Roman theologians who defined Christ's command to love as Gospel. Melanchthon placed the command to love in the category of a third use of the Law.

However, as noted above, a threefold use of the Law was already established in medieval exegesis. Luther had twice described a third use or office of the Law before Melanchthon (first in 1522 and again in 1528). The distinction arose out of the early exegetical tradition and medieval interpretation of 1 Tm 1:8–9, therefore, it cannot be attributed to the theological issues of the early 1530s as Wengert concluded. Nor does the third use of the Law emerge for the first time as a reaction to Agricola's antinomianism.

THE SECOND PERIOD OF THE *LOCI COMMUNES*

The second major edition of the Loci provided the earliest passage where Melanchthon spelled out the third office of the Law (*tertium officium legis*),[405] some thirteen years after Luther described it in the *Christmas Postil*. Ken R. Schurb provided a translation of the passage and some commentary in "Philip Melanchthon, the Formula of Concord, and the Third Use of the Law."[406]

> The third function of the law in those who are righteous by faith is that it also teaches them concerning good works, which works please God. It also prescribes certain works in which they might exercise obedience toward God. For although we are free from the law as far as justification is concerned, nonetheless the law remains as far as obedience is concerned. For it is necessary that those who are justified obey the law. Indeed, somehow they begin to do the law in

---

[404] See p. 91 of his book.
[405] CR 21:406.
[406] Schurb 221. See his commentary on the use of the Law in the 1535 *Loci*, pp. 218–27.

part. And that inchoate obedience pleases [God] because the persons are pleasing on account of Christ.

Melanchthon began by describing this use of the Law for "those who are righteous by faith" as Luther described a third type of persons responding to the Law.[407] Melanchthon focused more on the prescription of the Law whereas Luther focused more on the spontaneity of the righteous in using and fulfilling the Law. Like Luther, Melanchthon wrote of "exercise" with the Law. He was clearly following Luther's precedent though, not surprisingly, Melanchthon expressed himself more concisely and as though he were writing a definition.

Although Melanchthon mentioned a "third reason for the Law" in his 1534 Scholia on Colossians, Schurb rightly affirmed that the passage in the 1535 Loci is the place where the second generation of Lutheran theologians would have learned the distinction.[408] In this edition, Melanchthon devoted about twice as much space to describing the theological use of the Law as he devoted to the civil and righteous man's use of the Law.

THE THIRD PERIOD OF THE *LOCI COMMUNES*

As noted in Table 18, the third period of the *Loci* began with the 1543 edition. Melanchthon greatly expanded the content in this last version of the *Loci* as the text for the third use of the Law illustrates. It is cited below from the Preus translation that originally was thought to be based on the 1543 edition but actually comes from the 1559 edition, the last edition that Melanchthon edited before his death in 1560.[409]

---

[407] See p. 79.
[408] Schurb 206.
[409] Preus translated the text in CR 21. This volume presented the first period of the *Loci* with the 1521 edition and the second period of the *Loci* with the 1535 edition. In both of these cases, it represented the period with the first edition of that period. However, for the third period it skipped over the first edition (1543) and went to the last edition of the *Loci*. Preus did not notice this change in presentation and so concluded that he had translated the 1543 edition. For more on this issue, see Benjamin Mayes's preface to Philip Melanchthon's *The Chief Theological Topics: Loci Praecipui Theologici 1559*. Melanchthon provided four points on moral law that have interesting parallels with the uses of the Law. See Schurb 249–50.

The third use of the Law pertains to the regenerate. Insofar as the regenerate have been justified by faith, they are free from the Law. This must be said under this locus. For they are freed from the Law, that is, from the curse and the condemnation and the wrath of God which is set forth in the Law, that is to say, if they remain in the faith and fight against sin in confidence in the Son of God, and overcome the terrors of sin. Yet in the meantime it must be said that the Law which points out the remnants of sin, in order that the knowledge of sin and repentance may increase, and the Gospel also must proclaim Christ in order that faith may grow. Furthermore, the Law must be preached to the regenerate to teach them certain works in which God wills that we practice obedience. For God does not will that we by our own wisdom set up works or worship, but he wills that we be ruled by His Word, as it is written, "In vain do they worship Me by the commandments of men," Matt. 15:9. Again, "Your Word is a lamp unto my feet," Ps. 119:105. When human reason is not directed by the Word of God it is very likely to lack something. For it is seized by wicked desires or gives its approval to iniquitous works, as is apparent in the laws of the gentiles. The divine order that we are to obey God remains unchangeable. Therefore, even though we are free from the Law, that is from damnation, because we are righteous by faith for the sake of the Son of God, yet because it pertains to obedience, the Law remains, that is, the divine ordinance remains that those who have been justified are to be obedient to God. Indeed, they have the beginning of obedience which we shall discuss under its own locus as to how it is pleasing to God. These comments suffice to give instruction briefly regarding the threefold use of the Law. We shall return later to the second and third uses.

Melanchthon placed special emphasis on the freedom of the Christian in this last edition of the *Loci*. He also sought to clarify the roles of Law and Gospel in the Christian life, noting that the growth of faith does not stem from the Law but from the Gospel. Yet the believer has an ongoing need for the Law since human reason is weak to understand right and wrong without God's Word.[410] In Melanchthon's final edit of the *Loci*, he clearly gave more space to the civil and theological uses of the Law and covered the righteous man's use of the Law in a single paragraph.

LUTHERAN DOGMATIC TERMS

Chapter one illustrated some of the ways Lutheran dogmaticians have described the uses of the Law. Having come to the end of the chapter on Melanchthon, it seems helpful to provide specific illustration of the terms used by other Lutheran teachers. The following table traces the developments in terminology.

Table 19
Lutheran Dogmatic Terms for the Uses of the Law

Melanchthon's *Chief Theological Topics* (1559)

The terms are consistent with earlier editions except that the term "pedagogical" is added in the third period of *Loci* publication.

1. pedagogical or civil
2. second use
3. third use

Leonhard Hutter's *Compendium Locorum Theologicorum*

In 1610 Hutter's work replaced use of Melanchthon's *Loci* at Wittenberg University.

1. politicus
2. paedagogicus
3. didacticus

Martin Chemnitz's *Loci Theologici*

Since Chemnitz's *Loci* commented directly on the 1559 edition of Melanchthon's *Loci*, his terminology closely followed that of Melanchthon. Interestingly, Chemnitz devoted more space in his *Loci* to the first and third uses of the Law than to the second use of the Law.[411]

1. civil use
2. second use
3. third use

---

[410] See Schurb's commentary, pp. 253–67.

[411] This does not mean Chemnitz devoted less emphasis to the second use. One must always remember that teachers may be addressing specific circumstances and needs of their readers.

Johann Gerhard's *Loci Theologici*

Gerhard provided most of his terms in Greek, which are transliterated below.

1. politikos or paedagogicus
2. theologikos or elegktikos
3. theologikos didaktikos

Later Lutheran dogmaticians had a fourfold use, subdividing the second use of the Law: *usus elenchthicus* (rebuking sin) and *usus paedagogicus* (driving one toward Christ indirectly). Sometimes they included other terms. (See Richard A. Muller, *Dictionary of Latin and Greek Theological Terms* [Grand Rapids, MI: Baker, 1985], 320–21.)

CONCLUSION

Melanchthon's role in the doctrine of the use of the Law is best characterized as regularizing Luther's terminology, a contribution he seems to have shared with the editors for Luther's 1535 *Lectures on Galatians*. As Wengert noted, Melanchthon had a special fondness for enumerated categories, as his writing on "The Effects of the Law" illustrates in his *Commentary on Romans*.[412] Melanchthon had the term *usus* in his 1521 *Loci* article on the divine law. However, as noted earlier, Martin Bucer likely spread the term *tertius usus legis* through his Latin translation of Luther's 1522 postil (see p. 88). Melanchthon made this terminology a preferred dogmatic term by broadcasting it in editions of his *Loci*, from 1535 onward. As will be seen in the next chapter, Calvin picked up the same terminology for his first edition of the *Institutes* (1536).

Note that Luther wrote about the righteous man's use of the Law or faith's use of the Law, emphasizing the Christian's new relationship to the Law. Luther divided his third use between the prophetic use (Gospel) and the Christian fulfilling the Law without constraint. Melanchthon emphasized the law as teaching, what later dogmaticians would term the *usus didacticus*. Melanchthon's approach made the three uses consistently divine uses (cf. *Loci* heading) in which the Spirit applied the Law to the hearer. Luther more consistently held that the Spirit dwelling in the believer led him to spontaneously keep the Law and appreciate its teaching.

Witte described Melanchthon as holding the educational use of the Law as most important. This does not appear to be the case in the *Loci*, where Melanchthon explicitly wrote about three uses of the

---

[412] Pp. 140–143.

Law. From the 1535 edition forward, it appears that Melanchthon devoted significantly less space to the righteous man's use in the section of the locus on use of the Law. However, one must allow that Witte's point may be based on broader evidence. I look forward to further assessment of Melanchthon's emphases.

Melanchthon may have contributed a unique emphasis on *obedience*.[413] For example, Melanchthon used the term four times in his brief paragraph on third use of the Law in the 1535 *Loci*. However, as noted from the *Antinomian Disputations*, Luther also wrote about the role of the Law in the Christian's obedience, though he turned to that wording less often than Melanchthon did.

---

[413] In *Law and Gospel*, Wengert made a similar observation on pp. 199–200. See examples of Luther's use of the term, pp. 131, 151, 153, 155, 181, and 183.

CHAPTER EIGHTEEN

CALVIN ON THE USE OF THE LAW

Melanchthon mediated Luther and Calvin.

—Philip Schaff

This chapter and the next represent a departure from tracing the doctrine of the use of the Law in Lutheran thought, which I have pursued in chapters seven through seventeen. I include these chapters for three reasons. First, it seems important to note that Lutherans were not alone in recognizing the value of the distinctions that the Fathers made on the use of the Law. Christians in other traditions will likely wish to consider their reception of the ancient and medieval teaching. Chapters eighteen and nineteen provide some starting points for that consideration.

Second, these chapters also provide context for the Lutheran development of the Formula of Concord, taken up in chapter twenty. One of the characterizations of the Formula in the twentieth century was that it deviated from Luther's teaching and even introduced Calvin's teaching. Knowing something about Calvin's teaching will prove helpful for considering that question.

Third, Roman Catholics and Lutherans have in recent times held dialogues and even published joint statements on the doctrine of justification. Yet they did so while including little account of the use of the Law, which seems to be a major omission. By pointing out how sixteenth century Roman theologians received the ancient and medieval teaching on the use of the Law, one may highlight an opportunity for what one may hope would be a more fruitful dialogue with stronger roots in the history of doctrine.

MELANCHTHON'S INFLUENCE

John T. McNeill noted in the *Library of Christian Classics* edition of Calvin's *Institutes*, "In the 1535 and later editions, [Melanchthon] introduces the three uses of the law here expounded by Calvin."[414] As noted in the previous chapter, Melanchthon regularized the descriptions of the three uses of the Law. The effect of this can be seen clearly in John Calvin's first edition of the *Institutes of the Christian Religion* published in 1536. Calvin's comments on the doctrine of the use of the Law have much in common with Luther but they clearly stem from Melanchthon's *Loci*. They also include Melanchthon's emphasis on obedience as a significant term.

Despite clear dependence on Melanchthon's teaching, Calvin also presented the use of the Law differently from both Luther and Melanchthon, as this chapter will demonstrate.

THE 1536 INSTITUTES

From the start, Calvin described the uses of the Law differently from Luther and Melanchthon. He set them in order but did not specifically title them. Using the standard titles defined in Table 2, here is Calvin's order:

Theological use

Civil use

Righteous man's use

The reason for Calvin's order is not immediately apparent.

Luther had ordered the uses based on history and experience: (1) the giving of the Law to Moses, (2) the restoration of the Law after Israel's idolatry with the golden calf, and (3) the conquest of the

---

[414] *Calvin's Institutes of the Christian Religion*, John T. McNeill, ed; Ford Lewis Battles, trans. *The Library of Christian Classics*, vol. XX (Philadelphia: The Westminster Press, 1960), 354, n. 10. I also checked two works by Zwingli to see whether he wrote about the work of the Law: the *Sixty-Seven Articles* (1523) and *A Commentary on the False and True Religion* (1525). I did not find references to use of the Law in either work.

Promised Land under Joshua.[415] These events described how people experienced and related to the Law. The first two uses corresponded to what Luther called "the time of the Law"; the third corresponded to "the time of grace." This order owes much to Augustine's four stages of man from his study of Romans.[416] The uses had a definite sequence in Luther's teaching and Melanchthon followed Luther's order.

Calvin may have ordered the uses differently because he placed the teaching on the use of the Law in the midst of his teaching on justification.[417] In chapter one Calvin began with the knowledge of God, the Law, and the Commandments. He then began to teach on justification—but with the use of the Law dropped into the middle of the teaching. His comments on justification naturally included statements about the theological use of the Law,[418] which is where he began to explain the Law's use.[419]

> From these things [on justification and righteousness] one can gather what the function and use of the law are.[420] Now, it consists of three parts. First, while showing God's righteousness, that is, what God requires of us, [the law] admonishes each one of his unrighteousness and convicts him of his sin. . . .
>
> Then, since the law declares God will be the avenger, sets the punishment for transgressors, and threatens death and judgment, [the law] serves at least by fear of punishment to

---

[415] See p. 85.
[416] See p. 43.
[417] See Battles ed. (Eerdmans), 29–41.
[418] See Battles ed., p. 32. See also the Heidelberg Catechism (1563), which includes the theological use of the Law in its second question but suspends presentation of the Ten Commandments until the third part on thankfulness and good works (questions 86–115). This shows the necessity of the theological use in Reformed thinking, yet how the righteous man's use holds the greater emphasis and weight so that the Law is principally a tool for growing in obedience.
[419] Richard A. Muller notes that Calvin and Reformed theology hold a continuity between the Old and New Testaments that explains the moral law "as belonging to the divine promise of salvation" since the Law is a gracious gift of God. See *Dictionary of Latin and Greek Theological Terms* 121.
[420] "Ex his colligi potest, quale officium et quis sit usus legis" (CR 29:49). The Latin verbs are singular; he is more or less equating "office" and "use."

> restrain certain men who, unless compelled, are untouched by any concern for what is just and right. But they are restrained, not because their inner mind is stirred or affected, but because, being bridled, so to speak, they keep their hands from outward activity, and hold inside the depravity that otherwise they wantonly have indulged. . . .
>
> Lastly, to the believers, too, in whose hearts the Spirit of God already lives and reigns [the law] provides no unimportant use, warning then as it does, more and more earnestly what is right and pleasing in the Lord's sight. For even though they have the law written and engraved upon their hearts by the finger of God [Jer. 31:33; Heb. 10:16] that is, have been so moved and quickened that they long to obey the Lord's will, they still profit by the law because from it they learn more thoroughly each day what the Lord's will is like.

It is noteworthy that Calvin speaks of the Law serving to warn the righteous man as well as teach him. Boundaries between the uses are not especially clear at this early stage. There is something similar to Luther's idea of spontaneous love and service (Calvin's "they long to obey") but this spontaneous impulse seems not to be enough. The righteous need daily instruction. In contrast, Luther would more likely think of daily repentance leading back to fresh spontaneity. Luther's thinking stems from his view of the Christian life as righteous and sinner at the same time (*simul justus et peccator*). Calvin does not deny that the righteous are still sinners, but as will be seen further, he emphasized ongoing transformation and duty.

Calvin's emphasis on the righteous man's use of the Law as the "principle use" shows that he did not understand daily repentance and the state of the Christian life in the same way as Luther, who emphasized the theological use of the Law.[421]

---

[421] "There is one major distinction between the Lutherans and the Reformed in the discussion and application of the *usus legis*: the Reformed lay heavy stress on the *tertius usus legis* on the assumption that faith must spring forth and bear fruit of good works, as defined by the law in its normative function. The Lutherans, however, see here the danger of works-righteousness and insist that the *usus normativus* ultimately returns the believer, who remains *simul justus et peccator*, to the *usus paedagogicus* and from there again to Christ and his grace as the sole source of salvation. . . . This difference between the Lutherans and the Reformed arise out of the dialectical

THE 1559 INSTITUTES

The last edition of Calvin's Institutes, though significantly larger than his 1536 edition, retained the same order for the uses of the Law, as illustrated below.[422] Calvin also increasingly emphasized a positive view of the Law as a standard for the Christian life.[423]

> That the whole matter may be made clearer, let us take a succinct view of the office and use of the Moral Law. Now this office and use seems to me to consist of three parts. First, by exhibiting the righteousness of God,—in other words, the righteousness which alone is acceptable to God,—it admonishes every one of his own unrighteousness, certiorates, convicts, and finally condemns him. This is necessary, in order that man, who is blind and intoxicated with self-love, may be brought at once to know and to confess his weakness and impurity. (Inst. 2.7.6)

> The second office of the Law is, by means of its fearful denunciations and the consequent dread of punishment, to curb those who, unless forced, have no regard for rectitude and justice. Such persons are curbed not because their mind is inwardly moved and affected, but because, as if a bridle were laid upon them, they refrain their hands from external acts, and internally check the depravity which would otherwise petulantly burst forth. (Inst. 2.7.10)

---

relationship between law and Gospel in Lutheranism as opposed to the simple distinction of law and Gospel within the one *foedus gratiae* held among the Reformed." Muller 321. For another helpful overview from a Reformed theologian, see John P. Burgess, "Calvin's Third Use of the Law: An Assessment of Reformed Explications of the Ten Commandments" (Unpublished), 7–9. See also Stephen W. Ramp, "John Calvin on Preaching the Law," in *Word and World* (Vol. XXI, no. 3; Summer 2001) 262–269; Joel R. Beeke, "Use of the Law in Reformed Theology" (Unpublished) 1–19. By making the third use the principle use, Calvin prepared the way for the re-emergent doctrine of perfectionism and later controversies about signs of election in the Antinomian controversy among English Calvinists.
[422] John Calvin, *Institutes of the Christian Religion*, 3 Vols., Henry Beveridge, trans. (Edinburgh, 1845–46).
[423] Beeke 11.

> The third use of the Law (being also the principal use, and more closely connected with its proper end) has respect to believers in whose hearts the Spirit of God already flourishes and reigns. For although the Law is written and engraven on their hearts by the finger of God, that is, although they are so influenced and actuated by the Spirit, that they desire to obey God, there are two ways in which they still profit in the Law. For it is the best instrument for enabling them daily to learn with greater truth and certainty what that will of the Lord is which they aspire to follow, and to confirm them in this knowledge; . . . Then, because we need not doctrine merely, but exhortation also, the servant of God will derive this further advantage from the Law: by frequently meditating upon it, he will be excited to obedience, and confirmed in it, and so drawn away from the slippery paths of sin. (Inst. 2.7.12)

Calvin began with the accusing power of the Law, which removes from mankind their delusion of self-righteousness. The children of God (i.e., the elect) then flee to God for mercy and receive the righteousness of Christ. The reprobate are brought to despair of themselves but do not flee to God. They are restrained by the civil use of the Law, though unhappily so.

Luther, at this point, would write warnings against persons using the Law for self-justification. These warnings do not occur at this point in Calvin's *Institutes*. Calvin continued by arguing that the restraining function of the Law is useful for training the children of God before they are converted so that they are in the habit of outward obedience.

It appears that Calvin held the civil law as part of the moral law, so that the coming of the New Testament did not abrogate the Old Testament civil law. Calvin also wrote that the Law was given "to keep alive the hope of salvation in Christ until His advent" (heading of *Institutes*, bk. II ch. 7).[424] Wendel noted that in Calvin's thought, the Law as a whole prefigured the coming life and service of Jesus.[425]

---

[424] Beveridge translation. See François Wendel, *Calvin: Origins and Development of His Religious Thought*, Philip Mairet, trans. (New York: Harper and Row, 1963), 197.
[425] Wendel 198.

This may be Calvin's version of the prophetic use of the Law though it may also relate to Calvin's view of Law and Gospel as a continuum of one covenant of grace.

Under Calvin's third use of the Law there is a change from the 1536 edition. In both editions he writes about the Law teaching. This point remained much the same. In contrast, his second point about the Law warning has now changed to a role of exhortation. The believer meditates upon the Law (Ps 1) and is thus excited to obey it. The result of all this is finally very like restraint from sin.

Luther's emphasis on spontaneous love and service is nearly wholly absent. Calvin's third use begins by talking about the Spirit but ends with the righteous man exciting himself to obedience, a very different outcome.

CALVIN'S LEGACY

Calvinism has often been characterized as a severe or austere expression of Reformation theology. This stems in part from Calvin's personal character and family life. But it might also be associated with his doctrine of the Law, which elevated the third use of the Law as the most important.

One hundred years after Luther and Melanchthon grappled with Agricola's antinomian views, an antinomian controversy broke out among English Calvinists. Antinomian views from the medieval mystics had resurfaced among Anabaptist groups during the sixteenth century. These views flowed with the Rhine down to Holland and across the channel to England, where they have been identified in the Familists, Ranters, and Congregationalists. Such ideas seem to have influenced the views of some Puritans.

As I noted in the introduction, the Puritan Antinomian controversy came to light in the teachings and trial of Anne Hutchinson, a midwife in the early Massachusetts colony whose views were influenced by the preacher John Cotton.[426] Hutchinson became controversial while teaching women and men who gathered

---

[426] See Eve LaPlante's *American Jezebel: The Uncommon Life of Anne Hutchinson, the Woman Who Defied the Puritans* (New York: HarperOne, 2004). The subtitle is misleading since Hutchinson was a deeply committed Puritan herself who held to views that were controversial among the Puritans.

in her home. She questioned the value of striving for a holy, exemplary life as evidence of one's election to grace. She opposed the Puritan preachers who taught a "covenant of works" and claimed she could see who was elect and who was not. Like the Puritan preacher John Cotton, she emphasized a "covenant of grace" as the basis of election and assurance in contrast with moral striving. In this case, which almost tore the Massachusetts Bay Colony apart, Calvin's emphasis on grace was the favored doctrine of those charged with Antinomianism, while his doctrine of the Law was the favored doctrine of those who brought charges against Hutchinson.

CONCLUSION

Calvin developed his doctrine of the Law from Melanchthon and other influences. He consistently ordered the uses of the Law differently from Luther and Melanchthon, emphasizing the righteous man's use of the Law as the principle use. The different order and emphases in Calvin's uses of the Law likely stem from a variety of underlying differences in theology. Luther spoke from the vantage of (1) the Christian as righteous and sinner at the same time and (2) spontaneous love and service wherein the righteous man takes up the Law and uses it freely. Calvin emphasized ongoing transformation and stirring one's self to duty.

For the purpose of this historical survey, these points may suffice. Much more could likely be written about the differences between Luther, Melanchthon, and Calvin with further and deeper investigation. I commend this topic to future scholarship.

CHAPTER NINETEEN

THE COUNCIL OF TRENT (1545–63)

> If anyone says that Christ was given by God to men as a redeemer in whom to trust, and not also as a legislator whom to obey, let him be anathema.
>
> —The Council of Trent

In the very earliest movements of the Reformation, Luther and others sought a free council of the Church where dialogue could take place in safety. For example, after Cardinal Cajetan examined Luther at Augsburg, Luther appealed directly to Leo X on November 28, 1518. He requested a council where he might receive a fair hearing. Five years later, the Diet of Nuremberg similarly requested that a council take place in Germany.

Despite these appeals, the movement toward a council developed slowly. On June 2, 1536 Paul III issued a plan for a general council—not in Germany but in Mantua, Italy. It would take place on May 23, 1537. Luther wrote the Smalcald Articles in preparation for this gathering. Unfortunately, the plans fell through. In 1541 Charles V arranged for Roman theologians and Protestant theologians to gather at Regensburg (Ratisbon) to discuss differences and work for a settlement.[427] The *Regensburg Book*, containing twenty-three articles of doctrinal topics, introduced the idea of twofold righteousness as a

---

[427] Roman theologians included John Gropper, Julius von Pflug, and Johannes Eck, with Gasparo Contarini and Giovanni Morone as papal legates. Protestant theologians included Martin Bucer, Johannes Pistorius the elder, and Philip Melanchthon.

compromise between the Roman theologians and the Protestant theologians at the Council of Regensburg. Ultimately, other theologians did not well receive the *Regensburg Book*. Near the end of Luther's life, firm plans for a council began to take shape, though it was not the free council the Reformers had sought.

In this little chapter we will briefly consider the doctrine of the use of the Law found in two Roman theologians who contributed ideas about the doctrine of justification for the Council of Trent.[428] We will also review what the council finally taught about the use of the Law.

GASPARO CONTARINI

From an important family in Venice, Gasparo Contarini (1483–1542) was well positioned to become a leader. He was educated at the University of Padua, served as an ambassador, and witnessed the 1521 Diet of Worms where Luther defended his teachings before Emperor Charles V. As a papal legate for the Diet of Regensburg, Contarini's views on the use of the Law had an important influence.

In his *Scholia in Epistolas Divi Pauli* (c. 1542), Contarini demonstrated that he was familiar with the doctrine of the use of the Law. For example in the notes on Galatians 3 he wrote:

> But what usefulness does the Law offer to us? It offers this, that it shows us our sins, so in everyway we shall have turned, we should see that we are concluded under sin; so from [the Law] we hasten to be admonished to faith.[429]

Contarini had in view a theological or elenchtic use of the Law,[430] fostering a pedagogical use of the Law that led to faith. Like Luther and Melanchthon, he was writing about the use of the Law in keeping with the longstanding teaching of the Church. He also seems to have appreciated the role of the Law for forming a clearer doctrine of

---

[428] Other theologians of interest would be John Gropper and Reginald Pole.
[429] Gasparis Contarini Cardinalis, *Opera Omnia* (Venetiis: Damlanum Zenarium, 1589), 479. The Latin text is, "Sed quid vtilitatis nobis lex praestat? praestat hoc, quia ostendit nos peccatores, ut quoquouersum nos uerterimus, uideamus nos conclusos esse sub peccato; ut ex ea admoniti curramus ad fidem . . ."
[430] On the elenchtic use, see pp. 8, 198.

repentance and justification. Likewise, in his introduction to 1 Timothy, Contarini wrote:

> The Apostle immediately in the beginning restores this [point about the Law of Moses] in memory for Timothy. Moreover, he teaches the legitimate use of the Law, which strives to this end—so that he may make us free from the old Law, that is, from the coercion of the Law.[431]

Contarini went on to write about the "power of the Law" as well. He showed a good familiarity with the medieval categories and the Protestant emphasis on the theological use of the Law. As a Roman theologian who attacked the Protestants, yet also worked toward reconciliation,[432] his contribution to the sixteenth century discussion about the usefulness of the Law bears further investigation.

GIROLAMO SERIPANDO

The Augustinian Order of Hermits received a young Italian novice in 1507, only two years after they received Martin Luther. Seripando (c. 1492–1563) experienced the disarray of the order following the dispute over the Ninety-Five Theses. In 1524 when von Staupitz released Luther from the order, the disarray only continued. Augustinian monks in Germany and even in Italy continued to read Luther's writings and the writings of other Reformers. Church leaders suspected the Augustinians of spreading Luther's message. As a result, the general of the Augustinians banned Luther's writings within the order. However, on October 26, 1531, Clement VII granted special permission to Seripando so he could read books written by Luther and other Reformers.[433] Seripando also studied the works of St. Augustine, the namesake of the order.

---

[431] "Apostolus statim in exordio redigit Timotheo hoc in memoriam. In super docet usum legis legitimum, qui tendit ad hunc finem, ut nos liberos faciat a veteri lege; id est, a coactione legis" (p. 507).

[432] In his epistle on justification, Contarini defended the distinction of a twofold righteousness in the *Regensburg Book*. See Hubert Jedin, *A History of the Council of Trent*, vol. II, Ernest Graf, trans. (St. Louis: B. Herder Book Co., 1957), 258. Twofold righteousness was a compromise developed by Martin Bucer and John Gropper. Jedin, *Council of Trent* II:168.

[433] Hubert Jedin, *Cardinal Seripando: Papal Legate at the Council of Trent*, Frederic C. Eckhoff, trans. (St. Louis: B. Herder Book Co., 1947), 102. After

Seven years later while Luther was responding to the excesses of Agricola's Antinomianism, Paul III appointed Seripando as vicar general of the Augustinians. His chief task was to restore the order and clear the Augustinians of the charge that they were complicit with the Reformation. Again in 1543 Paul III urged Seripando to study the writings of the Reformers in preparation for a general council.

Seripando's Draft

Hubert Jedin described Seripando's development and influence before, during, and after the council.[434] Among those gathered at Trent, Seripando—as an Augustinian—had broad knowledge of Luther's views and even empathy for some of Luther's observations. He understood the importance of the doctrine of the Law for a discussion of justification.[435] However, the broader council did not focus on the doctrine of the Law but sought to deal more specifically with the doctrine of justification.

There were three main theological schools present at Trent: the Thomists, associated with the Dominicans; the Scotists, associated with the Franciscans; and the Augustinians. From 1290, the Augustinian Order based their theological studies on the writings of Giles of Rome (Aegidius Romanus, d. 1316),[436] who was a student of Thomas Aquinas. The Augustinians and Dominicans competed for position and resources in Germany, a rivalry that contributed to the development of the Reformation.[437] Their rivalry and different approaches to theology affected the outcome at Trent.

On August 11, 1546, Seripando presented a draft of a decree on justification. However, the council little discussed the text that day due to news and fears about the military progress of the Protestant Smalcaldic League. Seripando titled the second chapter of his draft to

---

studying the Protestant literature, Seripando published *Commentaria in epistolam Pauli ad Romanos et in epistolam ad Galatas* (Lugnuni, 1541).

[434] See *Cardinal Seripando*. Jedin was one of the most important Roman Catholic historians of the twentieth century.

[435] Anselm Forster touches on these ideas in *Gesetz und Evangelium bei Girolamo Seripando* (Paderborn: Bonifacius-Druckerei, 1963).

[436] Posset 16, 37.

[437] Posset 25.

describe the functions of the Law and the promises of Jesus Christ.[438] It was essentially Seripando's description of the distinction and use of Law and Gospel as preparatory to the doctrine of justification. However, the second draft of the decree, from August 19, dropped the chapter on the office of the Law.

CANONS AND DECREES

In the end, the Council of Trent made little mention of the doctrine of the Law. The decree concerning justification (January 13, 1547) stated:

> Not even the Jews by the very letter itself of the law of Moses, were able to be liberated, or to arise, therefrom; although free will, attenuated as it was in its powers, and bent down, was by no means extinguished in them.[439]

In this way the theologians at Trent noted the limitations for the Law as a means of justification. On this point they, like Luther, showed agreement with earlier theologians (chs. four through six). However, unlike Luther, in chapter XVI the council affirmed concerning the justified that "by those very works which have been done in God, [they] fully satisfied the divine law according to the state of this life."[440]

In the sixth session on justification, the theologians at Trent anathematized the Reformer's emphasis on grace and faith alone, as well as antinomianism. The canons and decrees made no explicit

---

[438] *Concilium Tridentinum* vol. 5, Stephanus Ehses, ed. (Friburg: Herder, 1964), 822.

[439] Sixth session, ch. I. *The Canons and Decrees of the Sacred and Oecumenical Council of Trent*, J. Waterworth, ed. and trans. (London: Dolman, 1848). From http://history.hanover.edu/texts/trent/trentall.html on 5.12.2011. There were very few representatives from Germany and none who could vote. At the session on justification, there were only 59 voting prelates. Jedin, *Council of Trent* II:483, "Thus a round hundred bishops and as many theologians participated in this first period of the Council of Trent. . . . In both groups Italy undoubtedly furnished an overwhelming majority." Jedin, *History*, p. 484. Thomism became the dominant theology of Trent and subsequent Roman Catholicism.

[440] *Canons and Decrees*, sixth session, ch. XVI.

mention of the use of the Law. Nor did the council concern itself with legalism.

> CANON XVIII. If any one saith, that the commandments of God are, even for one that is justified and constituted in grace, impossible to keep; let him be anathema.
>
> CANON XIX. If any one saith, that nothing besides faith is commanded in the Gospel; that other things are indifferent, neither commanded nor prohibited, but free; or, that the ten commandments nowise appertain to Christians; let him be anathema.
>
> CANON XX. If any one saith, that the man who is justified and how perfect soever, is not bound to observe the commandments of God and of the Church, but only to believe; as if indeed the Gospel were a bare and absolute promise of eternal life, without the condition of observing the commandments ; let him be anathema.
>
> CANON XXI. If any one saith, that Christ Jesus was given of God to men, as a redeemer in whom to trust, and not also as a legislator whom to obey; let him be anathema.[441]

Chemnitz, in the *Examen*, frequently mentioned the Law when responding to the Canons and Decrees. In what feels like a one sided conversation, he appealed to all the classic passages from Romans, Galatians, and 1 Timothy, showing the enduring influence and interest in the doctrine of the Law among the Reformers.[442]

After the Council of Trent, Seripando's teaching about the use of the Law continued to appear in print.[443] His *Commentarius in D. Pauli epistolas ad Galatas* went through numerous editions.[444] The teaching about use of the Law extended into the Roman Catholic

---

[441] *Canons and Decrees*, sixth session.
[442] Martin Chemnitz, *Examination of the Council of Trent*, Fred Kramer, trans. 4 Vols. (St. Louis: Concordia, 1971–86), Part 1, pp. 534–536; Part 2, pp. 575–76; 631–32.
[443] See Hieronymus Seripandius, *In Epistolam Pauli ad Galatas* (Antverpiae: Christophori Plantini, 1567), 49–50, 52
[444] Editions appeared in 1549[?], 1565, 1567, 1569, and 1586.

exegetical tradition but does not appear to have crossed over into its dogmatic tradition in a significant way.[445]

CONCLUSION

Remarkably, Luther's doctrine of the Law, so rooted in the long tradition of western theology, was not on the agenda at the Council of Trent. Luther could not begin discussion of the Gospel and justification without the doctrine of the Law. Melanchthon concluded already in 1521, "Christian doctrine must begin with the function of the Law."[446] The absence of the doctrine at Trent is a telling contrast.

Yet there were theologians at Trent who saw the Reformers' emphasis on the use of the Law and agreed that it was an important element in discussion of the doctrine of justification. Seripando went so far as to write the use of the Law into his draft for the council. And even though this portion of the draft did not survive the writing process, Seripando's publications continued to teach about the use of the Law. This is a moment in history that makes one wonder what might have happened if the council had started with the use of the Law in considering the doctrine of justification.

To leap forward to the present, one finds that in the *Joint Declaration on the Doctrine of Justification* there is only passing reference to the use of the Law as a Lutheran concern.[447] This hardly

---

[445] *The Catechism of the Council of Trent* mentions the power of the Law but provides no further reference to or teaching on the uses of the Law. Georg Kraus's article on "Law and Gospel" in the *Handbook of Catholic Theology*, Wolfgang Bienert and Frances Schüssler Fiorenza, eds. (New York: Crossroad, 1995) does not show awareness of the distinction of uses of the Law in the Roman Catholic tradition. He attributed the distinctions to Evangelical theologians. He also wrote that the distinction between Law and Gospel did not become essential to Evangelical theology and eventually became a meaningless distinction (p. 427). Kraus seems unaware of the enduring place of the Law and Gospel distinction in the Formula of Concord, to which Lutheran pastors subscribed at their ordination, and the renewed interest in Law and Gospel fostered by the nineteenth century confessional revival (e.g., Franke's *Theologie der Concordienformel* [1858] and Walther's *Die rechte Unterscheidung von Gesetz und Evangelium* [1897]). The distinction remains vibrantly alive among traditional Lutherans.
[446] LCC 19:83; CR 21:154.
[447] Lutheran World Federation and The Pontifical Council for Promoting Christian Unity, (Grand Rapids, MI: Eerdmans, 2000), 23.

does justice to the longstanding discussion of the biblical doctrine of the early and medieval Fathers. Although the use of the Law is certainly a Lutheran concern, it appears to be a broad catholic concern that could help to clarify the doctrinal positions of both Lutherans and Roman Catholics. One might even look forward to future dialogues that would begin with the doctrine of the Law before seeking to settle the doctrine of justification.

CHAPTER TWENTY

THE FORMULA OF CONCORD VI

> The children of God live in the law and walk according to the law of God.
>
> —Formula of Concord

In *Law, Life, and the Living God: The Third Use of the Law in Modern American Lutheranism*, Scott R. Murray described the modern debate surrounding Formula of Concord VI, "Concerning the Third Use of the Law."[448] In the course of the book, he noted a number of concerns scholars have raised about article VI, ranging from mild critique to forceful denouncement. For example, advocates of the only two uses consensus see Formula of Concord VI as a departure—even a significant departure—from Luther's doctrine of the Law.

In this chapter we will consider the relationship between Luther's doctrine of the Law and the teaching in article VI by referring to the Appendix D commentary on the title and *Affirmativa* of the article. The appended commentary references biblical passages, Luther's expressions, Luther's theology as described earlier in this book, and points from throughout Luther's writings. Since the only-two-uses consensus has enjoyed such wide popularity over the last sixty years, the idea that Luther taught a threefold use of the Law—and that this led to Melanchthon's doctrine and the doctrine in the Formula of Concord—will be challenged. This chapter will briefly consider some

---

[448] (St. Louis: Concordia, 2002), 9.

of the counter arguments likely to arise from defenders of the only-two-uses consensus.

THE DEVELOPMENT OF FC VI

After Luther's death, a second Antinomian controversy arose in 1556. This controversy was not the same as that raised by Johann Agricola in 1527 and reintroduced by Agricola and Jacob Schenck in 1537–1540. The first Antinomian controversy had focused on the roles of Law and Gospel in repentance. The second controversy was a milder disagreement about whether the Law still served a Christian after conversion, whether a Christian still needed the Law. Theologians who raised the issue were Andrew Poach (1516–1585), Anton Otto (b. c. 1505), Andrew Musculus (1514–1581), and Michael Neander (1525–1595).[449] FC VI was intended to settle the second Antinomian controversy by conciliating both sides.

Modern scholars often regard Melanchthon as the theologian whose work and influence stood behind Formula of Concord VI on the Third Use of the Law. This is reasonable given that the writers of the Formula were students of Melanchthon trained from his *Loci Communes*. With this background in place, we shall now consider the modern complaints about the doctrine of the article.

CONCERNS WITH FC VI

Having looked at the relationship between Luther's teaching, Melanchthon's teaching, and the background of FC VI, we can now address some of the modern concerns about the theology of FC VI. The following is a list of concerns mentioned in Murray's book, Schurb's dissertation, and the writings of some theologians in the Evangelical Lutheran Church in America. I provide brief observations.

  1. FC VI is a compromise document, therefore, it cannot serve well as a confession of the Church.

If a compromise document cannot serve as a confession of the Church, then that would exclude use of virtually all creeds and confessions since Nicea! If history demonstrates anything, it is that

---

[449] Poach, Otto, and Musculus studied at Wittenberg under both Luther and Melanchthon. Neander studied under Melanchthon.

theology is a difficult topic and that Christians often reach a consensus on teaching after hearing and ingesting different points of view.

2. The title of FC VI is not fully compatible with the contents.[450]

FC VI certainly includes more than the specific topic "the third use of the Law." However, as noted in Appendix D, the first paragraph describes the use of the Law by a Christian, which Luther associated with a third use. The rest of the article addresses issues raised by theologians who either rejected the third use of the Law or protested against points associated with the third use. As a consequence, the title seems appropriate enough.

3. The definition paragraph in FC VI is ambiguous; the German seems to refer to the third use of the Law with Christians but the Latin edition may say that all three uses of the Law apply to Christians.[451]

The only use defined explicitly with the term "reborn" is the third use of the Law. Therefore, the expression "should such a thing be urged upon reborn Christians, or not?" is referring to the reborn having the Law as "a definite rule." This observation agrees with the Latin text about "whether or not the law should be inculcated upon the reborn" (Schurb 92). The FC does not try to teach that the preacher can control the uses of the Law as though he could teach one use without other uses having their effects. Preachers cannot control the effects of the Law.

4. The focus of FC VI is on the first and second uses of the Law rather than the third use of the Law.[452]

The article opens with the third use, which stems from Luther's terminology and doctrine that ultimately informed Melanchthon's definition of the third use of the Law. The article certainly mentions other uses of the Law but does so in terms of the Christian life and the struggle the Christian faces (*simul justus et peccator*).

5. There is no distinct third use of the Law. It is really just an application of the first use or second use in the life of a believer.[453]

---

[450] Observation from David Scaer in Murray, p. 211, n. 188.
[451] Observation from Schurb 91–95.
[452] Observation from Charles Arand in Murray, p. 9.

This is one of the most commonly held views by advocates of the only-two-uses consensus (cf. Wengert, *Formula*, 91, 97–98). The history of the doctrine of the Law speaks against their opinion. For example, ancient and medieval interpreters described a prophetic use of the Law, which medieval theologians described as a third use. Thomas Aquinas wrote of four effects of the Law. Later Lutheran theologians distinguished two uses within the "second use" itself so that some of them ended up defining four uses of the Law. Luther and Melanchthon did not try to define all possible uses of the Law or try to make all possible distinctions. They were providing a simple, memorable understanding of the Law as it related to the doctrine of justification. Their efforts were guided by Augustine's four stages of man.

Those who assert that, since there are only two uses of the Law, therefore, there cannot be a third use of the Law, also fail to note that different subjects use the Law. God uses the law, the believer uses the Law, and even the devil may use the Law as he did during the temptation of Jesus (Mt 4; Lk 4). Observing that different subjects use the Law multiplies the number of potential uses one could distinguish. Luther's advice seems best, "Use the Law anyway you like only do not attribute justification to it" (*Lectures on 1 Timothy* [1528] LW 28:231).

The righteous man's use of the Law is different from the civil use because (A) the Holy Spirit is working through the righteous man to bring forth the fruit of the Spirit in keeping with the Law, (B) the righteous man takes up the Law and uses it willingly, (C) the righteous man uses the Law "without constraint" in active obedience, and (D) keeping the Law by grace through faith actually pleases God whereas civil righteous or outward obedience does not please God.

6. FC VI is incompatible with Luther's doctrine.[454]

The commentary in Appendix D substantially undermines this concern, showing the great compatibility with Luther's teaching. Also, the reader must bear in mind that FC VI addresses some issues that were raised after Luther's death. As a result, the article addresses more issues than Luther himself had occasion to address in his day.

---

[453] Observation from Elert and Bring (Schurb p. 94).
[454] A general assertion made by theologians who teach that Luther had only two uses of the Law.

Nevertheless, this fact does not mean that the article is in conflict with Luther's theology, otherwise all theological treatises written after 1546 (including those by advocates of the only-two-uses consensus) would automatically be incompatible with Luther's theology, which is a nonsensical argument.

7. The third use of the Law comes from Calvin.[455]

This is clearly a historical error as the preceding chapters demonstrate. Calvin did not write about the third use of the Law until after Luther and Melanchthon. FC VI does not reflect Calvin's ordering of the doctrine or his emphasis on the third use of the Law as the primary use of the Law. FC VI maintains Luther's and Melanchthon's approaches in distinction from Calvin's approach.

8. The Law cannot properly be equated with the immutable will of God because the Gospel is also the will of God and the chief will of God.[456]

This observation is true but misleading. Both Law and Gospel are the Word of God. Therefore, both Law and Gospel are the will of God. But note that FC VI does not teach that *only* the Law is the will of God or that the Law is the chief will of God. To read the article as though it taught that the Gospel was not the will of God is an incorrect reading of the text.

James Nestingen expresses a similar concern that the FC defines the Law as the definitive expression of God's will.[457]

9. FC SD VI 24 describes an *eschatological limit* when "people are perfectly renewed in the resurrection. Then they will need neither the proclamation of the law nor its threats and punishment, just as they will no longer need the gospel, for both belong to this imperfect life."[458]

The wording of the passage seems to contradict the point that the Law is "the unchanging will of God" (FC SD VI 17) or the "eternal will" of God as both Luther and Melanchthon described it. It also implies

---

[455] Observation from Ickert and Schwanz in Murray, p. 203, n. 33.

[456] Observation associated with Jungkuntz in Murray, p. 188.

[457] See "Changing Definitions: The Law in Formula VI," in CTQ 69:3–4 (2005): 267.

[458] Observations connected with summaries from Elert and Jungkuntz in Murray, pp. 94, 190.

that the Gospel will no longer be needed in eternity, which conflicts with the description of the Gospel as eternal in Rv 14:6.[459] However, these concerns would stem from a misreading of the text, which actually teaches that *the need to proclaim* the Law and the Gospel will end when the saints are perfected in eternity (cf. Jer 31:34). It does not state that the doctrines themselves, which stem from God's nature, will go away.[460]

> 10. FC VI obscures the role of the Law and is contradictory. It teaches on the one hand that a third use of the Law is necessary for the regenerate. On the other hand, it teaches that the regenerate need the Law because their regeneration is incomplete in this life. The taming of the Law for the regenerate leads to a covert antinomianism since FC VI does not allow the Law to accuse and condemn appropriately, nor does it bring the accusation of the Law to an end.[461]

FC VI describes the complexity of a Christian as saint and sinner at the same time. It does not teach that the Law is tame toward sin but that Christians still need the accusation of the Law insofar as they are sinners. Insofar as Christians are righteous, they may use the Law in the freedom of the Spirit. The circumstances described in FC VI are indeed complex but they are not contradictory.

CONCLUSION

FC VI captured the manner of Ps 119 where the psalmist celebrated the Law of Moses and the benefits it brought to his life. It aptly described how believers may hear and see and use the Law. This is the manner of teaching about the third use of the Law that Lutherans would cultivate in light of FC VI.

In this chapter we have seen how indebted FC VI is to the teaching of Scripture as Luther described it. The article is certainly

---

[459] Murray's book also states, "The Formula of Concord raises the hypothetical case of the 'perfect saint' only to illustrate the real need for an informatory function of the Law.... The Law has a transitory character in the Formula. The Formula states that both Law and Gospel will be unnecessary at the resurrection" (p. 94). It is not clear whether these observations are from Elert or from Murray.

[460] Schurb 110–111.

[461] Observation from Forde in *Christian Dogmatics* 2:460.

also compatible with Melanchthon's teaching, though it is not a rehearsal of Melanchthon's 1559 *Loci*. Schurb has noted:

> The theology of the third use in article VI of the Formula of Concord was indeed "Melanchthonian." But it must immediately be added that the Formula reflected a definite stage in the development of Melanchthon's thinking. It reiterated Melanchthon's theology of the Law from the time after 1521, but before the synergistic and "Majoristic" ideas came into the 1535 and 1543 Loci. That is, the Formula mirrored Melanchthon's thinking on the Law as of the time when he wrote the Augsburg Confession and the Apology, as shown in those confessional documents.[462]

There are different emphases and concerns in Luther, Melanchthon, and the authors of the Formula of Concord. Yet there also seems to be substantial unity from Luther, to Melanchthon, to the writers of the Formula. Theologians or historians who wish to maintain that FC VI is incompatible with Luther's teaching should produce specific, documented examples that take into account the breadth of Luther's teaching rather than base their assessment primarily on the 1535 *Lectures on Galatians*. The pattern of Luther's dialectic and rhetoric is important to maintain in this matter as well as Luther's verbs in his commentaries and catechisms on the Law. The *Antinomian Disputations* are especially important for noting this continuity between Luther, Melanchthon, and later Lutheran tradition. Advocates of the only-two-uses consensus must not overlook these observations in future critiques of FC VI.

---

[462] Schurb 287.

PART THREE

TOWARD A NEW CONSENSUS

CHAPTER TWENTY-ONE

CURRENT QUESTIONS AND ANSWERS

> The law has been given for . . . a sure guide . . . to light their way . . . to follow the Spirit. . . . In this manner the children of God live in the law and walk according to the law of God.
>
> —Formula of Concord

In "the Three Uses of the Law," John Witte Jr. described how the teaching of the Reformers influenced the legal practice of western society. Jurors made deterrence, retribution, and rehabilitation the goals of criminal punishment, likely drawing on threefold descriptions of the Law in Protestant theology.[463] The Reformation is commonly described as Luther's rediscovery of the Gospel. However, in view of the Reformer's interest in the use of the Law and the proper distinction between Law and Gospel, and western society's responses to those teachings, one might also describe the Reformation as a rediscovery of the Law.

For the past sixty years or longer, the facts about the doctrine of the Law as taught during the Reformation have been either misunderstood or unappreciated. It appears that Elert's discovery in the Second Antinomian Disputation and Ebeling's influential article misdirected researchers unintentionally, which led to the only-two-uses consensus. Misunderstanding of the history led to misunderstanding of the doctrine.

---

[463] *God's Joust, God's Justice: Law and Religion in the Western Tradition* (Grand Rapids: Eerdmans, 2006), 263–92.

Another likely historical factor that contributed to the rise of the only-two-uses consensus was the ecumenical environment in pre-war and post World War II Germany. In 1935 Lutheran theologians reacted sharply to Karl Barth's essay *Evangelium und Gesetz*. When post-war efforts arose to unite the Lutheran and Reformed churches, these tensions were renewed. Theologians like Elert seem to have striven for a greater distinction between Lutheran and Reformed views in an effort to preserve Lutheran identity. Ironically, Lutheran churches that participated in the union with the Reformed tended to embrace the only-two-uses consensus whereas the more conservative Lutherans tended to retain and teach the validity of the threefold use of the Law.

QUESTIONS ON THE HISTORY OF DOCTRINE

Many things about the history of the doctrine of the Law remain to be investigated. Here is a list of questions to consider:

- What Old Testament and New Testament texts relate specifically to the ongoing role of the Law in the life of a person declared righteous by grace through faith alone?
- What was the contribution of intertestamental Judaism to Jesus' and Paul's interests and arguments about the doctrine of the Law?
- What is the relationship between the biblical and classical traditions on the usefulness of the Law?
- How did misunderstanding of the Law lead to misunderstanding of justification in early Christianity?
- How did the focus on Pauline theology reemerge in western Christianity with Tyconius, Ambrosiaster, Augustine and others?
- What is the relationship between the doctrine of the Law in the exegetical tradition and the dogmatic tradition of scholasticism?
- How did Petrus Aureoli and Nicholas of Lyra end up with a threefold use? Did other medieval theologians reach the same conclusion?

What did Luther learn about the Law in scholastic training? What did he reject and what did he retain?

Are there other as yet unrecognized passages in Luther where he taught a threefold use?

What more could we learn about Melanchthon's teaching on three uses of the Law and how it stemmed from and related to Luther's teaching?

How did other Wittenberg theologians receive Luther's teaching on the use of the Law?

What did later Reformed theologians teach about the use of the Law and how did their teaching relate to Calvin's teaching?

What terms, phrases, and arguments of Melanchthon contributed to Formula of Concord VI?

Did the doctrine of the Formula of Concord VI settle the matter in Lutheran history before the new issues raised in the twentieth century?

What is the broader relationship of the Lutheran doctrine to the Reformed and the Roman Catholic traditions?

Given the teaching of the Fathers, why is the doctrine of the use of the Law not more explicit in Roman Catholic theology?

How did the threefold consensus form at the end of the nineteenth century?

How precisely did the only-two-uses consensus form and why was it so strongly embraced in the twentieth century?

Should the discoveries about the doctrine of the Law affect the catechetical, practical, or ecumenical efforts of the Lutheran Church and other traditions?

ANSWERS TO CURRENT QUESTIONS

New data provides a new opportunity for understanding and for a new consensus. In the preface, I noted that a series of papers in the *Concordia Theological Quarterly* Vol. 69 (2005) prompted my research. Scholars prepared these papers in dialogue with and response to Scott Murray's book, *Law, Life, and the Living God: The Third Use of the Law in Modern American Lutheranism*, which challenged established opinions about the use of the Law. For the conclusion, I return to these papers and the questions the authors raised, presenting them with the authors' names and the page numbers where the questions appeared in the journal. Murray's book continues to serve as a valuable critique of modern Lutheran teaching about the use of the Law. I will address the questions his work raised in view of the broader history of the use of the Law.

    1. "Which laws apply? . . . How shall we promote the Law?" (Larry M. Vogel, p. 201).

Divine law, natural law, the Law of Moses, ecclesiastical laws, and human laws of various regions—Christian theologians have supported a broad variety of law for the sake of good order. They have done so with the understanding that any good and useful law must stem from the divine law, the eternal and immutable will of God.

One must also note that human laws come and go over time as the needs of people change. Even the Law of Moses, given by God, was temporal in character since it was designed especially for Israel. The question is perhaps not, "Does the Law apply?" but "How does the Law apply?" For example, the new covenant has abrogated the Law about circumcision (Genesis 17; etc.). Yet the passages about circumcision from the Old Testament still stand for our benefit and edification today (cf. 1 Corinthians 10:6, 11–12). Abrogated ceremonies still apply to our lives by teaching us about God's ways, even though Christians do not perform these ceremonies physically. All good and valid laws—rooted in the divine law—apply. (The moral law is fulfilled in Christ but never set aside.) God's people promote them as they apply them in view of the new covenant. In Luther's words, "Law vigorously preached . . ."

    2. If the Law is a disciplinarian leading us to Christ, then what becomes of the Law for us once we are in Christ? Is the Christian wholly lawless? Does the Law remain a guide for the Christian? (Mark C. Mattes, pp. 271–272)

God's Law is eternal so it does not suddenly go away once we are in Christ. Also, God placed the Law in the hearts of human beings at the time of creation (Rm 2:15). As a result, the natural, moral law is ever with us and is always a part of our thinking. In view of this, a

Christian is not "wholly lawless"; if the Law remains a natural part of a Christian's thinking, then it also is influencing or guiding the Christian in some way.

3. Are we dealing with an article of faith intimately related to every other article of faith . . . ? (Carl L. Beckwith, p. 294)

The experience of the Church Fathers shows that the doctrine of the Law is intimately related to every other article. The Law of God is eternal. It stems from who God is and how He relates to His creation. He built it into the hearts of mankind. He reintroduced it through Moses. He used it to judge and to lead Israel. Jesus taught the Law and came to fulfill it. The Law is a servant of the Gospel; it is to drive us to repentance. It is bound to be involved in the life of every Christian. Because we are sinners, it always accuses us. Throughout our lives, it always teaches us and remains useful to us. God will enable us to keep the Law perfectly in eternity.

4. Did Luther teach that there is a function of the Law for the Christian? Did Lutheranism teach that there is a function of the Law for the Christian? (Lawrence R. Rast Jr., p. 188).

Luther clearly taught that the accusatory function of the Law would always be useful to the Christian since in this life, the Christian always has the sinful nature and needs the Law to humble him. The Christian life is one of ongoing repentance and trust in God's forgiveness.

It is also now clear historically that Luther taught about a threefold function of the Law. His training in patristic and scholastic theology introduced him to this way of thinking. Luther ultimately saw that this teaching came from the apostle Paul. Melanchthon and other Reformers learned the threefold use of the Law from Luther. It became a standard part of pastoral training at Wittenberg during Luther's lifetime. There is as yet no evidence that Luther repudiated this approach to teaching about the Law. His own teaching tended to follow a pattern of teaching two uses of the Law of Moses, misuses of the Law of Moses, followed by descriptions of how a Christian used the Law in his life in an ongoing way.

5. Having begun by the Gospel, are we now perfected by the Law? (Larry M. Vogel, p. 198).

This is an adaptation of a question from Paul (Gal 3:3) and the answer is clearly, "No." The Law has no power to perfect. It is the Gospel that makes the Christian complete or perfect through the inherited righteousness in Christ. It is Christ's perfect righteousness that silences the accusations of the Law in our consciences, fills us with God's Holy Spirit, and makes us heaven bound. Christians begin to keep the Law in this life through the sanctifying work of the Holy Spirit who leads them to serve God and their neighbors spontaneously. Such Christian life and service is never lawless since the natural, moral law is always available to mankind, though only Christians gladly use and fulfill it as a result of the Gospel.

6. Was the Formula faithful to Luther? (Lawrence R. Rast Jr., p. 188)

Evidence suggests that the writers of the Formula of Concord were intimately familiar with Luther's teaching about the doctrine of the Law (see Appendix D). The terms, phrases, and fuller argument are clearly indebted to Luther as seen in the 1522 postil, the 1528 *Lectures on 1 Timothy*, the 1535 *Lectures on Galatians*, and the 1537–40 *Antinomian Disputations*. Without question, Luther expressed himself at times in ways that may be judged as conflicting with the Formula of Concord—such conflicting statements were in fact the reason why colleagues and students of Luther became confused and why the *Antinomian Disputations* became necessary. Luther must be understood in view of his own writings, especially his mature statements by which he rejected and condemned the opinions of the Reformation era Antinomians. His teaching helped to create the Formula of Concord and comports well with its content and argument. The burden of proof rests with those who wish to drive a wedge between Luther and the Formula.

7. Should Lutheranism teach that there is a third use? Is the phrase "third use of the Law" necessary? Is the phrase beneficial in the 21st century? (Larry M. Vogel, pp. 191–92).

Yes. The teaching clearly has deep roots in biblical and Christian doctrine over the centuries. The phrase "third use of the Law" is embodied in the confessional writings and is part of the Lutheran Church's enduring heritage. Advocates of the only-two-uses approach misjudged the history of the doctrine due to inadequate evidence and undue focus on the 1535 *Lectures on Galatians*. Knowing that the phrase actually comes from our catholic heritage makes it beneficial for the twenty-first century, especially as Lutherans dialogue with other Christians who share this inheritance.

8. The Church has been a vibrant and living soul in the world. How could it be otherwise for those who hold the Christian faith? (Larry M. Vogel, p. 214).

Because Christians are sinners, they fall miserably and contribute to the misery of life in a sinful, broken world. The history of the Church is replete with examples of such painful, destructive, and self-destructive intentions and actions. But, thanks be to God, who calls us to repentance through His Law and delivers us from evil through the Gospel of Jesus Christ, who alone is the Savior of the world, especially of those who believe (1 Tm 4:10). With His good gifts and Spirit, the Church continues to be a vibrant witness to eternal truth—the doctrine of the Law and the doctrine of the Gospel—which shape our lives in Christ Jesus and thereby change our world. The Scripture warns that at the end there will be apostasy and it remains to be seen how death-filled and dark the world will become in that hour. Yet we have the enduring promise of the eternal God and Savior that the gates of hell shall not prevail against His Church. The Lord dwells in Zion. Heaven is already our home.

PROBLEMS WITH MODERN CRITIQUES

As I have studied the history of the doctrine of the Law up to the Reformation, I have also read various modern critiques of the western tradition and proposals to amend its problems. However, I believe that there is a basic problem with the available modern critiques: they have not rightly understood or represented the history of doctrine. Consequently, they may be proposing the wrong theological solutions for the churches today.

In order to illustrate my concern about potential misunderstandings of the history of doctrine, I will draw attention to the work of one theologian: Gerhard O. Forde. I have chosen Forde because he wrote the locus on "Christian Life" in the Braaten and Jenson, *Christian Dogmatics*.[464] As the commonly used dogmatic in the largest North American Lutheran church body (the Evangelical Lutheran Church in America), great numbers of theological students have read and ingested this locus. Forde is certainly not the only theologian that I could critique, nor do I wish to make him a unique contributor to modern issues. I chose his locus because its broad use makes it an obvious choice.

An Introduction to Forde's Locus. Forde began his locus concerned that he was doing something risky, since writing about the Christian life entails temptations to flout piety. One must run the gauntlet between hypocrisy and despair over one's works while potentially failing to write anything helpful. Despite these risks, Forde launched into a sharp critique of western Christian thought in which he sought to answer Paul's basic question: "Are we to continue in sin that grace may abound?" (Rm 6:1) and Forde's own question about whether a Christian has anything more to do since Christ has already given him life (p. 396; Forde's question forecasts a passive approach to the Christian life). Forde's approach in this locus was consistent with his earlier writings as one can see from reading *A More Radical Gospel*.[465]

Forde may be commended for working from Scripture, especially early in the locus. He may also be commended for his concern that the western model of theology has wrongly centered on the Law rather than justification apart from the Law (*Christian Dogmatics* 2:404–405, 409). Forde's work in the locus and elsewhere well illustrates the inherent connection between the doctrine of the Law and the doctrine of the Gospel since what one teaches about the atonement directly affects what one teaches about the Law and the Christian life.[466] Forde used strong rhetoric and argued passionately for his conclusions, which makes his locus interesting to read.

Forde's Critique. Forde's goal early in the locus was to dismantle the western synthesis between justification and the Law so

---

[464] Vol. 2 (Philadelphia: Fortress Press, 1984), 391–469. My colleague, Robert Baker, has also offered a critique for some of Forde's writings in *Natural Law: A Lutheran Reappraisal*, 135–56
[465] This is a collection of Forde essays from 1970–92.
[466] Forde also wrote the locus on "The Work of Christ," *Christian Dogmatics* 2:1–99.

that he could provide "justification by faith" as a new model (*Christian Dogmatics* 2:406). His approach entailed the rejection or redefinition of many basic features of the western tradition. For example, Forde questioned the following:

1. The Law as an eternal standard according to which salvation is measured (*Christian Dogmatics* 2:403)
2. Justification by grace as a way of satisfying or fulfilling the Law (*Christian Dogmatics* 2:407)
3. Descriptions of the Law in terms of functions (*Christian Dogmatics* 2:415)
4. Law as an eternal, ontological structure (*Christian Dogmatics* 2:416)
5. The forensic model of describing justification (*Christian Dogmatics* 2:427)
6. The traditional model of the order of salvation (*Christian Dogmatics* 2:428)
7. The use of natural law as the structural model of the theological system (*Christian Dogmatics* 2:447)
8. Distinctions between moral, ceremonial, and civil laws (*Christian Dogmatics* 2:447)
9. The idea that a Christian as a new man can use the Law (*Christian Dogmatics* 2:449)

Forde's critique proposed a thorough reorientation of doctrine, which would affect the views of Protestants and Roman Catholics, if adopted. In the background is Forde's rejection of vicarious satisfaction as the doctrine of the atonement taught by Anselm of Canterbury (c. 1033–1109).

For reading the locus, it is important to note that modern theologians like Forde tend to think and write about the Law abstractly as a principle rather than concretely as the Law of Moses, natural law, moral law, etc. There is a tendency to reduce the Law to threat, guilt, fear, and the like. This creates an important and somewhat confusing barrier between his writing about the Law and that of earlier theologians.

What Forde Misunderstood. A basic problem with Forde's critique is that he has not understood or accurately represented western teaching on the history of the use of the Law and possibly other points of theology. For example, like many other modern theologians, Forde viewed Luther as teaching only two uses of the Law and Melanchthon as the theologian who introduced a third use of the Law. As a Protestant theologian trained in the only-two-uses approach during the mid twentieth century, he was trained to work with these views.

Forde described the traditional distinction of moral and ceremonial laws as having no basis in biblical teaching when, in fact, such passages clearly do exist (e.g., 1Sm 15:22; Mi 6:6–8; Mt 23:23; Col 2:16–23). Forde questioned the role of the Law as an eternal standard in western theology without dealing with basic biblical statements about the eternality of God's nature, which points to the Law as something more than a passing feature of our world or experience (e.g., God's confession of Himself in Ex 34:6–7, which includes a statement of the Law). Other biblical texts also point to the eternal or everlasting character of the word of the Law (e.g., Ps 119:44, 160; Lk 21:33). Before one could accept Forde's critique, one would need to account for these canonical passages and produce evidence that God's Law is, in fact, temporal since biblical statements about the temporal role of the Law are about the Law given at Sinai, not the eternal will of God.[467]

Forde assumed that Luther made a radical departure from the western tradition's doctrine of the Law and did not fully recognize how Luther actually stood within that tradition and continued that tradition. Forde tended to choose features of Luther's theology as a basis for his critique of the western tradition. At times, he attributed things to Luther that clearly go back to earlier western theologians, such as Augustine (e.g., the idea that the Law has uses), so that Forde inaccurately isolated Luther from his forbearers. His locus tended to romanticize Luther as an innovative theologian in contrast with theologians who appear like drones of the western system such as Thomas Aquinas and Lutheran Orthodox theologians (*Christian Dogmatics* 2:404, 426–29).

---

[467] Modernist theologians tend to reduce the Law to mere accusation. This is, I think, a psychologization of the Law. It hides the Law and makes it temporal by assuming that when the Gospel is applied, the Law has ended and gone away. Reducing the Law to accusation is a partner to Gospel reductionism.

What Forde Omitted. Forde's critical approach to the western system invites the reader to critique Forde's thought more closely. As one reads this locus carefully, one notices startling omissions in Forde's approach. For example, Luther's teaching was important for Forde's critique of the western system but citation of Luther became less important as Forde moved further into the locus to provide an eschatological perspective on the Christian life. A most surprising omission is the almost complete lack of argument from the Lutheran Confessions.

The reader should also note what passages Forde actually referenced from Scripture. Most of his argument flows from five chapters of the New Testament: Rm 3; 6–8 and Gal 3. In itself, the focus on Romans and Galatians is not surprising. Citation of these passages is in keeping with his stated purpose to write about the source of the Christian life rather than the Christian life itself (*Christian Dogmatics* 2:397). However, the limited range of citation means that Forde inevitably stayed away from discussion of the Mosaic Law, which was a major concern for the apostle in Romans and Galatians, and from the paraenetic sections of Paul's epistles where Paul described what the Christian life looked like because of justification. Forde criticized the western tradition's emphasis on the order of salvation (*Christian Dogmatics* 2:428–29) but ironically failed to note that the very chapters he cited from Romans were important to the early development of the order of salvation in western theology (e.g., Augustine's "stages of man").

Another factor in Forde's argument from Scripture is that he stayed away from Ephesians, Colossians, 1 Timothy, 2 Timothy, and Titus. This is possibly due to the influence of modern biblical criticism, which has questioned the Pauline authorship of these canonical letters and thereby muted their use in modern theology. Given that western Christianity consistently interpreted Gal 3 along with 1Tm 1, a reader may see how the critical views of modern theologians disconnects them from theologians of the past. Also, Ephesians 2 is an obvious passage to cite regarding the relationship between grace and faith. Forde wanted to drive a wedge between them as part of the rejection of his characterization of the western system (*Christian Dogmatics* 2:407) so he stayed away from Ephesians 2.

Often Forde attacked the positions of unstated theologians so that one cannot tell what positions he was actually rejecting. For example, when he wrote about the third use of the Law as a transformation of the Law into a "more or less neutral guide"[468] and as an introduction of covert antinomianism, one wonders what theologians are actually arguing that the Law is neutral. For Forde, the suggestion that the Law serves as a guide necessarily introduces legalism. He wrote, "Insofar as law brings knowledge, it does not bring knowledge of the good but knowledge of sin" (*Christian Dogmatics* 2:419). For Forde, a third use of the Law also introduces a covert antinomianism because the Law is "tamed" and so no longer accuses. Do these ideas really follow necessarily? (They certainly do not reflect Luther's doctrine of the Law.) Who is arguing for such things?

Forde's description of the western tradition also makes one ponder whether what he wrote is an accurate presentation or whether it is a characterization meant to entice the reader to reject the western tradition in favor of a radical new position. As stated above, Forde has strong rhetoric. His approach makes it difficult to distinguish when he is working for effect and when he is stating historical fact. A general order for his writing is sharp, radical critique of an existing doctrine, followed by a proposed new approach, which ultimately returns to features of the existing doctrine (cf. his closing comments about the role of the civil use of the Law in Christian vocation, which is an attempt to bring the use of the Law back into the Christian life).[469]

Luther made daily repentance a hallmark of the Christian life. Forde distanced his locus from a discussion of repentance. Instead, he introduced modern terminology such as "progress" in writing about the Christian life, while seeking to undermine the idea of the believer progressing toward holiness through a system. These terms and depictions serve his arguments but also serve to separate him from Luther and earlier theologians who work with the biblical call to repent and thereby emphasize the theological use of the Law. In contrast, Forde's approach attributed aspects of the theological use of the Law to justification. Here are examples from the locus.

---

[468] *Christian Dogmatics* 2:451.
[469] Another example of this is the essay "In Our Place" in *A Moral Radical Gospel*.

One is justified by hearing and believing God's judgment, and such hearing and believing leads to the realization and confession that we are sinners. (*Christian Dogmatics* 2:408)

When God says, "I forgive you, I declare you just for Jesus' sake," sin is unmasked and attacked at once. (*Christian Dogmatics* 2:409)

The word of justification is precisely that kind of word. It kills the old exactly because it pronounces that there is nothing to do. (*Christian Dogmatics* 2:410)

The death inflicted by the word of justification which reduces us to nothing is the real death, the true spiritual death. (*Christian Dogmatics* 2:411)

Only one way remains open: to grasp justification and sanctification as a dynamic unity in the light of the eschatological nature of the divine action. Justification by faith means the death of the old and the resurrection of the new. (*Christian Dogmatics* 2:430)

The progress is the coming of the kingdom of God among us. That is why the complete sanctification is always the same as justification and cannot be something more added to it or separated from it. (*Christian Dogmatics* 2:435)

Justification is the end and goal, it is death and resurrection. (*Christian Dogmatics* 2:457)

The justification proclamation is an attack on the old being, on whatever folly it happens to be engaged in. (*Christian Dogmatics* 2:463)

In these passages, Forde was trying to make the point that because God justifies us in Christ, we can never justify ourselves. However, his attempt to describe the doctrine "radically," as he stated repeatedly, tended to confuse the work of the Law and the work of the Gospel. Justification becomes an instrument of death and becomes mixed with sanctification.

Eschatological perspective. In place of the western system, Forde proposed "eschatological perspective," which he saw in Luther's writings (*Christian Dogmatics* 2:449–50). As I read Forde's locus, I wrestled with the question of just what he meant by this eschatological perspective since he did not provide an explicit definition nor have I found one in other writings. Forde seemed to mean that we understand theology and the Christian life from their goal rather than see them as a process working step-by-step or part-by-part, though he acknowledged that Luther wrote about the Christian life in both ways, depending on what he was writing about (*Christian Dogmatics* 2:432). In Forde's view, Christ has fulfilled the Law so that it has reached its goal (*telos*) and comes to an end (*finis*). Since Christ completed our redemption, the Christian has rest from the accusations of the Law and from the need for works. Faith in God's work ends the need for all else, so that one may now simply live as a new being. Forde's eschatological emphasis seemed to dominate his thought and perhaps even replace the role that justification has traditionally played in Lutheran theology.

I find that Forde's locus ended in a confusing way. He began to describe the civil use of the Law as the "proper use" of the Law that Christians can enact in this world (*Christian Dogmatics* 2:458–59), although earlier he had criticized the idea that Christians could use the Law (*Christian Dogmatics* 2:449). Luther, by contrast, focused on the theological use of the Law as the proper use, since that use was designed to call sinners to repentance. This issue raises once again the lack of focus on repentance in Forde's writing about the Christian life. Also, instead of Forde describing Christians calling people of the world to repentance through the proclamation of the Law, he described Christians quietly serving their neighbors by civil use of the Law. (What suddenly happened to his emphasis on "radical"?) The civil use of the Law he envisioned was not rooted in biblical standards but in the wisdom of the ages and of specialists (*Christian Dogmatics* 2:458). His eschatological perspective seems to domesticate the Law by suspending its proclamation for repentance and fulfillment.

The reader is left thinking that if he takes steps to fulfill the Law in this life, Forde's eschatological approach condemns him as a legalists or absolutist. Likewise, if the reader does not take steps to fulfill the Law, Forde's approach condemns him as an antinomian or relativist (*Christian Dogmatics* 2:466–69). Luther's teaching that the Holy Spirit and faith lead the Christian to spontaneously do good works and use the Law is noted (*Christian Dogmatics* 2:439) but not significant to Forde's thought, which is much more concerned about the dangers of works righteousness. Ultimately, Forde's locus urged a Christian passivity that hopes for the fulfillment of the Law but that is limited from action due to concerns about appearing or becoming self-righteous. His conclusion returned to these risks, which he described on the first page of the locus. His locus is most helpful when he works with Luther's point that a Christian is both sinner and saint at the same time. For example, he noted:

> There are only two possibilities vis-à-vis law as the expression of the will of God. It is either an enemy or a friend, but never a neutral guide.... The new being, however, is to be incarnated in down-to-earth fashion in the concrete calling of the Christian in this world. In that battle—in the calling in this world, in the flesh—the law of God is ultimately not an enemy or an emasculated guide but a true and loved friend. (*Christian Dogmatics* 2:451–52)

Although Forde contended against the western "system" as he understood it, he also finally saw the wisdom in returning to elements of that tradition.

A SECOND EXAMPLE

Bickle and Nordlie's 1992 publication of *The Goal of the Gospel: God's Purpose in Saving You*[470] introduced a different problem with the doctrine of the Law. Just as Forde felt the risks of publishing a locus on the Christian life, Bickle and Nordlie saw themselves taking a risk. They wrote:

> At times we may say something that at first sounds bizzare or even wrong. But please bear with us. We do not pretend to have discovered new doctrines. Instead we have found in the Scriptures a different emphasis or balance between doctrines than we had ever seen before. In response to this, we have since been developing a new approach to teaching obedience and the Christian life in our church. We believe this new

---

[470] St. Louis: Concordia, 1992. Note that the book was withdrawn from publication.

approach is more biblical than previous, traditional practice.[471]

The editor for the book likewise saw a risk. In the foreword he stated candidly, "Concordia offers it in order to contribute to the conversation the Lord has originated and invited us to join. *The Goal of the Gospel* is not the last word."[472] The editor's hesitancy was prescient, since the doctrinal review process for The Lutheran Church—Missouri Synod soon withdrew the book due to doctrinal concerns. I will briefly characterize the book and summarize how it misapplied the doctrine of the Law, which led to confusion about the doctrine of justification.

Content. The book essentially has three parts. First, it tells the story of how Bickel and Nordlie began their research in view of concerns about spiritual indifference at their congregation. Second, it relates their study of biblical teaching on obedience and sanctification. Third, the largest part of the book is their study of the "Goal of the Gospel in Romans," a running commentary on Paul's letter that amplifies passages on sanctification and thoughts on mission work.

I would commend the authors for turning to the Scriptures when faced with troubles in their congregation. They cite numerous passages of Scripture throughout. The emphasis on mission work and sharing the Gospel of salvation is likewise important and commendable. The book might have been well received and used among evangelical Christians, except for significant weaknesses that appropriately led to its withdrawal.

The Weaknesses. The book started with a false premise that undermined its message throughout. The authors stated:

> Ultimately we will see that the goal of the Gospel has three facets. It includes (1) obedience to God's revealed will; (2) world evangelization through the proclamation of the Gospel; and (3) living to the glory of God. We will touch on all three themes repeatedly in this book, at times referring to each one as the goal of the Gospel. When doing so, we do not wish to imply that any one of these three facets is the only goal of the Gospel. Obedience, world evangelization, and the

---

[471] *Goal of the Gospel* 14.
[472] *Goal of the Gospel* 7.

glory of God are too intimately linked to be treated as three separate goals.[473]

Just before this passage, the authors had acknowledged, "Yes, Paul does say that the goal or result (*telos*) of the Gospel is eternal life" but this truth about justification was soon overwhelmed in a massive emphasis on obedience. As a result, the promised salvation in Jesus Christ appeared as a servant to sanctification. The term "goal of the Gospel" finally became an expression for the Law and Law-motivation for good works such as mission work.[474] Phrases including "Gospel" often appeared in statements of the Law so that Law and Gospel were not clearly distinguished.

Distinguishing Law and Gospel. When Bickel and Nordlie noted the problem of indifference in their congregation and sought to address it, they rightly diagnosed a problem with Christians today. God does indeed want His people active in service to their neighbors, especially in proclaiming the life-giving Gospel of salvation in Jesus Christ (Ps 145:4–13). However, the congregation needed to hear a clear message of God's Law, which would reveal their sins of indifference and drive them to repentance. The "goal of the Gospel" term masked the use of the Law, which would finally confuse people about the blessings of the Gospel.

CONCLUSION

The doctrine of the use of the Law has raised many questions for theologians today. A greater understanding of the history of doctrine will likely help answer some of those questions. This book provides a start at answering the questions, which I hope others will pursue.

I provided a critique of Gerhard Forde's locus on the Christian life as a way of illustrating how misunderstanding of the history of doctrine could contribute to misstatements in theology. Perhaps I have critiqued Forde's locus too harshly. I did not study under him and have perhaps missed some subtleties of his thought (though if I am having difficulty understanding him, I am likely not alone). I acknowledge that my perspective as a confessional Lutheran limits the appeal of his modernist theology of the Christian life, especially

---

[473] *Goal of the Gospel* 15–16.
[474] See p. 246. "So what motivated Paul to go to Spain? The full Word of God, including both the Gospel and the goal of the Gospel."

the way that it omits significant, traditional elements such as theological use of the Law and daily repentance. I do believe that he was right to focus on the doctrine of justification as the appropriate basis for understanding the Christian life. Yet, I do not think one arrives at an appropriate understanding of doctrine and life by writing about the Law abstractly, reducing the uses of the Law, or by excluding the Law from the eternal nature of God. Thankfully, when Forde stepped away from his rhetoric, one can see him siding more closely with Luther's doctrine of the Law and its application to the Christian life.[475]

Bickle and Nordlie's *Goal of the Gospel* illustrates a different problem. In this case, the issue is not history of doctrine but use of terms. Preachers may decide that they are proclaiming the righteous man's use of the Law, forgetting the caveat of the Confessions that "The Law always accuses," even if one dresses it up with the term "Gospel." Because Christians are complex—righteous and sinners at the same time— preachers cannot readily control how Christians will hear their proclamation of the Law or how they might abuse their liberty in the Gospel. This is why Luther so greatly emphasized distinguishing Law and Gospel. This distinction not only helps the hearers recognize the differences between the two doctrines but also helps preachers keep track of their emphases and exhortations, maintaining the dominance of the Gospel in Christian teaching.

By *dominance* of the Gospel, I do not mean simply that a message contains more Gospel than Law. Some preachers might adopt that as a goal but it is not always what we see in the Scriptures, Luther's sermons, or the messages of other faithful teachers. The proclamation of the Law often takes more space, depending on the state of the hearers. (For example, this is what happened in the Book of Jeremiah and in Luther's Large Catechism, since the latter devoted about half its content to the Ten Commandments.) By dominance, I mean that the proclamation of the Law serves the purpose of the

---

[475] A noteworthy example appears in the article "The Normative Character of Scripture for Matters of Faith and Life: Human Sexuality in Light of Romans 1:16–32" in *Word & World*, vol. XIV, no. 3 (Summer 1994):305–14. Forde's rhetoric obscured his point in the article, especially the litany of unanswered questions at the end (pp. 311–12). Thankfully, his point is rescued by the inclusion of "Addendum: On the First Use of the Law," where his thought is presented in a much more plainspoken manner.

Gospel: our forgiveness, life, and salvation in Christ alone. This requires sensitivity to the hearers, addressing their sins appropriately with the Law so that the Gospel may do its life-giving work. It also means proclaiming the Gospel vigorously as our only hope and comfort. We trust the Holy Spirit to apply the Word we proclaim, likewise trusting that God's Word will bear abundant fruit as He promises.

Chapter Twenty-Two

Conclusions

> Use the Law as you wish. Read it. Only keep this use away from it, that you credit it with the remission of sins and righteousness.
>
> —Martin Luther

We have come a long way in our walk through the history of the doctrine of the Law, striding through some 2,500 years of biblical and Christian thought up through the sixteenth century. We have seen especially how the idea that the Law has uses for human life was more and more described over time, culmination in the great importance it played in the Reformation. We began with a story about how supporters of Rome burned Luther's works and how Luther and his friends burned copies of canon law in response. These actions showed how deeply each side felt about the issues and how the matter of Law was central to the Reformers. The fires that started in the sixteenth century have continued to smolder or flair even to our day though, thankfully, inter-Christian relationships have greatly improved as the warmth of friendship replaced the fires of anger.

As stated at the beginning, this book is only a survey. Many paths remain to be explored. Thank you for walking this way with me as a friend of the Law and a child of the Gospel. In this final chapter, I will draw together observations made along the way to provide a more comprehensive view of what a new consensus on the use of the Law could look like.

Ancient and Medieval Background

We must abandon the idea that the use of the Law is a concept created by Luther and the Reformation. Likewise, we may acknowledge that it predated the ancient and medieval Fathers who developed our Latinate terms. The idea that the Law has uses is apparent in biblical and non-biblical culture. I would not be surprised to see examples of the idea in the most ancient literature, like the writings of the Egyptians and Mesopotamians. I think this because law is a basic element of civilization and people have thought about the usefulness of laws for a very long time—what is fair and good. As a theologian, I would argue that the use of the Law stems from the natural law God has placed in the hearts of mankind. So, how to make and use laws has always been with us, since every new born eventually cringes or rebels when a parent says "No!" and every young child wonders, "Is that fair?" There is no such thing as a lawless era of mankind, except in the sense of rebellion against God's natural, moral law. When the biblical writers mention times "without law" or "before the law," they are describing time with reference to God giving the Law to Moses on Mt. Sinai.

One of the weaknesses of the only-two-uses consensus is that it worked with a heroic vision of the Reformation that credited Luther with the discovery of the use of the Law. This suggested that Luther's approach was the only valid way of writing about the use of the Law. Melanchthon was viewed as the creator of the third use of the Law, which made him either a hero or a villain, depending upon one's theology. John Agricola and others like him likewise became either heroes or villains by providing an antinomian vision for the Christian life. Our survey demonstrates that all the Reformers were late comers to the issue. As a result, there have been many ways among God's people to write about the topic. We may embrace and explore this breadth as part of our inheritance.

The roots of Christian terminology about the use of the Law are found in the biblical teaching of the Old and New Testaments with intertestamental Judaism contributing through its emphasis on the Law of Moses and positive descriptions of life under the Law. The Letters of Paul are key for the development of the Christian terms and distinction of uses; especially important are Romans, Galatians, and 1 Timothy. Intertestamental Judaism, Jesus, and Paul described the righteous as having a new status with respect to the Law of Moses.

Believers were no longer servants of the Law or merely chastened by the Law but lived in freedom, victory, friendship, and sonship.

It was the Scripture-interprets-Scripture study of Rm 1:20; 2:15; 5:20; Gal 3:19–24; and 1 Tm 1:8–9 that forged the term *usefulness of the Law* in the Latin Fathers. Augustine was the earliest one we have discovered using this term. Scholars like Ebeling suspected that Augustine was the source but did not adjust their search for the way terms change over time, which would have allowed him to discover the relationship between *usefulness* (*utilitas*) and *use* (*usus*). Incidentally, both John Calvin and Johann Gerhard were aware of the root of the term in Augustine since they both refer to Augustine's letter to Asellius while writing about the use of the Law.[476] The historians of doctrine apparently were not consulting these dogmatic works while investigating the history of terms.

Augustine and other Latin Fathers noticed that there were different uses of the Law and described them informally. One can find at least four uses described in Augustine. But Augustine did not enumerate or define the uses. Augustine's Stages of Mankind may have contributed to organizing the idea about the usefulness of the Law since the stages correspond with the typical order of uses. Ambrosiaster introduced the expression "friend of the Law," which described one aspect of the Christian life. This term and idea beautifully summarizes the biblical ideas about and the early Christian reflection upon the believer's change in status with respect to the Law. I believe this friendship analogy provides a very helpful means for teaching people about the beneficial yet limited role of the Law for the Christian life. I chose it as the title of my book as a way of commending this expression to the Church.

Medieval interpreters began to order the uses of the Law and enumerate them in their commentaries. These developments seem to stem from the University of Paris where one finally sees regular terms, order, and definition. Oddly, I have not found that this regular teaching on the use of the Law made it into the medieval dogmatic tradition. The fact that the teaching on usefulness of the Law appeared in the exegetical literature rather than the dogmatic literature may explain why historians of the only-two-uses consensus did not

---

[476] For example, see Johann Gerhard, *Loci Theologici*, Preuss ed. (Berlin: Gust. Schlawitz, 1865), 3:105. See also Calvin's 1559 *Institutes* bk. II, ch. 7, para. 9.

notice Luther's debt to medieval theology in this matter, even though Heinrich Denifle pointed it out already in 1905.

The medieval theologians made many helpful contributions toward clarifying the doctrine of the Law. However, they also unhelpfully continued to describe the Gospel as a new law, which contributed to confusion about the doctrines of justification and sanctification. They tended to write about the Christian life as one of sanctified keeping of the Law without acknowledging the complexity of the Christian as a sinner.

LUTHERAN REFORMATION

Luther clearly learned and used the medieval terms for the usefulness of the Law. He likely acquired them from his extensive interaction with Nicholas of Lyra's postils. The only-two-uses historians did not recognize this connection to medieval theology and described the idea that the Law has uses as a distinctly Protestant idea. The earliest expression they identified in Luther's writings was the 1521 mention of the function of the Law. We have noted that Luther was using the medieval terms as early as 1513–15 when he first lectured on Psalms. This is important for gaining perspective on Luther's 1522 postil on Galatians. Instead of working with the terms for only about a year before writing about a threefold use of the Law, we see that Luther had been using the terms for at least six years. In other words, the threefold statement was not merely a spontaneous observation that could be readily abandoned as Ebeling thought. Luther's views were maturing over those years and the 1522 statement was a product of that maturation.

We likewise noticed that Luther distinguished himself from the late medieval definition by including both a prophetic use of the Law (which actually corresponded with the Gospel) as well as statements about the role of the Law in the believer's life. His Law and Gospel distinction from the early lectures had adjusted the way he talked about the usefulness of the Law. Here is the Reformation insight that deserves our attention. The distinction of the uses of the Law and the distinction of Law and Gospel grew up together to provide a more helpful way of seeing justification and sanctification.

Luther worked with the Augustinian and medieval categories he had learned in order to address basic theological problems about how God saves us and sanctifies us, even though sin still clings to us (*simul justus et peccator*). Justification, as the chief topic of theology and the chief issue of the Reformation, dominates in Luther's writings. As a result, he wrote most often about the civil and theological uses of the Law rather than the righteous man's use of the Law. However, Luther continued to hold to a righteous man's use—a third use. This is evident especially from his *Lectures on 1 Timothy*, and his postils. The only-two-uses consensus focused too strongly on Luther's *Lectures on Galatians* of 1531 and 1535. As a consequence, the twentieth century consensus failed to understand Luther's theology of the Law for the Christian life.

In view of this failure, I am concerned that generations of Lutheran pastors and perhaps also Protestant pastors in mainline denominations have been trained with a deficient doctrine of the Law. I believe this problem has contributed to the current struggles over moral questions in denominations like the Evangelical Lutheran Church in America, whose 2009 statement on sexuality worked with an only-two-uses theology, while merely noting in their statement (that is, burying) the use of the Law for the Christian life. Similar issues appear in The Lutheran Church Missouri Synod due to the teachings of the Valparaiso University theologians, whom Scott Murray describes in his book.[477] These issues continue to the present as Elert's theology remains important for this school of thought. (However, Gottfried G. Krodel's translation of Johannes Heckel's work provides helpful caveats to these trends.)[478]

The idea that the natural, biblical doctrine of the Law condones homosexual activities is plainly wrong to any honest interpreter of Holy Scripture. Protestant theologians who change biblical teaching by using the Gospel to silence the proclamation of the Law or who reduce the Law to a whisper are misleading God's people, introducing great shame and vice, and hindering appropriate calls to repentance.[479] Claiming that the only-two-uses approach actually stems from Luther or Reformation theology is likewise false or misleading. Luther plainly taught that God wanted preachers to proclaim both Law and

---

[477] Murray 91–95.
[478] See epilogue, pp. 255–56.
[479] In the *Antinomian Disputations*, Luther did speak of softening the preaching of the Law (p. 153). This refers to exhortation that acknowledges believers want to keep the Law inherently. It does not mean a loosening of the moral code.

Gospel *vigorously*. Subsuming the Law under the Gospel, subordinating it into silence and whispers, is like subordinating one nature of the person of Christ to another. Such teaching endangers souls. Good Lord, deliver us!

Alongside the excesses of liberal Protestantism, one finds a pitfall for more conservative, evangelical teachers. I have illustrated this issue from the example of a publication within The Lutheran Church Missouri Synod, a well intentioned book that confused the terminology of Law and Gospel. While I applaud the effort to encourage good works and mission outreach, it is necessary to distinguish the Law and the Gospel also here. One may certainly remind the congregation of their calling to proclaim the Gospel to all people. God expects His people to speak His word to others (Ps 145). However, we should plainly acknowledge that this expectation is a proclamation of the Law. At the same time, we may rejoice that the Gospel equips God's people to carry out His mission and that our bold confession of salvation is the work of His grace. Here and throughout the Christian life, the preacher has cause to proclaim both messages from the Lord, which are distinctly useful.

Only-two-use theologians have also tended to blame or credit Melanchthon with creating the third use of the law, which is now clearly incorrect. Mischaracterization of the Formula of Concord has followed, attributing its doctrine to Melanchthon or even preposterously to Calvin. We can now see the important role Melanchthon played in regularizing the dogmatic terminology for the Lutheran Reformation and for suggesting threefold use of the Law to Calvin, who finally developed the terms and distinctions in his own way. In the view of this author, Luther, Melanchthon, and the Formula of Concord stand tight on the doctrine of the use of the Law, though one should allow for differences in expression and emphasis.

Ecumenical Dialogues

This history matters greatly to current ecumenical discussion. As stated in the previous chapter, Elert's advocacy for the only-two-uses consensus developed while Lutheran and Reformed churches in Europe were seeking greater unity. Elert likely formed his opinions as a contrast to the threefold use of the Law in Calvinism, desiring to keep Lutheran theology distinct.

The current dialogues between Roman Catholics and Lutherans also enter into the matter. The *Joint Document on the Doctrine of Justification* failed to say anything substantial about the use of the Law, which Melanchthon described as the beginning of Christian doctrine. In fact, it appears that Roman Catholic theologians have not continued in the long tradition of working with the usefulness of the Law, despite its appearance in Augustine, Peter Lombard, Thomas Aquinas, Nicholas of Lyra, and even some papal legates at the Council of Trent. This happened even though it was a Roman Catholic historian—Heinrich Denifle—who pointed out Luther's continuity with the late medieval tradition on the doctrine of the Law. One would hope that any future dialogue on the Gospel and justification would start with a careful discussion of the doctrine of the Law.

A further concern comes with the switch from talking about Law and Gospel to talking about Lutheran or Christian ethics. *Ethics* essentially means "customs," or community standards of right and wrong. This way of approaching the Law introduces the following problems: (1) self-willed standards are more readily embraced than divinely willed standards, (2) as communities change, the standards change in a fluid and likely deceptive manner, and (3) the encroachment of ethics upon Christian freedom will turn things that are adiaphora into matters of necessity because the community will urge conformity. Rather than writing about ethics, the Church would be better served by writing about how God's Law applies and what the love of Christ compels Christians to do. Biblical ways of thinking will keep matters of right, wrong, and freedom clearer for God's people.

THE PARISHES TODAY

Servants of the Word daily proclaim the doctrine of the Law, as the counter point to the saving Gospel in the Law and Gospel dialectic. As the doctrine of justification is chief among doctrines of the Church in its practical bent, so the doctrine of the Law serves the purposes of the Gospel and should grow in importance in our eyes. With today's moral license or antinomianism, a clearer account of the doctrine of the Law and its use rises in importance. Luther's Law and Gospel distinction remains the best theological paradigm for preachers today. When properly understood, it can serve as a simple two-step message used in sermons and evangelism. With the uses of the Law, it can help people understand the complexities of life in a sinful world and the Christian life of daily repentance and mortification of the sinful nature. Learning the terms and distinctions is a first step toward practicing this life-long art of Evangelical theology.

The only-two-uses understanding of Luther's theology has blunted his theology of the Gospel, disallowing the righteous man's use of the Law as a means to praise God for the gifts of the Holy Spirit, faith, and joyous spontaneity in service to others. A gospel that cannot change people's lives is not even a helpful social gospel, much less the Gospel of Him who died and rose again. The only-two-uses consensus would leave believers as enemies of the Law and even estrange them from the Righteous One who gives the Law. I doubt that Elert and Ebeling intended this to happen. Yet it seems to have happened nonetheless. There is an almost paranoid fear of works righteousness in some quarters today, which tends toward an endless questioning of motives. When Christians do something helpful and kind, they may find themselves chided for trusting in their own righteousness or trying to gain God's favor through works. Whatever happened to putting the best construction on the actions of others—even acts of civil righteousness? Must God's people sit back and let the world go to hell just so that they can appear appropriately humble? God forbid.

God intends that the one He has declared righteous by grace through faith may enjoy freedom in his conscience and that the righteous man may, through the sanctifying work of the Spirit, bear the fruit of the Spirit to the praise of God's surpassing grace. In view of this, Luther taught that God's people may daily take up the commandments of God's Law, sing them on the way to their work, and actually use them for the benefit of their neighbors. He did not see this active, Spirit-led use of the Law as a return to works righteousness but as an example of the free and joyful work of the Gospel in our lives. My hope is that the eyes of God's people today, enlightened by the Gospel, may see the Law anew as a friend, a companion, and a counselor for life together in the communion of saints while maintaining the Gospel and the Sacraments as the only means for "the forgiveness of sins, the resurrection of the body, and the life everlasting."

Epilogue

As I prepared the manuscript for the printer, Franz Posset brought to my attention the recently published translation of Johannes Heckel's *Lex Charitatis: A Juristic Disquisition on Law in the Theology of Martin Luther*, Gottfried G. Krodel, trans. and ed. (Grand Rapids: Eerdmans, 2010). I had looked at the German edition of Heckel's book early in my research. Finding very little on the use of the Law, I set it aside so that I could focus on investigating primary resources.

I am pleased to see this new edition, which is especially helpful for Luther's teaching on natural law and the relationship between divine law and secular law. Heckel described Luther's development with reference to Scholastic theology (pp. 44–46). As I have noted, Luther worked with the Scholastic terms and ideas but went beyond them. Heckel's thesis was that the reformation of the church required a reformation of the doctrine of the law (p. 12). Because modern theologians focused on the "law of faith," they have neglected Luther's doctrine of the law (p. 88). The result is misunderstanding of Luther's theology, especially its application in a believer's life. I agree with these general points of history and concern, which I find compatible with my research.

On the use of the Law, Heckel followed the general conclusions of the only-two-uses consensus that dominated the latter half of the twentieth century. However, I noticed in one of his footnotes that he turned up an even earlier passage from Luther on the use of the Law. In commenting on Ps 25:8 during the *First Lectures on the Psalms* (1513–15), Luther wrote about the application of the Law to sinners. He used the term *usus legis* (WA 3:144.3; see Heckel 324, nt. 183). Here one sees a still earlier appearance of the term in Luther, before those in his lectures on Galatians that I had noticed. Also, this passage confirms that Luther had the term *usus legis* at the very beginning of his career as a theologian, making it still more likely that it comes from a medieval writer and not from Luther or Melanchthon as assumed by theologians of the only-two-uses consensus.

Anyone who reads Heckel's work will find a deep and rich investigation of Luther's doctrine of the Law. However, I will provide one caveat. At times Heckel summarized and tended to blend Luther's thought into a single view point without distinguishing how Luther's views changed over his career or how his statements differed depending on what problem he was addressing. In other words, Heckel tended to cite Luther as though he were settled in his doctrine of the Law rather than distinguish what Luther taught (A) before the conflicts with Rome, (B) after the conflicts with Rome, Erasmus, and the Anabaptists, and ultimately (C) in opposition to the Antinomians. Heckel was aware of such development in Luther's thought (pp. 19–21) but he did not describe it throughout. In view of this, the reader should carefully note the dates for the many quotations from Luther in Heckel's footnotes and be prepared to distinguish Luther's development and consistency. This is especially the case when Heckel cited Luther's earliest writings alongside Luther's latest writings. Nonetheless, Heckel's book is most valuable.

Appendix A

The Law of Moses in Early Judaism and Christianity

During the intertestamental period, Israelites described the Law of Moses as wisdom. Rabbis enumerated c. 613 commandments within the Law of Moses. Alongside the written Law of Moses was the oral law, later committed to writing in the 63 tractates of the Mishnah and the Tosephta, though not accepted by all Jews.

The LORD epitomized the Law in the Ten Commandments (lit. "Ten Words"; Ex 20:1–17; Dt 5:6–21). The commandments could be subdivided into two tables or two general commands directing or prohibiting certain actions toward the LORD and toward mankind, as first century scribes taught (Mt 25:39; Mk 12:33; Lk 10:27). Finally, Jesus and St. Paul epitomized the broad complexity of the Law in the one command to love.

Table 20
<u>The Summary of the Law</u>
Torah as the embodiment of wisdom (cf. Ps 119; Ecclus 39:1–11)
The written Law of Moses in c. 600 laws; the oral law

	First Table	Second Table
Focus on Ten Commandments:	1 2 3	4 5 6 7 8 9 10
	Love the LORD	Love your neighbor
	(Dt 6:5; Mt 22:37)	(Lv 19:18; Mt 22:39)

Simplified to "love" (Jn 14:15; Rm 13:8–10)

Appendix B

Luther's Phrases for the Use of the Law

The following chart sketches examples of Luther's expressions from throughout his career. Luther's earliest phrases for the use of the Law come from his study of Romans, Augustine, and Scholastic theology. The phrase *usus legis* does not stem from Melanchthon's application of *usus* in the locus on the Law in the 1521 *Loci Communes* (see p. 191) or from Bucer's 1525 translation of Luther's *Weihnachtspostille* where Ebeling found the earliest recognized example of *usus legis*.

As noted in chapter eleven, the frequent occurrence of *usus legis* in the 1535 *Lectures on Galatians* is unusual for Luther and seems to be the result of Rörer's regularization of Luther's expressions. Luther, in fact, had a wide variety of expressions that were shaped by the particular texts he was expounding, as illustrated in Appendix C.

Date	English	German/Latin
1513–15	use of the Law	usus legis (WA 3:144)
1515	work of the Law (LW 25:240)	opus legis (WA 56:253–54)
1516/17	usefulness of the Law	legis utilitatem (WA 57:20)
1519	usefulness of the Law (LW 27:269)	utilitate legum (WA 2:522)
1521	office of the Law (LW 44:302)	officium legis (WA 8:609)
1522	three-fold use of the Law (cf. Lnk 6:272)	dreyerley brauch des gesetzes (WA 10/I.I:456)
1528	functions of the Law (LW 28:235)	officia legis (WA 26:17)

APPENDIX B

1531	use of the Law	usum legis (WA 40 I:476)
	function of the Law	officium legis (WA 40 I:477)
1535	use of the Law (LW 26:308)	usus legis (WA 40 I:479)
	Law is useful (LW 26:313)	legem . . . utilem (WA 40 I:485)
1536	office and use of the Law (Lnk 8:254)	Gesetz ampt und brauch (WA 22:37)
1537	office and force of the Law	Ampt oder Kraft des Gesetzes (SA III II 4)
1538	power of the Law (Silcock 268)	vi legis (WA 39 I:426)
	use of the Law (Silcock 303)	usum legis (WA 39 I:441)

1545	use of the Law (LW 8:170)	usus legis (WA 44:703)

Appendix C

Variety in Luther's Descriptions of the Law

The following chart provides a sampling, by no means complete, of Luther's many different ways of describing the Law and its uses. All the examples below are drawn from chapter 3 of the 1531 *Lectures on Galatians* (WA 40 I).

This is a mere snapshot of the complexity of Luther's self-expression. In many cases the expressions below are paired with *usus legis* or *officium legis*. The variety illustrates why the fixation on *usus legis* in modern research was misplaced and misleading.

English	German	Page in WA 40 I
curse of the Law	maledicto legis	443
condemnation of the Law	legis damnationem	448
land of the Law	terra legis	469
use of the Law	usum . . . legis	476
office of the Law	legis officium	477
power of the Law	vim legis	502
end of the Law	finis legis	506
theology of the Law	legis theologia	511
time of the Law	tempus legis	524
work of the Law	opere . . . legis	531
nature of the Law	natura legis	534
matter of the Law	materiam legis	535

Appendix D

Commentary on Formula of Concord VI

We shall cite article VI, note particular terms or phrases in italic, and present comments and cross references to other relevant passages. The order of citation will be (1) additional Scripture passages not listed in the article, (2) Luther, and (3) Melanchthon.

FC Epitome VI, the Title

Concerning the Third Use of the Law

Use of the Law. Cf. "the law is good, if one *uses it lawfully*" (1 Tm 1:8–9), which is the historical source of the expression. "The work of the law" (Rm 2:15), a Pauline expression for the theological use of the Law, is likewise important to the history of the term.

Third Use of the Law. The German title of article VI closely parallels Luther's German phrase in the 1522 *Weihnachtspostille*:

Daß dreyerley brauch des gesetzes sind

Vom dritten Brauch des Gesetzes Gottes[480]

The Latin title in the Epitome, "de tertio usu legis divinae," was a rendering of the German. It is similar to the wording in Bucer's translation of Luther's 1522 postil, "triplicem legis usum."[481] In Luther's *Lectures on 1 Timothy*, George Rörer recorded ".3.

---

[480] BKS 962.
[481] WA 10/1.1 456, Latin note 3.

APPENDIX D

officium."⁴⁸² Melanchthon wrote in 1534, "God gave the law for these three reasons: to coerce the flesh and to terrify or humble. The third reason pertains to the righteous, that they may practice obedience" (*Scholia on Colossians*; trans. by Wengert, pp. 195–96). In the 1535 Loci, Melanchthon wrote of the *tertium officium legis* (CR 21:406).

Luther was the Wittenberg theologian who introduced wording about a threefold or third use, which spread mainly through the twenty-eight editions of his postil published during his lifetime and also through Melanchthon's *Loci* of 1535 and later editions.

FC EPITOME VI 2

Affirmative Theses⁴⁸³

The Correct Christian Teaching concerning this Controversy

1. We believe, teach, and confess that, although people who truly believe in Christ and are genuinely converted to God have been liberated and set free from the curse and compulsion of the law through Christ, they indeed are not for that reason without the law. Instead, they have been redeemed by the Son of God so that they may practice the law day and night (Ps. 119[:1]). For our first parents did not live without the law even before the fall. This law of God was written into the heart, for they were created in the image of God.

The opening thesis asserts the Christian's ongoing need for and use of the Law of God by noting that (1) redemption leads to the keeping of the Law and (2) all believers have the Law of God at all times since God wrote the natural law into human hearts at creation (Rm 2:15). The latter observation is based on the fact that Luther and other theologians equated the moral law of both testaments with the natural law.⁴⁸⁴ In other words, the thesis describes the use of the Law

---

⁴⁸² WA 26:17. The periods around the numeral indicate that it is an abbreviation for *tertium*.

⁴⁸³ The Arabic numerals in the headings for the commentary are based on the marginal number system in the Book of Concord, which can be confused with the paragraph numbers found in manuscripts of the Formula of Concord since in this case they differ only slightly (e.g., margin number 2 applies to *Affirmativa* 1).

⁴⁸⁴ See *one single law* in the next section.

APPENDIX D

by believers, who were the third kind of persons noted in Luther's threefold use of the Law. "The third are thoroughly righteous. . . . He must not by any means preach the Law to the third class as an instrument of righteousness; this were perversion. . . . The third keep [the Law]" (*Church Postil*, Lenker 6:273).

liberated and set free from the curse and compulsion of the law through Christ. Cf. 2Co 9:7 (Ger.). Luther wrote, "Otherwise the whole essence of this controversy has to do with the necessity or freedom of works of the Law, not with what works of the Law are. For the works of the Law and the Law itself were not put to death and done away with though Christ in the sense that one may not do them at all (as St. Jerome, instructed by his teacher Origen, contends in more than one passage) but only in such a way that one believes salvation to be apart from them through Christ alone. He is the end of the Law. . . . But you must know that these works should not be done under compulsion of the Law—for the taskmaster was overcome by the Child" (*Lectures on Galatians* [1519] LW 27:202–203). See also *Lectures on Galatians* (1535) LW 26:84–85; 26:369–71; *Lectures on Galatians* (1519) LW 27:213; 27:233–34; 27:347. Melanchthon wrote, "They are freed from the Law, that is, from the curse and the condemnation and the wrath of God which is set forth in the Law" (1559 *Loci*).

without the law. Phrase found in Rm 2:12; 3:21; 7:8–9; 1Co 9:21. St. Paul used the phrase to describe (1) the state of the Gentiles and the uninstructed who did not know the Law of Moses and (2) the state of the righteous, who are no longer under the Law's coercion, though they still have the natural law (1Co 9:21). FC VI used the latter sense. See also Gn 2:16–17; 3:3 before God gave the Law of Moses. This expression is critical for understanding the relationship between Luther and the writing of the Formula. Luther wrote, "For the just man lives as though he had need of no Law to admonish, urge, and constrain him; but spontaneously, *without any legal constraint*, he does more than the Law requires. And so the Law cannot accuse and condemn the just; nor can it disturb their consciences" (*Lectures on Galatians* [1535] LW 27:96, emphasis added). See also LW 27:48; Disp. 1, arg. 7; Disp. 1, Arg. 32. See Melanchthon, *Romans*, 98–99.

practice the law day and night. Cf. Ps 1:2; 119:1; cf. Lm 2:9 (Ger.); 1 Tm 4:7. Luther wrote, "We must repeat the text that we have already treated above in connection with the First Commandment in order to show how much effort God desires us to devote to learning how to teach and practice the Ten Commandments" (LC Concl. of Com. 319). See also LC longer preface (*Triglotta* 567); LC longer preface 18. Melanchthon wrote that the Law "prescribes certain works in which they might exercise obedience toward God" (1535 *Loci*; Schurb 221). Note the subjunctive ("might"), which illustrates the voluntary nature of the believer's service.

law . . . written into the heart. Drawn from Rm 2:15, "The work of the law is written on their hearts," a favorite passage for Luther and Melanchthon. The natural law in the heart, the Ten Commandments, and the moral law are more or less interchangeable for Luther and Melanchthon. See Schurb 139–140, nt. 76. Cf. Pr 3:3; 7:3; Jer 31:33; Heb 8:10; 10:16. See *Lectures on Romans* (1515–16) LW 25:186–88; Melanchthon, 1521 *Loci*, p. 50; *Romans*, p. 89.

created in the image of God. Drawn from Gn 1:26–27. Cf. Eph 4:24; Col 3:10. Luther wrote, "When Adam was first created, not only was the law possible for him, but it was also delightful. He performed this obedience, which the law required, with a perfect will and a cheerful heart, and indeed perfectly" (Disp. 1, Arg. 1). See also Luther's *Lectures on Genesis* (1535–45) LW 1:92–97, where he described the tree of the knowledge of good and evil serving as the Law.

FC EPITOME VI 3–4

2. We believe, teach, and confess that the proclamation of the law is to be diligently impressed not only upon unbelievers and the unrepentant but also upon those who believe in Christ and are truly converted, reborn, and justified through faith.

3. For even if they are reborn and "renewed in the spirit of their minds" [Eph. 4:23], this rebirth and renewal is not perfect in this world. Instead, it has only begun. Believers are engaged with the spirit of their minds in continual battle against the flesh, that is, against the perverted nature and character which clings to them until death and which because of the old creature is still lodged in human understanding, will, and all human powers. In order that people do not resolve to perform service to God on the basis of their pious imagination in an arbitrary way of their own choosing, it is

necessary for the law of God constantly to light their way. Likewise, it is necessary so that the old creature not act according to its own will but instead be compelled against its own will, not only through the admonitions and threats of the law but also with punishments and plagues, to follow the Spirit and let itself be made captive (1 Cor. 9[:27]; Rom. 6[:12]; Gal. 6[:14]; Ps. 119[:1]; Heb. 13[:21]).

This thesis rejects the errors of Johann Agricola that arose during the First Antinomian Controversy in 1528. The second paragraph provides specific reasoning based on Luther's *simul justus et peccator* distinction, which he described already in the 1515 *Lectures on Romans* when he wrote, "I am at the same time a sinner and a righteous man, for I do evil and I hate the evil which I do" (*Lectures on Romans* [1515–16] LW 25:63, commenting on Rm 7:16). This was a foundational insight for Luther's doctrine of the use of the Law, to which he returned frequently (e.g., the 1525 sermons on 1 Timothy and the *Antinomian Disputations*). See also Melanchthon, *Romans*, 160–62.

proclamation of the law . . . also upon those who believe. See Col 1:23–29; cf. Is 3:10–11 (Ger.). The Scripture is replete with examples of the Law being taught to Christians. The paraenetic conclusions to Paul's letters are a prime example of this practice. Luther wrote, "The law is indeed taught to Christians, but with some privilege, because they triumph over these things, and do not yield, either to sins, if ever they are put before them, or to the Law" (Disp. 3, Arg. 5). See also Disp. 1, Arg. 21; Disp. 3, Arg. 2; Disp. 3, Arg. 24; and Luther's practice of providing admonition after the sermon (see p. 182). Melanchthon wrote, "Later we add also the teaching of the law, . . . *because God requires good works*" (Ap IV 188).

not perfect . . . only begun. See Phil 3:12; 2 Tm 3:16–17. Luther wrote, "Impelled by him, they begin to fulfill the law also in this life, and in the future life their obedience of the law will be supremely delightful and perfect, that is, they will do it with body and soul, as the angels do now" (Disp. 1, Arg. 1). See also *Church Postil*, Lenker 6:193; Disp. 1, Arg. 5; Disp. 3, Arg. 4. Melanchthon wrote, "They begin to do the Law in part" (1535 *Loci*; Schurb 221).

continual battle. Cf. 1 Tm 6:12; Rm 7:23. Luther wrote, "The Law must be taught and inculcated in order that we might be summoned to the battle, lest we become lazy and sluggish, and we perish" (Disp. 3, Arg. 4). See also Disp. 1, Arg. 32; Disp. 3, Arg. 2; Disp. 3, Arg. 5; Disp. 3, Arg. 13. Melanchthon wrote concerning Rm 7, "He is not speaking about small affections and temptations but about very severe impulses. He uses powerful words—war service and captivity—to indicate that the impulses are vehement, like those we experience in calamities or in death. How difficult it is to obey! Our whole nature rages, is angry, and resists" (*Romans* 160). He also wrote, "[The regenerate] fight against sin in confidence in the Son of God" (1559 *Loci*).

perverted nature . . . clings to them. See Gal 5:17; Rm 7:14, 21, 23. Luther wrote, "Although the Galatians had been illuminated, were believers, and had received the Holy Spirit through the preaching of faith, there still remained in them this shred of their old vices, this tinder that so easily caught the flame of false teaching" (*Lectures on Galatians* [1535] LW 26:189). See also LC III 101; *Lectures on Genesis* (1535–45) LW 7:237; LW 8:5–6.

service . . . of their own choosing. The Book of Concord frequently cites, "In vain do they worship me, teaching as doctrines the commandments of men" (Is 29:13; Mt 15:9; Mk 7:7). See also Col 2:23. Luther wrote, "Nowhere has God promised that He intends to justify men and save them on account of religious orders, observances, and forms of worship that have been thought up and established by men. In fact, as all Scripture attests, nothing is more abominable to God than such self chosen works and forms of worship" (*Lectures on Galatians* [1535] LW 26:397). See also *Lectures on Genesis* (1535–45) LW 4:102; 4:124; *Lectures on Galatians* (1519) LW 27:141. Melanchthon wrote, "God does not will that we by our own wisdom set up works or worship, but he wills that we be ruled by his Word" (1559 *Loci*).

necessary for the law. "Do we then overthrow the law by means of faith? By no means! On the contrary, we uphold the law" (Rm 3:31). Luther wrote, "Now political laws, human traditions, ecclesiastical ceremonies, and even the Law of Moses are matters located outside Christ; therefore they do not count for righteousness in the sight of God. It is, of course, permissible to use them as *good and necessary things*, but in their proper place and time. But if they are summoned into the discussion of justification, they do not count for anything at all but get in the way" (*Lectures on Galatians* [1519] LW 27:138–39, emphasis added). See also *Lectures on Genesis*

(1535–45) LW 8:170; *Lectures on 1 Timothy* (1528) LW 28:232; LW 28:231–32; LC Close of Com. p. 121 above. Melanchthon wrote, "It is also taught that such faith should yield good fruit and good works and that a person must do such good works as God has commanded for God's sake but not place trust in them as if thereby to earn grace before God" (AC VI 1; cf. AC XX); "It is necessary that those who are justified obey the law" (1559 *Loci*; see also *Romans* 104–105).

light their way. A biblical analogy as in Pr 6:22–23, "When you walk, they will lead you. . . . The commandment is a lamp and the teaching a light . . . the way of life." Luther typically used the light analogy to describe the accusatory function of the Law as in Jn 3:19–21. However, the analogy also turned easily toward encouragement. For example, he wrote, "The ungodly must be battered by the light of the law in order that in their terror they finally learn to seek Christ, and the law is also to be taught to the godly in order to admonish and encourage them to stay in the fight and contest, so that they do not allow themselves to be conquered however much their flesh may afflict and scoff at them" (Disp. 3, Arg. 5). See also *Church Postil*, Lenker 6:273–74; *Commentary on Psalm 101* (1534/1535) LW 13:151; *Lectures on Galatians* (1535) LW 26:115–16; 26:320; *Lectures on 1 Timothy* (1528) LW 28:210; *Preface to the Old Testament* (1523, 1545) LW 35:245–46.

admonitions and threats of the law. Cf. Col 1:28; 2 Tm 3:16–17. "Here therefore it is necessary to be constantly admonished lest we forget God's commandment, especially since the law of God is the highest wisdom and so as the source, origin, and wellspring of all virtues and disciplines toward God and human beings, it is infinite because sin is infinite" (Disp. 3, Arg. 24). See also LC Close of com.; Table of Duties; Disp. 1, Arg. 21; Disp. 3, Arg. 2; Disp. 3, Arg. 5. Melanchthon wrote, "Paul says [Rom. 4:15]: 'The law brings wrath.' He does not say that through the law people merit the forgiveness of sins. For the law always accuses and terrifies consciences" (Ap IV 38).

follow the Spirit. Cf. Rm 8:1, 4, 13; Gal 5:16. Luther wrote, "He gives the Holy Spirit to those who believe in him that they may take pleasure in the law of the Lord, according to Psalm 1[:2], and thus their hearts may be restored through it, and this Spirit gives them the will to do it" (Disp. 1, Arg. 6). See also Disp. 1, Arg. 1; Disp. 2, Arg. 16; Disp. 3, Arg. 13. See Melanchthon, *Romans* 163, 167, 174.

FC Epitome VI 5–6

4. Concerning the difference between works of the law and fruits of the Spirit, we believe, teach, and confess that works performed according to the law remain works of the law and should be so called, as long as they are coerced out of people only through the pressure of punishment and the threat of God's wrath.

5. Fruits of the Spirit, however, are the works that the Spirit of God, who dwells in the believers, effects through the reborn; they are done by believers (in so far as they are reborn) as if they knew of no command, threat, or reward. In this manner the children of God live in the law and walk according to the law of God—what St. Paul in his epistles calls it the law of Christ and the law of the mind. And yet they are "not under the law but under grace" (Rom. 7[:23]; 8[:1, 14]).

In this section of the article, the writers address specific concerns about a specific set of Bible passages and expressions within those passages.

works of the law. From Rm 3:20; Gal 2:16. The Reformers used this expression to mean both the actions demanded (coerced) by the Law and the works people do in their attempt to satisfy the Law. Luther wrote, "Yes, the entire Law [of Moses], including the Law of the Decalog, is also fatal without faith in Christ. Moreover, no Law should reign in the conscience except that of the Spirit of life, by which we are delivered in Christ from the Law of the letter and of death, from its works, and from sins. This does not mean that the Law is evil; it means that it cannot contribute anything to justification" (*Avoiding the Doctrines of Men* [1522] LW 35:139).

fruits of the Spirit. From Gal 5:22–23. Cf. Gal 5:16. Luther wrote, "Paul does not say 'works of the Spirit,' as he had said 'works of the flesh'; but he adorns these Christian virtues with a worthier title and calls them 'fruit of the Spirit.' For they bring very great benefits and fruit, because those who are equipped with them give glory to God and by these virtues invite others to the teaching and faith of Christ" (*Lectures on Galatians* [1535] LW 27:93). See also LW 27:65, 131; *Lectures on 1 Timothy* (1528) LW 28:233.

as if they knew no command. Cf. Gal 5:23; 1 Tm 1:8–9. The clause is a comparative. Believers know the command yet fulfill it spontaneously. The emphasis here is not on what the Law does but on what the believers do with the Law because they have God's grace and Spirit. Luther wrote, "There is now no Moses, no Law; only Joshua, Christ who leads by faith and fulfills all Moses' commandments. Thus is suggested the class to whom no Law is given, as Paul says, and who becomes righteous, not through works, but through grace; that is, their good works are not performed through constraint of the Law. Moses is not in evidence with them" (*Church Postil*, Lenker 6:274). Moses gave the Law to Israel twice: when the covenant was instituted (Ex 19–24) and at the renewal of the covenant after the idolatry with the golden calf (Ex 34). For Luther, these events corresponded to the first two uses of the Law. See "law of Christ" below. See also *Lectures on Galatians* (1535, 1519) LW 27:96, 378.

walk according to the law. Cf. Ex 16:4; Ps 1:1–2; 119:1; Ezk 36:27; Mi 4:2; 6:8; Rm 6:4; 8:1, 4; Gal 5:16; Eph 5:9; Phil 3:16; 2 Jn 6. A major biblical theme based on a common Semitic expression for manner of life or behavior. Luther wrote, "It [the Gospel] uses the office of the law to go after and expose the vices and to prepare for life, how the new people, saints, out to walk in the new life" (Disp. 3, Arg. 21).

law of Christ. From Gal 6:2. Cf. Jn 13:34 where Jesus sets a new standard for what love is. See also Jn 15:9–10. Luther wrote, "The Law of Christ is the law of love. After redeeming and regenerating us and constituting us as His church, Christ did not give us any new law except the law of mutual love (John 13:34)" (*Lectures on Galatians* [1535] LW 27:113; also p. 114). In medieval theology, after Moses had twice given the Law (Ex 19–24; 34), there was a third giving of the Law: the new covenant, in which Christ was a new Moses and the Gospel was a new Law (see below). Luther rejected this thinking but did note Christ's command to love, which focused on the essence of the Law (Rm 13:8–10) and pointed to Christ as the highest example of the Law's fulfillment. See Melanchthon, *Romans* 223–24.

law of the mind. From Rm 7:23. Luther wrote, "*The Law of my mind,* that is, to love, which is the spiritual law, yes, the spirit itself" (*Lectures on Romans* [1515–16] LW 25:65). See Melanchthon, *Romans* 161–62.

Appendix D

FC Epitome VI 7

6. Therefore both the repentant and unrepentant, for the reborn and those not reborn, the law is and remains one single law, the unchangeable will of God. In terms of obedience to it there is a difference only in that those people who are not yet reborn do what the law demands unwillingly, because they are coerced (as is the case with the reborn with respect to the flesh). Believers, however, do without coercion, with a willing spirit, insofar as they are born anew, what no threat of the law could ever force from them.

one single law. Related to Ex 12:49; Nm 15:15–16. Luther wrote concerning Gal 5:14, "No less carefully must one understand that very popular distinction which is made among natural law, the written law, and the law of the Gospel. For when the apostle says here that they all come together and are summed up in one, certainly love is the end of every law, as he says in 1 Tim. 1:5. . . . Therefore there is one law which runs through all ages, is known to all men, is written in the hearts of all people, and leaves no one from beginning to end with an excuse . . . only this one [law], which the Holy Spirit dictates unceasingly in the hearts of all" (*Lectures on Galatians* [1519] LW 27:354–55).

unchangeable will of God. On the constancy of God and His will, see Ex 34:4–7; Ps 102:25–27; Num 23:19; Mal 3:5–7. See also references to the everlasting covenant in nt. 388. Luther wrote, "There is bestowed upon us [through Christ] the sense that the fulfilling of the Law may now for the first time be successfully attempted and perfectly realized, and this is the eternal, fixed and unchangeable will of God" (*Church Postil*, Lenker 5:188). See also *Lectures on Galatians* (1535) LW 26:12. The basic function of the Law is to "teach what I should do—for that is the proper function of the Law" (LW 26:91; cf. *Lectures on 1 Timothy* [1528] LW 28:235). Melanchthon wrote, "Our opponents are fine theologians. They focus on the second table and civil works; they pay no attention to the first, as though it were irrelevant, or at best they require only outward observances. They do not at all consider that eternal law" (Ap IV 131); "The divine order that we are to obey God remains unchangeable" (1559 *Loci*).

obedience to [the Law]. For Luther, related biblical expressions are "keeping," "fulfilling" (*Lectures on Romans* [1525] LW 25:250), and "observing" the Law. E.g., "The third class [the righteous] observe it both externally and with the heart. This class is the tables of Moses, written upon outwardly and inwardly by the finger of God himself" (*Church Postil*, Lenker 6:273). He also wrote, "If your flesh becomes lascivious, repress it by the Spirit. . . . when you do this, you walk by the Spirit; that is, you follow the Word and will of God. . . . Unless he follows the Spirit as his guide and obeys the Word of God when it gives him correct and faithful warning about his duty, he will gratify the desires of the flesh" (*Lectures on Galatians* [1535] LW 27:70; see also p. 73). Cf. *Lectures on Galatians* [1535] LW 26:12. Melanchthon wrote in the 1559 Loci, "The Law must be preached to the regenerate to teach them certain works in which God wills that we practice obedience." *The Chief Theological Topics* 123.

coerced . . . with respect to the flesh. Cf. *Prefaces to the Old Testament* (1523, 1545) LW 35:240.

Believers . . . without coercion, with a willing spirit. Cf. Ps 51:12–13; Mt 26:41; Jn 14:12, 15; Rm 7:22; 2 Co 9:7 (Ger.); Gal 5:1, 13. Luther wrote about the command to love, "These are the brief commandments which Christ calls 'My commandments.' 'And these,' He says, 'I impose on you only if you love Me and gladly keep them for My sake. For I do not want to be a Moses, who drives and plagues you with menace and terror; but I give you commands which you can and will surely observe without coercion if you love Me at all. If love is wanting, it is useless for Me to give you many commandments; for they would not be observed anyhow. Therefore if you want to keep My commandments, see that you love Me, and think of what I have done for you.'" (*Sermons on John* [1533–34/1538–39] LW 24:102). See also *On the Jews and Their Lies* (1543) LW 47:214.

insofar as they are born anew. Cf. Jn 3:5–6, 18–21; Rm 7:22–25. Luther wrote, "The inward and the outward man, or the new man and the old, are not distinguished according to the difference between soul and body but according to dispositions. . . . Therefore the whole man is a spiritual man insofar as he savors the things that are of God (Matt. 16:23)" (*Lectures on Galatians* [1519] LW 27:367; see also 363, 379). Cf. *Lectures on Genesis* (1535–45) LW 7:36; *Sermon on the Mount* (1530–32) LW 21:66; *Lectures on Romans* (1525) LW 25:339.

APPENDIX D

Melanchthon wrote, "Insofar as the regenerate have been justified by faith, they are free from the Law" (1559 *Loci*).

APPENDIX E

THE MODERN DEBATE ON THE USE OF THE LAW

The Confessional Revival, in response to the 1830 Prussian Union, brought new focus on the Formula of Concord, which described how Lutheran doctrine differed from Reformed doctrine. Some important publications and an event on the doctrine of the Law for this period are as follows:

1858   Frank. *Theologie der Concordienformal.*
1884/85   Walther's lectures on the proper distinction between Law and Gospel.

According to Werner Elert, the three-uses consensus developed from the research of Gustav Kawerau, who did not recognize the textual problems in the second Antinomian Disputation, which included the expression "third use" of the Law (p. xiii). Important publications of this period are as follows:

1895   Kawerau. *Disputationen Dr. Martin Luthers.*
1897   Walther. *Die Rechte Unterschiedung . . .*
1905   Denifle. *Die abendländischen Schriftausleger.*
1916   A. Pieper. *Über den Unterschied der reformierten und lutherischen . . .*
1921   Holl. *Geschichtliche Aufsätze zur Kirchengeschichte I.: Luther.*
1927   Aner. "Gesetz und Evangelium" in *Religion in Geschichte und Gegenwart.*
1929   Walther. *The Proper Distinction between Law and Gospel.* Dau translation.
1933   Seeberg. *Lehrbuch der Dogmengeschichte.* 4th ed.

APPENDIX E

The rise of National Socialism caused scholars to reinvestigate the doctrine of the Law as the ecumenical movement encouraged greater dialogue and cooperation between Lutheran and Reformed theologians. Lutheran theologians sharply criticized Barth's 1935 essays, "Evangelium and Gesetz." This generated investigation of Reformation history and theology as theologians reacted to one another. Important publications of this period are as follows:

1935	Barth. *Evangelium und Gesetz.*
1937	Schlink. *Gesetz und Evangelium.*
1943	Bring. *Gesetz und Evangelium.*
1948	Elert. *In Zwischen Gnade und Ungnade. Gesetz und Evangelium.*
1950	Ebeling. *Zur Lehre vom triplex usus legis.*
1952	Althaus. *Gebot und Gesetz.*
1953	Heckel. *Lex Charitatis: Eine juristische Untersuchung über das Recht in der Theologie Martin Luthers.*
1958	Schultz. *Gesetz und Evangelium in der lutherischen Theologie des 19. Jahrhunderts.*
1958	Haikola. *Usus Legis.*
1960	Barth. *Gospel and Law.* English translation.
1961	Barth. *Evangelium und Gesetz* reprinted in German.
1962	Althaus. *Die Theologie Martin Luthers.*
1963	Ebeling. Essay translated in *Word and Faith.*
1963	Althaus. *The Law and Gospel in Luther.*
1966	Althaus. *The Divine Command.* Trans. by Schroeder.
1967	Elert. *Law and Gospel.* Trans. by Schroeder.
1968	Joest. *Gesetz und Freiheit.*
1969	Forde. *The Law-Gospel Debate.*
1970	Langemeyer. *Gesetz und Evangelium.*
1972	Fagerberg. *A New Look at the Lutheran Confessions.*

The four-hundredth anniversary of the Formula of Concord encouraged new studies. The only-two-uses consensus was firmly established in Luther scholarship while conservative Lutherans continued to argue that Luther's teaching was compatible with a threefold use of the Law. Some recent publications are as follows:

1977	Meyer. *Normen Christlichen Handelns.*
1978	Lazareth. *Foundation for Christian Ethics.*
1978	*Contemporary Look at Formula of Concord.* Anniversary studies of FC.

1980	Schuetze. *No Other Gospel.*
1981	Haikola. *Usus Legis* reprint.
1981	Peters. *Gesetz und Evangelium.*
1986	Barth. *Evangelium und Gesetz* reprint.
1997	Wengert. *Law and Gospel.*
2002	Murray. *Law, Life, and the Living God.*
2002	Witte. *Law and Protestantism.*
2004	Gieschen, ed. *The Law in Holy Scripture.*
2006	Witte. *God's Joust, God's Justice.*
2008	Kolb and Arand. *The Genius of Luther's Theology.*
2008	Witte. *The Reformation of Rights.*
2010	Heckel. *Lex Charitatis: A Juristic Disquisition on Law in the Theology of Martin Luther.*
2016?	*Antinomian Disputations* forthcoming in *Luther's Works.* Silcock, trans.

BIBLIOGRAPHY

The bibliography has two parts: (1) works cited or referenced for the book and (2) resources on the topic of Law and Gospel. To make the second part of the bibliography most convenient, works on Law and Gospel that appeared in the works cited list are repeated in the second list. For further bibliographic aid, interested readers should also consult *Theologische Realenzyklopädie* Bd. XIII (Berlin: Walther de Gruyter, 1984), 40–147.

WORKS CITED OR REFERENCED

Agricola, Johannes. "One Hundred Thirty Common Questions," Timothy Wengert, trans. in *Sources and Contexts of the Book of Concord* Robert Kolb and James A. Nestingen, eds. Minneapolis: Fortress Press, 2001.

Aland, Kurt, ed. *Hilfsbuch zum Lutherstudium*. 4th ed. Bielefeld: Luther-Verlag, 1996.

Alexander, Donald L. ed. *Christian Spirituality: Five Views of Sanctification*. Downers Grove: InterVarsity Press, 1988.

Althaus, Paul. *The Theology of Martin Luther*. Philadelphia: Fortress Press, 1966.

Ambrosiaster. *Lectures on Galatians–Philemon*, Gerald L. Bray, trans. In *Ancient Christian Texts*, Thomas C. Oden and Gerald L. Bray, eds. Downers Grove, IL: IVP Academics, 2009.

Aner, Karl. "Gesetz und Evangelium, dogmengeschichtlich," *Religion in Geschichte und Gegenwart*, 2nd ed. Tübingen, 1927.

Ante-Nicene Fathers: Translations of the Writings of the Fathers down to 325 A.D. Alexander Roberts and James Donaldson, eds. Grand Rapids, MI: Eerdmans, reprint 1980–87.

Arand, Charles P. *That I May Be His Own: An Overview of Luther's Catechisms*. St. Louis: Concordia, 2000.

Aristotle. *The Politics*. With an English Translation by H. Rackham. In *Loeb Classical Library*. London: W. Heinemann, 1932.

———. *The Works of Aristotle Translated into English*. Vol. X. W. D. Ross, ed. Oxford: Clarendon Press, 1921.

Augustine. *The Works of Saint Augustine: A Translation for the 21st Century, Letters (156–210)*. Hyde Park, New York: New City Press, 2004.

———. *The Works of Saint Augustine: A Translation for the 21st Century, Sermons (148–183)*. New Rochelle, New York: New City Press, 1992.

Augustine on Romans. Paula Fredricksen Landes, trans. Chico, CA: Scholars Press, 1982.

Aveling, Frances. "Antinomianism." In *The Catholic Encyclopedia: An International work of Reference on the Constitution, Doctrine, Discipline, and History of the Catholic Church*. 15 vols. Herbermann, Charles G. et al. eds. New York: The Encyclopedia Press, 1907.

Beckwith, Carl L. "Looking into the Heart of Missouri: Justification, Sanctification, and the Third Use of the Law." *Concordia Theological Quarterly* 69:3–4 (2005): 293–308.

Beeke, Joel R. "The Place of the Third Use of the Law in Reformed Theology." Unpublished. Available online.

Bekenntnisschriften der evangelisch-lutherischen Kirche, Die. 10th ed. Göttingen: Vandenhoeck & Ruprecht, 1991.

Bickle, Philip M. and Robert L. Nordlie. *The Goal of the Gospel: God's Purpose in Saving You*. St. Louis: Concordia, 1992.

Biel, Gabriel. *Collectorium circa quattuor libros Sententiarum*. Wildridus Werbeck and Udo Hofmann, eds. Tübingen: J. C. B. Mohr, 1979.

Bonner, Gerald. *St. Augustine of Hippo: Life and Controversies*. Norwich: The Canterbury Press, 1986.

Braaten, Carl E. and Robert W. Jenson, eds. *Christian Dogmatics*. 2 Vols. Philadelphia: Fortress Press, 1984.

Brecht, Martin. *Martin Luther*. 3 Vols. Minneapolis: Fortress, 1985–93.

Bright, John. *A History of Israel* 4th ed. Louisville: Westminster John Knox Press, 2000.

Burce, Willard L. trans. "The Distinction between the Law and Gospel: A Sermon by Luther, January 1, 1532." *Concordia Journal* 18 (April, 1992): 153–63.

Burgess, John P. "Calvin's Third Use of the Law: An Assessment of Reformed Explications of the Ten Commandments." Paper delivered to Society of Christian Ethics, 2001. Available online.

Calvin, John. *Institutes of the Christian Religion*. Henry Beveridge, trans. 3 Vols. Edinburgh, 1845–46.

Calvin's Institutes of the Christian Religion. John T. McNiell, ed. Ford Lewis Battles, trans. In *The Library of Christian Classics* Vol. XX. Philadelphia: The Westminster Press, 1960.

Cambridge History of the Bible. 3 Vols. Cambridge: University Press, 1963–70.

Canning, Raymond, "Uti/frui." In *Augustine through the Ages: An Encyclopedia*. Allen D. Fitzgerald et al., eds. Grand Rapids: Eerdmans, 1999.

Canons and Decrees of the Sacred and Oecumenical Council of Trent. J. Waterworth, ed. and trans. London: Dolman, 1848.

Carson, D. A. and Moo, Douglas J. *An Introduction to the New Testament*. 2nd ed. Grand Rapids, MI: Zondervan, 2005.

Catechism of the Council of Trent, Published by Command of Pope Pius V. J. Donavan, trans. Baltimore: Fielding Lucas, Jr., [1829].

Charles, Henry. *A History of the Inquisition of the Middle Ages*. New York: Harper & Brothers, 1887.

Chemnitz, Martin. *Examination of the Council of Trent*. 4 Vols. Fred Kramer, trans. St. Louis: Concordia, 1971–86.

Cicero. *Laws*. Clinton Walker Keyes, trans. In *The Loeb Classical Library*. Cambridge, MA: Harvard University Press, 1928.

Concilium Tridentinum. Vol. 5. Stephanus Ehses, ed. Friburg: Herder, 1964.

Concordia Triglotta. St. Louis: Concordia, 1921.

Contarini, Cardinalis Gasparis. *Opera Omnia*. Venetiis: Damlanum Zenarium, 1589.

Denifle, Heinrich. *Die abendländischen Schiftausleger bis Luther über Justitia Dei (Rom. 1,17) und Justificatio*. Mainz: Kirchheim & Co., 1905.

Dictionary of Medieval Latin from British Sources. Fasc. VI. D. R. Howlett et al., eds. Oxford: Oxford University Press, 2001.

Dictionary of the Middle Ages. Joseph R. Strayer, ed. New York: Charles Scribner's Sons, 1983.

Digest of Justinian, The. Vol. 1. Charles Henry Monro, trans. Cambridge: Cambridge University Press, 1904.

Digesta Iustiniani Augusti. Vol. 1. Th. Mommsen, ed. Berlin: Weidmann, 1868.

Ebeling, Gerhard. *Luther: An Introduction to His Thought*. R. A. Wilson, trans. London: Collins, 1970.

———. "On the Doctrine of the *Triplex Usus Legis* in the Theology of the Reformation." *Word and Faith*, James W. Leitch tr. Philadelphia: Fortress Press, 1963.

———. "Zur Lehre vom *triplex usus legis* in der reformatorischen Theologie." *Theologische Literaturzeitung* 75 (1950): 235–246.

Elert, Werner. "Eine theologische Fälschung zur Lehre vom tertius usus legis." *Zeitschrift für Religions- und Geistes geschichte* 1 (1948): 168–70.

———. *Law and Gospel*. Facet Books: Social Ethics Series. Edward H. Schroeder, tr. Philadelphia: Fortress Press, 1971.

———. *The Structure of Lutheranism*. Vol. 1. St. Louis: Concordia, 1962.

Engelbrecht, Edward. *One True God: Understanding LC II 66*. St. Louis: Concordia, 2007.

Erasmus, Desiderius. *In epistolam Pauli ad Galatas Paraphrasis*. Argentina, 1520.

———. *Paraphrases in Novum Testamentum* (1522). In *Opera Omnia*. Lugduni: Petri Vander, 1706.

Fagerberg, Holsten. *A New Look at the Lutheran Confessions, 1529–1537*. Gene J. Lund, trans. St. Louis: Concordia, 1972.

Forde, Gerhard O. *A More Radical Gospel: Essays on Eschatology, Authority, Atonement, and Ecumenism.* Mark Mattes and Steven Paulson, eds. Grand Rapids: Eerdmans, 2004.

———. "The Normative Character of Scripture for Matters of Faith and Life: Human Sexuality in Light of Romans 1:16–32." In *Word & World* Vol. XIV, No. 3 (Summer 1994):305–14.

Forster, Anselm. *Gesetz und Evangelium bei Girolamo Seripando.* Paderborn: Bonifacius-Druckerei, 1963.

Franke, Fr. H. R. *Die Theologie der Concordienformel: historisch-dogmatisch Entwickelt und Beleuchtet.* 3 Vols. Erlangen: Theodore Blaesing, 1863.

Frend, W. H. C. *Martyrdom and Persecution in the Early Church: A Study of a Conflict from the Maccabees to Donatus.* New York: Anchor Books, 1967.

Gerhard, Johann. *Loci Theologici.* Preuss ed. Berlin: Gust. Schlawitz, 1865.

Gibson, Margaret. "The Latin Apparatus." In *The Eadwine Psalter: Text, Image, and Monastic Culture in Twelfth-Century Canterbury.* Margaret Gibson, T. A. Heslop, Richard W. Pfaff, eds. University Park, PA: The Pennsylvania State University Press, 1992.

Gratian. *The Treatises on Laws (Decretum D. D. 1–20) with Ordinary Gloss.* Augustine Thompson, O. P. and James Gordley, trans. Washington, D. C.: The Catholic University of America Press, 1993.

Green, Lowell C. *How Melanchthon Helped Luther Discover the Gospel.* Fallbrook, CA: Verdict Publications, 1980.

———. "The 'Third Use of the Law' and Werner Elert's Position." Paper for Symposium on the Lutheran Confessions, Fort Wayne. Final Version—January 25, 2005. Available online.

Handbook of Catholic Theology. Wolfgang Bienert and Frances Schüssler Fiorenza, eds. New York: Crossroad, 1995.

Hasler, Victor Ernest. *Gesetz und Evangelium in der alten Kirche bis Origenes.* Zurich/Frankfort am Mein: Gotthelf-Verlag, 1953.

Heckel, Johannes. *Lex Charitatis: A Juristic Disquisition on Law in the Theology of Martin Luther.* Gottfried G. Krodel, trans. and ed. Grand Rapids: Eerdmans, 2010.

Herrmann, Erik. " 'Why then the Law?' Salvation History and the Law in Martin Luther's Interpretation of Galatians 1513–1522." PhD Diss. St. Louis: Concordia Seminary, 2005.

Jedin, Hubert. *A History of the Council of Trent.* Vol. II. Ernest Graf, trans. St. Louis: B. Herder Book Co., 1957.

———. *Cardinal Seripando: Papal Legate at the Council of Trent.* Frederic C. Eckhoff, trans. St. Louis: B. Herder Book Co., 1947.

Joest, W. *Gesetz und Freiheit: Das Problem des tertius usus legis bei Luther und die neutestamentliche Parainese.* Göttingen: Vanderhoeck and Ruprecht, 1951.

Kawerau, Gustav. "Antinomistische Streitigkeiten." In *Realenzyklopaedie für die protestantische Theologie und Kirche.* Bd. 1. Leipzig: J. C. Hinrichs'sche Buchhandlung, 1896.

———. *Disputationen Dr. Martin Luthers.* Göttingen, 1895.

Klug, Eugene F. "Article VI. The Third Use of the Law." *A Contemporary Look at the Formula of Concord.* Robert D. Preus and Wilbert H. Rosin, eds. St. Louis: Concordia, 1978.

Koenker, Ernest B. "Man *simul justus et peccator*" in *Accents in Luther's Theology.* Heino O. Kadai, ed. St. Louis: Concordia, 1967.

Kolb, Robert. *Martin Luther: Confessor of the Faith.* Oxford: Oxford University Press, 2009.

Kolb, Robert and Charles Arand. *The Genius of Luther's Theology.* Grand Rapids: Baker Academic, 2008.

Kolb, Robert and Timothy J. Wengert, eds. *The Book of Concord: The Confessions of the Evangelical Lutheran Church.* Minneapolis: Fortress Press, 2000.

Kraus, Georg. "Law and Gospel." In *Handbook of Catholic Theology.* Wolfgang Bienert and Frances Schüssler Fiorenza, eds. New York: Crossroad, 1995.

LaPlante, Eve. *American Jezebel: The Uncommon Life of Anne Hutchinson, the Woman Who Defied the Puritans.* New York: HarperOne, 2004.

Lazareth, William. "Antinomians: Then and Now." *Lutheran Forum* 36 (Winter 2002). Available at http://archive.elca.org/

———. "Introduction." In *The Divine Command* by Paul Althaus. Philadelphia: Fortress Press, 1966.

Lerner, Robert E. *The Heresy of the Free Spirits in the Late Middle Ages.* Berkeley: University of California Press, 1972.

Lohse, Bernhard. *Martin Luther: An Introduction to His Life and Work.* Robert C. Schultz, trans. Philadelphia: Fortress Press, 1986.

Loofs, Friedrich. *Leitfaden zum Studium der Dogmengeschichte.* 4th ed. Halle am Salle, 1906.

Lull, Timothy, F. ed. *Martin Luther's Basic Theological Writings*, 2nd ed. Minneapolis, MN: Augsburg Fortress, 2005.

Luther, Martin. *Dr. Martin Luther's sämmtliche Werke.* Vols. 67. Erlangen: Carl Heyder, 1827.

———. *Dr. Martin Luther's sämmtliche Werke.* 2nd ed. Vols. 26. Frankfurt am Main: Heyder & Zimmer, 1866.

———. *Geist aus Luther's Schriften.* 4 Vols. Darmstadt: Druck und Verlag von Karl Wilhelm Leske, 1828–31.

———. *Luther's Works: American Edition* (LW). Vols. 1–30: Edited by Jaroslav Pelikan. St. Louis: Concordia, 1955–76. Vols. 31–55: Edited by Helmut Lehmann. Philadelphia/Minneapolis: Muhlenberg/Fortress, 1957–86. Vols. 56–75: Edited by Christopher Boyd Brown. St. Louis: Concordia, 2009–.

———. *Luthers Werke: Kritische Gesamtausgabe. Schriften.* 73 vols. in 85. Weimar: H. Böhlau, 1883–.

———. *Luthers Werke: Kritische Gesamtausgabe. Bibel.* 12 vols. in 15. Weimar: H. Böhlau, 1906–.

———. *Sermons of Martin Luther.* John Nicholas Lenker, ed. 8 vols. Grand Rapids, MI: Baker Book House, reprint 1989.

———. *Sermons of Martin Luther: The House Postils* 3 Vols. Eugene F. A. Klug, ed. Grand Rapids, MI: Baker Books, 1996.

Lutheran Study Bible, The. Edward A. Engelbrecht, gen. ed. St. Louis: Concordia, 2009.

Lutheran World Federation, The and The Pontifical Council for Promoting Christian Unity. *Joint Declaration on the Doctrine of Justification.* Grand Rapids, MI: Eerdmans, 2000.

Mansi, J. D. ed. *Sacrorum Conciliorum Nova et Amplissima Collectio.* Vol. XXV. Paris: Hubert, 1782.

Mattes, Mark C. "Beyond the Impasse: Re-examining the Third Use of the Law." *Concordia Theological Quarterly* 69:3–4 (2005): 271–92.

Maurer, Wilhelm. "Formula of Concord." In *The Encyclopedia of the Lutheran Church.* Vol. II. Julius Bodensieck, ed. Minneapolis: Augsburg Fortress, 1965.

McDonnell, Ernest W. *The Beguines and Beghards in Medieval Culture, with Special Emphasis on the Belgian Scene.* New York: Octagon Books, 1969.

Melanchthon, Philip. *The Chief Theological Topics: Loci Praecipui Theologici 1559.* J. A. O. Preus, trans. St. Louis: Concordia, 2011.

———. *Corpus Reformatorum. Philippi Melancthonis opera quae supersunt omnia.* Karl Bretschneider and Heinrich Bindseil, eds. 28 vols. Halle: A. Schwetschke and Sons, 1834–60.

———. *Loci Communes Theologici.* Wilhelm Pauck, ed. Lowell J. Satre, trans. *Library of Christian Classics* 19. Philadelphia: Westminster, 1969.

———. *Commentary on Romans.* Fred Kramer, trans. St. Louis: Concordia, 1992.

———. *Melanchthons Werke in Auswahl.* Vol. II. Robert Stupperich, ed. Gütersloh, 1952.

Muller, Richard A. *Dictionary of Latin and Greek Theological Terms.* Grand Rapids: Baker, 1985.

Murray, Scott R. *Law, Life, and the Living God: The Third Use of the Law in Modern American Lutheranism.* St. Louis: Concordia, 2002.

Natural Law: A Lutheran Reappraisal. Robert Baker, gen. ed. St. Louis: Concordia, 2011.

Nestingen, James A. "Changing Definitions: The Law in Formula VI." *Concordia Theological Quarterly* 69:3–4 (2005): 259–70.

Nicene Post-Nicene Fathers. Series 1. Philip Schaff, ed. Grand Rapids, MI: Eerdmans, reprinted 1986–89.

Nicholas de Lyre. *Postilla super totam Bibliam*. De Venetiis: impensis Octaviani Scoti, 1488.

Oxford Classical Dictionary. 3rd ed. Simon Hornblower and Antony Spawforth, eds. Oxford: Oxford University Press, 1996.

Oxford Dictionary of the Christian Church. 3rd ed. Oxford: Oxford University Press, 1997.

Oxford Encyclopedia of the Reformation. Hans J. Hillerbrand, ed. 4 vols. Oxford: Oxford University Press, 1996.

Oxford English Dictionary. Oxford: Oxford University Press, 1989.

Patrologiae cursus completus: Series Latina. Jacques-Paul Migne, ed. 221 vols. Paris & Turnout, 1859–1963.

Pelagius's Expositions of Thirteen Epistles of St. Paul. Vol. II. Cambridge: Cambridge University Press, 1926.

Petrus Aureoli. *Compendium Biblie Totius*. Argentinae: [1514].

Philo with an English Translation by F. H. Colson and Rev. G. H. Whitaker. Vol. IV. In *The Loeb Classical Library*. London: William Heinemann, LTD, 1932.

Plato. *The Republic, with an English Translation by Paul Shorey*. In The Loeb Classical Library. Cambridge, MA: Harvard University Press, 1935.

———. *Laws*. R. G. Bury, trans. In *The Loeb Classical Library*. Cambridge, MA: Harvard University Press, 1926.

Plummer, Eric. *Augustine's Commentary on Galatians*. Oxford: Oxford University Press, 2003.

Posset, Franz. *The Front-Runner of the Catholic Reformation: The Life and Works of Johann von Staupitz*. Hants, England: Ashgate Publishing Limited, 2003.

———. *The Real Luther: A Friar at Erfurt and Wittenberg.* St. Louis: Concordia, 2011.

Quasten, Johannes. *Patrology.* 4 Vols. Allen, TX: Christian Classics, 1996.

Quintilian. With an English Translation. Harold Edgeworth Butler. Cambridge. Cambridge, Mass., Harvard University Press; London, William Heinemann, Ltd. 1920.

Ramp, Stephen W. "John Calvin on Preaching the Law." *Word & World* Vol. XXI, No. 3. Summer 2001.

Rast, Lawrence R. "The Third Use of the Law: Keeping Up to Date with an Old Issue." *Concordia Theological Quarterly* 69:3–4 (2005): 187–90.

Scaer, David P. "The Third Use of the Law: Resolving the Tension." *Concordia Theological Quarterly* 69:3–4 (2005): 237–58.

Schloemann, Martin. *Natürliches und Gepredgtes Gesetz bei Luther.* Berlin: Alfred Töpelmann, 1961.

Schurb, Ken R. "Philip Melanchthon, the Formula of Concord, and the Third Use of the Law." Unpublished Doctoral Dissertation. The Ohio State University, 2001.

Schwiebert, E. G. *Luther and His Times.* St. Louis: Concordia, 1950.

Seeberg, Reinhold. *Lehrbuch der Dogmengeschichte.* 4th ed. Vol. IV. Leipzig, 1933.

Seripandus, Hieronymus. *Commentaria in epistolam Pauli ad Romanos et in epistolam ad Galatas.* Lugnuni, 1541.

———. *In Epistolam Pauli ad Galatas.* Antverpiae: Christophori Plantini, 1567.

Silcock, Jeffrey G. "Law and Gospel in Luther's *Antinomian Disputations*, with Special Reference to Faith's Use of the Law." Th.D. diss., Concordia Seminary, 1995.

Simons, Walter. *Cities of Ladies: Beguine Communities in the Medieval Law Countries, 1200–1565.* Philadelphia: University of Pennsylvania Press, 2001.

Smith, Louis A. "God's Law, God's Gospel, and Their Proper Distinction: A Sure Guide through the Moral Wasteland of

Postmodernism." *Concordia Theological Quarterly* 69:3–4 (2005): pp. 221–234.

Sources and Contexts of the Book of Concord. Robert Kolb and James A. Nestingen, eds. Minneapolis: Fortress Press, 2001.

Theological Dictionary of the New Testament. 10 Vols. G. Kittel and G. Friedrich, eds. Grand Rapids, MI: Eerdmans, 1967.

Theological Dictionary of the Old Testament. 15 Vols. G. Johannes Botterweck and Helmer Ringgren, eds. Grand Rapids, MI: Eerdmans, 2006.

Thomas Aquinas. *Commentary on Saint Paul's Epistle to the Galatians*. F. R. Larcher, trans. Albany, NY: Magi Books, Inc., 1966.

———. *The Summa Theologica*. Fathers of the English Dominican Province, trans. Benziger Bros., 1947.

Thucydides, with an English Translation by Charles Forster Smith. In *The Loeb Classical Library*. London: William Heinemann, 1930.

Tyconius: The Book of Rules. William S. Babcock, trans. Atlanta, GA: Scholars Press, 1989.

Vogel, Lawrence M. "A Third Use of the Law: Is the Phrase Necessary? *Concordia Theological Quarterly* 69:3–4 (2005): 191–220.

Walther, C. F. W. *Die rechte Unterscheidung von Gesetz und Evangelium*. St. Louis: Concordia, 1897.

Wendel, François. *Calvin: Origins and Development of His Religious Thought*. Philip Mairet, trans. New York: Harper and Row, 1963.

Wengert, Timothy J. *A Formula for Parish Practice: Using the Formula of Concord in Congregations*. Grand Rapids: Eerdmans, 2006.

———. *Harvesting Martin Luther's Reflections on Theology, Ethics, and the Church*. Grand Rapids, MI: Eerdmans, 2004.

———. *Law and Gospel: Philip Melanchthon's Debate with John Agricola of Eisleben over Poenitentia*. Grand Rapids: Baker Books, 1997.

Witte, John. *God's Joust, God's Justice: Law and Religion in the Western Tradition*. Grand Rapids: Eerdmans, 2006.

———. *Law and Protestantism: The Legal Teachings of the Lutheran Reformation*. Cambridge: Cambridge University Press, 2002.

Wortkonkordanz zum Decretum Gratiani. Timothy Reuter und Gabriel Silagi, bearb. München: Monumenta Germaniae Historica, 1990.

WORKS ON LAW AND GOSPEL

Althaus, Paul. *Gebot und Gesetz: Zum Thema "Gesetz und Evangelium."* Gütersloh, 1952.

Aner, Karl. "Gesetz und Evangelium, dogmengeschichtlich," *Religion in Geschichte und Gegenwart*, 2nd ed. Tübingen, 1927.

Barth, Karl. *Epistle to the Romans*. 6th ed. Translated by Edwyn Hoskyns. London: Oxford University Press, 1933.

———. *Evangelium und Gesetz*. Theologische Existenz Heute 32. Edited by Karl Barth and Eduard Thurneysen. Munich: Chr. Kaiser, 1935.

———. "Gospel and Law." In *Community, State, and Church*. A. M. Hall, trans. Garden City: Doubleday Anchor, 1960.

Beckwith, Carl L. "Law, Life, and the Living God: The Third Use of the Law in Modern American Lutheranism." *Pro Ecclesia* 12 (Summer 2003).

———. "Looking into the Heart of Missouri: Justification, Sanctification, and the Third Use of the Law." *Concordia Theological Quarterly* 69:3–4 (2005): 293–308.

Beeke, Joel R. "The Place of the Third Use of the Law in Reformed Theology." Unpublished. Available online.

Bente, F. *Gesetz und Evangelium: Busze und gute Werke*. St. Louis: Concordia, 1917.

Berman, Harold Joseph. *Faith and Order: The Reconciliation of Law and Religion*. Grand Rapids: Wm. B. Eerdmans Publishing, 1993.

Bring, R. *Gesetz und Evangelium und der dritte Brauch des Gesetzes in der lutherischen Theologie*. Publications of the Luther-Agricola Society in Finland, No. 4. Helsinki, 1943.

Bugenhagen, Johann. *Annotationes . . . in Epistolas Pauli, ad Galatas, Ephesios, Philippenses, Colossenses, Thessalonicenses primam & secundam, Timotheum primam & secundam, Titum, Philemonem, Hebraeas.* 2nd ed. Basel: Adam Petri, 1525.

Burgess, John P. "Calvin's Third Use of the Law: An Assessment of Reformed Explications of the Ten Commandments." Paper delivered to Society of Christian Ethics, 2001. Available online.

Chemnitz, Martin. "De Operibus Renatorum." In *Loci Theologici.* Frankfurt and Wittenberg: Sumptibus haeredum D. Tobiae Mevii, & Elerdi Schumacher, 1653.

Diem, Hermann. "Evangelium und Gesetz" oder "Gesetz und Evangelium"? *Evangelische Theologie.* 3 (1936). In Kinder, Ernst und Klaus Haendler. *Gesetz und Evangelium: Beiträge zur gegenwärtigen theologischen Diskussion.* Darmstadt: Wissenschaftliche Buchgesellschaft, 1986.

Ebeling, Gerhard. "On the Doctrine of the *Triplex Usus Legis* in the Theology of the Reformation." *Word and Faith*, James W. Leitch tr. Philadelphia: Fortress Press, 1963.

———. *Wort und Glaube.* Vol. 1. Tübingen: J. C. B. Mohr, 1960.

———. "Zur Lehre vom triplex usus legis in der reformatorischen Theologie." *Theologische Literaturzeitung* 75 (1950): 235–46.

Echternach, Helmut. "Zum Problem des tertius usus legis." In *Bekenntnis Zur Kirche.* Berlin: Evangelische Verlagsanstalt, 1963.

Elert, Werner. "Eine theologische Fälschung zur Lehre vom tertius usus legis." *Zeitschrift für Religions- und Geistes geschichte* 1 (1949).

———. *Law and Gospel.* Facet Books: Social Ethics Series. Edward H. Schroeder, trans. Philadelphia: Fortress Press, 1971.

———. *Zwischen Gnade und Ungnade: Abwandlungen des Themas Gesetz und Evangelium.* München: Evangelischer Presseverband für Bayern, 1948.

Forde, Gerhard O. "Fake Theology: Reflections on Antinomianism Past and Present." *Dialog* 22 (Autumn 1983).

———. "Law and Gospel as the Methodological Principle of Theology." In *Theological Perspectives*. Decorah: Luther College Press, 1967.

———. *The Law-Gospel Debate: An Interpretation of Its Development*. Minneapolis: Augsburg, 1969.

Forell, George W. "Law and Gospel." In *Marburg Revisited*. Paul C. Empie and James I McCord, eds. Minneapolis: Augsburg, 1966.

Forster, Anselm. *Gesetz und Evangelium bei Girolamo Seripando*. Paderborn: Bonifacius-Druckerei, 1963.

Geihsler, Walter. "The Law and the Gospel." In *The Abiding Word*. Vol. 1. Theodore Laetsch, ed. St. Louis: Concordia, 1946.

Gollwitz, Helmut. "Zur Einheit von Gesetz und Evangelium." *Antwort*. Zurich Evangelischer Verlag, 1956.

Green, Lowell C. "The 'Third Use of the Law' and Werner Elert's Position." Paper for Symposium on the Lutheran Confessions, Fort Wayne. Final Version—January 25, 2005. Available online.

Haikola, Lauri. *Gesetz und Evangelium bei Matthias Flacius Illyricus: Eine Untersuchung zur lutherischen Theologie vor der Konkordienformel*. Theologica Lundensia 1. Lund: C. W. K. Gleerup, 1952.

———. *Usus Legis*. Schriften der Luther-Agricola-Gesellschaft A 20. Helsinki, 1981.

Hamann, Henry P. "Article V: Law and Gospel." In *A Contemporary Look at the Formula of Concord*. Robert D. Preus and Wilbert Rosin, eds. St. Louis: Concordia, 1978.

Hanko, Ron. "Book Review of *Law and Gospel: Philip Melanchthon's Debate with John Agricola of Eisleben over Poenitentia*." Available online.

Hasler, Victor Ernest. *Gesetz und Evangelium in der alten Kirche bis Origenes*. Zurich/Frankfort am Mein: Gotthelf-Verlag, 1953.

Heckel, Johannes. *Lex Charitatis: A Juristic Disquisition on Law in the Theology of Martin Luther*. Gottfried G. Krodel, trans. and ed. Grand Rapids: Eerdmans, 2010.

Hermann, R. *Zum Streit um die Überwindung des Gesetzes: Erörterungen zu Luthers Antinomerthesen*. Weimar, 1958.

Herrmann, Erik. "'Why then the Law?' Salvation History and the Law in Martin Luther's Interpretation of Galatians 1513–1522." PhD Diss. St. Louis: Concordia Seminary, 2005.

Joest, W. *Gesetz und Freiheit: Das Problem des tertius usus legis bei Luther und die neutestamentliche Parainese.* Göttingen: Vanderhoeck and Ruprecht, 1951.

Klug, Eugene F. "Article VI. The Third Use of the Law." *A Contemporary Look at the Formula of Concord.* Robert D. Preus and Wilbert H. Rosin, eds. St. Louis: Concordia, 1978.

Krötke, Wolf. *Das Problem "Gesetz und Evangelium" bei W. Elert und P. Althaus.* Zürich: EVZ-Verlag, 1965.

Lange, Jonathan G. "Using the Third Use: Formula of Concord VI and the Preacher's Task." *Logia* 3 (January 1994).

Lazareth, William. "Antinomians: Then and Now." *Lutheran Forum* 36 (Winter 2002). Available at http://archive.elca.org/

———. "Introduction." In *The Divine Command* by Paul Althaus. Philadelphia: Fortress Press, 1966.

Leith, John H. "Creation and Redemption: Law and Gospel in the Theology of John Calvin." In *Marburg Revisited.* Paul C. Empie and James I. McCord, eds. Minneapolis: Augsburg, 1966.

Lohse, Bernhard. *Luthers Theologie in ihrer historischen Entwicklung und in ihrem systematischen Zusammenhang.* Göttingen: Vandenhoeck & Ruprecht, 1995.

Luther, Martin. *D. Martin Luthers Epistelauslegung.* Eduard Ellwein, ed. Vanderhoeck & Ruprecht, 1980.

———. *Der Galaterbrief.* Hermann Kleinknecht, ed. Vanderhoeck & Ruprecht, 1987.

McDonough, Th. M. *The Law and the Gospel in Luther: A Study of Martin Luther's Confessional Writings.* Oxford Theological Monographs. Oxford: Oxford University Press, 1963.

Malysz, Piotr J. "The Third Use of the Law in Light of Creation and the Fall." *The Law in Holy Scripture.* Charles A. Gieschen, ed. St. Louis: Concordia, 2004.

Marquardt, Kurt. "The Third Use of the Law as Confessed in the Formula of Concord." Symposium, January 2005.

Mattes, Mark C. "Beyond the Impasse: Re-examining the Third Use of the Law." *Concordia Theological Quarterly* 69:3–4 (2005): 271–92.

Maurer, Wilhelm. *Der junge Melanchthon zwischen Humanismus und Reformation.* Vandenhoeck & Ruprecht, 1967.

Melanchthon, Philipp. *Melanchthon on Christian Doctrine: Loci Communes, 1555.* Clyde Leonard Manschreck, tr. Grand Rapids: Baker Book House, 1965.

Montgomery, John Warwick. "The Third Use of the Law," from *The Suicide of Christian Theology.* Minneapolis: Bethany Fellowship, Inc., 1970.

Moo, Douglas J. "The Law of Christ as the Fulfillment of the Law of Moses: A Modified Lutheran View." *Five Views on Law and Gospel.* Greg L. Bahnsen, ed. Grand Rapids: Zondervan, 1996.

Mühlen, Karl Heinz zur. "Law." In *Oxford Encyclopedia of the Reformation.* Vol. 2. Oxford: Oxford University Press, 1996.

Murray, Scott R. *Law, Life, and the Living God: The Third Use of the Law in Modern American Lutheranism.* St. Louis: Concordia, 2002.

———. "The Third Use of the Law: The Author Responds to His Critics." *Concordia Theological Quarterly* 72:2 (April 2008): 99–118.

Nestingen, James A. "Changing Definitions: The Law in Formula VI." *Concordia Theological Quarterly* 69:3–4 (2005): 259–70.

Pieper, Francis. *Christian Dogmatics.* 3 vols. St. Louis: Concordia, 1951–1953.

Ramp, Stephen W. "John Calvin on Preaching the Law." *Word & World* Vol. XXI, No. 3. Summer 2001.

Rast, Lawrence R. "The Third Use of the Law: Keeping Up to Date with an Old Issue." *Concordia Theological Quarterly* 69:3–4 (2005): 187–90.

Scaer, David P. "The Third Use of the Law: Resolving the Tension." *Concordia Theological Quarterly* 69:3–4 (2005): 237–58.

Schlink, E. *Gesetz und Evangelium*. Theologische Existenz Heute 53. Edited by Karl Barth and Eduard Thurneysen. Munich: Chr. Kaiser, 1937.

———. "Gesetz und Paraklese: Antwort." *Festschrift für Karl Barth*. Zürich, 1956.

Schloemann, Martin. *Natürliches und Gepredgtes Gesetz bei Luther*. Berlin: Alfred Töpelmann, 1961.

Schroeder, Edward. *Sabbatheology Newsletter*. Thursday Theology #336. November 18, 2004.

Schuetze, Armin W. "On the Third Use of the Law: Luther's Position in the Antinomian Debate." In *No Other Gospel*. Edited by Arnold J. Koelpin. Milwaukee: Northwestern, 1980.

Schulken, Christian. *Lex efficax*. Tübingen: Mohr Siebeck, 2005.

Schultz, Robert C. *Gesetz und Evangelium in der lutherischen Theologie des 19. Jahrhunderts*. Arbeiten zur Geschichte und Theologie des Luthertums 4. Edited by Wilhelm Maurer, Karl H. Rengstorf, and Ernst Sommerlath. Berlin: Lutherisches Verlaghaus, 1958.

Schurb, Ken R. "Philip Melanchthon, the Formula of Concord, and the Third Use of the Law." Unpublished Doctoral Dissertation. The Ohio State University, 2001.

Seehawer, Johannes. *Zur Lehre vom Brauch des Gesetzes und zur Geschichte des späteren Antinomismus*. Rostock: Carl Boldt'sche Hof-Buchdruckerei, 1887.

Siirala, A. *Gottes Gebot bei Martin Luther*. Helsinki, 1956.

Silcock, Jeffrey G. "Law and Gospel in Luther's *Antinomian Disputations*, with Special Reference to Faith's Use of the Law." Th.D. diss., Concordia Seminary, 1996.

———. "Luther and the Third Use of the Law, with Special Reference to His Great Galatians Commentary." S.T.M. Thesis, Concordia Seminary, 1993.

Smith, Louis A. "God's Law, God's Gospel, and Their Proper Distinction: A Sure Guide through the Moral Wasteland of Postmodernism." *Concordia Theological Quarterly* 69:3–4 (2005): 221–34.

Sommerlath, Ernst. *Gesetz und Evangelium*. Luthertum Heft 17. Berlin: Lutherisches Verlagshaus, 1955.

Sonntag, Holger trans. *Solus Decalogus Est Aeternus: Martin Luther's Complete Antinomian Thesis and Disputations*. Minneapolis: Lutheran Press, 2008.

Tyconius: The Book of Rules. William S. Babcock, trans. Atlanta, GA: Scholars Press, 1989.

Vogel, Lawrence M. "A Third Use of the Law: Is the Phrase Necessary? *Concordia Theological Quarterly* 69:3–4 (2005): 191–220.

Walther, C. F. W. *Law and Gospel: How to Read and Apply the Bible*. A Reader's Edition. Charles P. Schaum, gen. ed. Christian C. Tiews, trans. St. Louis: Concordia, 2010.

———. *The Proper Distinction between Law and Gospel*. St. Louis: Concordia, 1929.

———. *Die rechte Unterscheidung von Gesetz und Evangelium*. St. Louis: Concordia, 1897.

Wengert, Timothy J. *Law and Gospel: Philip Melanchthon's Debate with John Agricola of Eisleben over Poenitentia*. Grand Rapids: Baker Books, 1997.

Witte, John. *God's Joust, God's Justice: Law and Religion in the Western Tradition*. Grand Rapids: Eerdmans, 2006.

———. *Law and Protestantism: The Legal Teachings of the Lutheran Reformation*. Cambridge University Press, 2002.

Scripture Index

Readers should note the nearly constant reference to two biblical chapters throughout the book: Galatians 3 and 1 Timothy 1. The history of the use of the Law clusters around the interpretation of these two passages, which were used to interpret one another already in the earliest years of the Church. Due to the constant reference to these two chapters, not every reference to them was included.

Genesis
1:26–27, 264
2:16–17, 265
3:32, 63
16:1–6, 23
ch. 17, 230
19:30–38, 46
26:4b–5, 13
chs. 42–43, 172

Exodus
12:49, 272
16:4, 271
19–24, 271
20:1–17, 257
24:8, 61
32:19, 85, 93
ch. 34, 271
34:4–7, 272
34:6–7, 236
34:34–35, 93

Leviticus
6:4–7, 14

19:18, 257
24:8, 184

Numbers
15:15–16, 272
23:19, 272

Deuteronomy
5:6–21, 257
6:5, 257
6:24–25, 14

1 Samuel
15:22, 236
17:7, 24, 32, 94

2 Samuel
23:5, 184

1 Chronicles
16:17, 184

Psalms
ps. 1, 24, 207

1:1, 16
1:1–2, 271
1:2, 75, 152, 265, 269
19:7–11, 14
ps. 25, 14
25:14, 15
32:8, 15
33:11, 15
37:3–4, 15
41:9, 21
51:12–13, 273
55:14, 15
73:23–26, 15
102:25–27, 272
105:10, 184
107:11, 16
111:1, 16
ps. 119, 14, 24, 124, 257
119:1, 264, 265, 267, 271
119:24, 16
119:44, 236
119:63, 16
119:77, xi
119:97, 74
119:105, 196
119:160, 236
145:4–13, 2, 43

Proverbs
1:30, 15
ch. 3, 15
3:1, 16
3:3, 266
3:11, 22

3:11–12, 15
ch. 6, 15
6:23–24, 15, 269
7:3, 266
7:4, 15
22:20, 15
27:6, 15

Isaiah
3:10–11, 267
5:19, 15
29:13, 268
55:3, 184
61:8, 184

Jeremiah
31:31–34, 16
31:33, 102, 124, 204, 266
31:34, 222
32:40, 184

Lamentations
2:9, 265

Ezekiel
16:60, 184
36:27, 271
37:26, 184

Micah
4:2, 271
6:6–8, 236
6:8, 158, 271

Scripture Index

Malachi
3:5–7, 272

Ecclesiasticus
2:15, 16
15:1, 16
39:1–4
39:1–11, 257

2 Maccabees
11:31, 17

Matthew
5:17–18, 184
15:9, 196, 268
16:23, 271
19:17, 184
22:37, 257
22:39, 257
23:23, 117, 236
23:24, 76
25:39, 257
26:41, 273

Mark
7:7, 268
12:33, 257

Luke
10:27, 257
19:20, 116
21:33, 236

John
3:5–6, 273
3:18–21, 273
3:19–21, 158
13:31–35, 21
13:34, 29, 271
14:12, 271
14:15, 21, 257, 273
15, 52
15:2, 116
15:9–10, 271
15:12–13, 21
15:14–17, 22
15:16, 52
20:19–31, 178

Acts
15:10, 61, 107

Romans
chs. 1–5, 26
1:18–20, 17
1:20, 26, 249
2:12, 41, 265
2:12–16, 24, 25
2:14, 60
2:14–15, 17
2:15, 22, 24, 26, 33, 75, 124, 190, 191, 230, 249, 263, 264, 266
ch. 3, 237
3:20, 43, 61, 74, 270
3:21, 265
3:31, 268

4:15, 267
5:20, 26, 38, 43, 59, 61, 75, 78, 249
chs. *6–8*, 237
6:1, 234
6:4, 271
6:12, 154, 267
6:12–19, 155
ch. *7*, 128
7:6, 154
7:7, 74
7:8–9, 265
7:14, 268
7:16, 112, 267
7:21, 268
7:22, 273
7:22–25, 273
7:23, 267, 268, 270
7:25–8:2, 159
8:1, 269, 270, 271
8:2, 64, 154
8:4, 269, 271
8:12–17, 48
8:13, 269
8:14, 270
8:15, 155
12:1–2, 155
13:8–10, 257, 271
13:10, 112
14:1, 76

1 Corinthians
1:2, 160
6:11, 155
9:21, 265
9:27, 267
10:6, 11–12, 230

2 Corinthians
1:1, 160
3:13–15, 85
3:17, 64
9:7, 263, 271

Galatians
2:16, 268
ch. *3*, 23, 26, 30, 39, 42, 46, 47, 54, 99
3:3, 232
3:13, 154, 181
3:19, 23, 24, 26, 34, 36, 39, 40, 42, 48, 55, 58, 59, 66, 67, 78
3:19–24, 26, 249
3:19–29, 24
3:22–23, 67
3:22–24, 66
3:23–29, 5, 80, 88, 168
3:24, 11, 23, 80
ch. *4*, 23, 46
4:5, 181
5:1, 273
5:13, 273
5:14, 272
5:16, 269, 270, 271
5:16–24, 167, 182
5:17, 152, 268
5:18, 64
5:22–23, 270

5:23, 271
6:2, 271
6:14, 267

Ephesians
1:1, 160
ch. 2, 237
4:23, 266
4:24, 266
5:9, 271

Philippians
1:1, 160
3:12, 267
3:16, 271

Colossians
1:23–29, 267
1:28, 268
2:14, 191
2:16–23, 236
3:10, 266

1 Timothy
ch. 1, 26, 42, 46, 76
1:3–11, 24, 25, 103
1:5, 102, 272
1:6–8, 16
1:8, 10, 25, 26, 46, 109, 111
1:8–9, 26, 38, 39, 42, 47, 48, 54, 56, 67, 78, 83, 84, 85, 88, 89, 99, 100, 101, 102, 107, 116, 118, 158, 177, 194, 249, 263, 271
1:8–11, 40
1:9, 42, 43, 60, 64, 107
3:2, 99
4:7, 23, 115, 119, 265
4:10, 233
5:9, 99
6:12, 267

2 Timothy
2:3–4, 158
3:16–17, 267, 269
4:2, 116

Hebrews
8:10, 266
10:1, 61
10:16, 204, 266
12:18–24, 27
13:13–14, 27
13:21, 267

1 Peter
1:2, 155

2 John
6, 271

Revelation
14:6, 184, 222

TOPICAL INDEX

abrogation of the Law, 37, 76, 188, 206
accusations of the Law, 39
actions of the Law, 50
admonition, 183–84. *See also* exhortation.
Agricola, John, 3, 63, 106, 108, 121, 147, 193, 218
allegory, Law and, 23
Ambrose, 37
Ambrosiaster, 39–43, 51, 52
amicus legis, 52
analogy, 26, 113, 158
Anselm of Canterbury, 235
Anselm of Laon, 55–57
antinomianism, 3, 63, 64–66, 77, 106–108, 122, 147–62, 183, 207–208, 218, 222, 238, 240
Antiochus IV Epiphanies, 16
Antiochus V Eupator, 17
Apocrypha, 16
Apologists, 27–34
Arand, Charles, xiv
Aristotle, 18, 60, 62
Asellius, letter of, 48
athlete, 117
Augustine, 36, 37, 43–49, 51, 236, 249
Augustinians, 211

Baker, Robert, 20, 234
Baptism, 41, 54
barbarians, 35–36
Bar Kochba Revolt, 27
Barth, Karl, 228
Beckwith, Carl L., xvii, 231
Bede, 60
Beguines and Beghards, 62–64
Bickle and Nordle, 241–43
Biel, Gabriel, 37, 69, 86, 92
book burning, 3, 17, 35, 187
Books of Moses, 171
Brecht, Martin, 3, 165
Bright, John, 15
Brown, Christopher, 183
Bucer, Martin, 79, 88
Cajetan, 209
Calvin, John, 3, 201–208, 221, 249
canon law, 49, 53, 69
catechisms, 121–25
Cerdon, 28
ceremonial law, 61, 86
Charles V, 209
Chemnitz, Martin, 214
Christian life, 20, 31, 38, 44, 52, 111, 135, 167, 177, 183
Christmas Postil, 79
church and state, 35, 53

TOPICAL INDEX

Church Postil, 164, 178
Cicero, 18, 191
civil law, 86, 95
civil use of the Law, 10, 39, 42, 51, 96, 105, 156, 173, 220, 240
classes of mankind, 84, 191
classical ideas of law, 19, 31, 42, 50, 59
Clement of Alexandria, 30–31
Clement VII, 211
clerk, 53–54
commandments, 123
companion, 52
consensus, current, 5–9
Concordia Theological Quarterly, xi, 229
conscience, 131
Contarini, Gasparo, 210–11
Corpus Juris Civilis, 49
Cotton, John, 207
Council of Vienne, 64
council, requests for, 209
Creuziger, Caspar, 165, 168
Cyprian, 37
Decretum Gratiani, 57
Denifle, Heinrich, 68, 252
Diocletian, 35
Dionysius Exiguus, 53
divine use of the Law, 82
doctrine, history of, xiv, xv, 4, 13
Donatist controversy, 37, 46

Ebeling, Gerhard, 5, 7, 36, 81–83, 88, 113, 144, 150, 156, 157, 163, 169, 227
Eck, John, 129
ecumenical dialogues, 228, 252
elect and reprobate, 206
Elert, Werner, xii, 140, 156, 157, 227
enjoying and using, 44
enumeration, 9, 47, 57, 62, 130–35
Erasmus, Desiderius, 37, 88, 103
eschatological perspective, 239
eternal law, 104, 236
ethics, 252
Evangelical Lutheran Church in America, xii, 251
evolution of doctrine, 8
exclusive terms, 5, 135
exercise, 23, 115, 116, 122, 194
exhortation, 31, 155, 207. *See also* admonition.
Fagerberg, Holsten, 36
Faustus the Manichaean, 45, 49, 52
Forde, Gerhard, 6, 233–41
forgery, 4, 156–57, 161
Formula of Concord, 217
Formula of Concord VI, 9, 218, 220, 261–72
Frederick the Wise, 164
freedom, 23, 27, 99, 106, 196

Frend, W. H. C., 35
friends of the Law, 41, 49, 52, 59, 79, 181, 241, 254
friendship, 21
frui and *uti*, Augustine on, 44
function of the Law, 6, 14, 33, 36, 79, 110, 11, 114, 139, 176, 191, 193, 206, 215, 231, 250. *See also* office of the Law; officium legis; use of the Law; usefulness of the Law.
Gerhard, John, 249
Gerichius, Cyriachus, 157
Giles of Rome, 37, 212
Glossa Ordinaria, 55, 58, 106
Gnostics, 28, 63, 64
God, nature of, 29
Gospel, xiii, xiv, 4, 7, 8, 25, 27, 32–34, 44, 48, 51–52, 84, 89, 106, 107, 114–115, 119, 131, 145, 149, 159–60, 166–67, 176, 179, 184, 196, 198, 207, 214–15, 221–22, 231–34, 242–45, 250, 253–54
grace, 29, 43–44, 47, 48, 51, 86, 89, 94, 105–106, 125, 174, 203, 207, 208, 237, 253–54, 269
Gratian, 57–58
Green, Lowell, 8, 188
guardian, Law as, 23
Hagar and Sarah, 23, 39
Heckel, Johannes, 255–56
Hercules, 128

history of doctrine, xvi, 243, 228
Holy Spirit, 38, 47, 82, 103, 105, 112, 142–43, 145, 151–55, 159, 161, 176, 182, 207, 232
House Postil, 166
human use of the Law, 40, 83, 85, 95, 97, 109
Hutchinson, Anne, 207
iconoclasm, 91, 95
imperial legal code, 36
Ingolstadt, University of, 187
instruction of the Law, 191
Instructor, 31
interpretation, 42, 66–67
Irenaeus of Lyons, 29–30, 51
Isidore of Seville, 49–50, 51, 57, 62
Israel, 26, 44
Jedin, Hubert, 212
Jerome, 42–43, 51
Jesus, teaching of, 21–22, 51
Johannes de Caseli, 37
John Chrysostom, 136
Joseph, 172
Joshua, 86, 112, 113
Judaism, 16–17, 22, 255
Judaizers, 111
justification, 4, 31, 39, 47, 109, 112, 129, 136, 139, 143–44, 163, 166, 191, 194, 203, 212, 215, 235, 238
Justin Martyr, 28–29
Justinian, 49

TOPICAL INDEX

Karlstadt, Andreas, 91–92, 95
Keen, Ralph, 8
Klug, Eugene, 156–157
Kolb, Robert, xiv
Kramer, Fred, 188
Law and early Christianity, 27
Law and Gospel, distinction of, 4, 25–25, 28, 33, 51, 52, 132, 139, 143, 144, 176, 222, 242, 243, 251, 253
Law and love, 44
Law and promise, 37, 39
Law motivation, 124
Law of love, 22
Law of Moses, 29, 41, 43, 91–98, 255
Law, abuse of, 46, 94, 142
Law, benefits of, 14–15, 48, 89
Law, categories of, 78
Law, companionship of, 16
Law, compulsion of, 17, 18
Law, constraint of, 86
Law, definitions of, 15, 18–19, 50. *See also* Law of Moses.
Law, instruction of, 15, 18, 19, 30–31
Law, manifold use of, 97
Law, medieval doctrine of, 69, 101
Law, permanence of, 30
Law, persuasion of, 18
Law, pupils of, 93
Law, purposes of, 32
Law, sum of, 257

Law, threefold descriptions of, 92–95
Law, unity of, 9
Lazareth, William, xiii
legalism, 4, 6, 64–66, 184, 240, 253
Leipzig, University of, 187
Lenker edition, 80
Leo X, 209
Lerner, Robert E., 64
Loci Communes, 189–92, 194–97
Logos, 31
Lohse, Bernhard, 165
Lot, allegory of, 46
love, 21, 44–45
Luther, Martin, consistency of, 175–85
Luther, Martin, life of, 3, 73–74, 248
Luther, Martin, preaching of, 92
Luther, Martin, rhetoric and dialectic of, 83–88
Luther, Martin, teaching of, 73–174, 89, 128, 192, 222, 227
Luther, Martin, uniqueness of, 176
Luther, Martin, variety of expression, 95, 259
Luther, most influential writings of, 165, 169
Luther, Martin, use of the Law, 250

Lutheran Church—Missouri Synod, 242, 251
Lutheran Confessions, 83, 261–72
Lutheran Study Bible, The, xiv
magistrate's use of the Law, 10, 95–97
Magna Glossatura, 58
Manichaeanism, 45
Marcion of Sinope, 28, 31
Marius Victorinus, 36–37
martyrs, 35
mathematical trap, 132
Mattes, Mark C., 230
Mayes, Benjamin, 195
McNeill, John T., 202
medieval terms, 70
Melanchthon, Philip, 3, 8, 81, 88, 108, 139, 147, 160, 161, 187–99, 223, 251
Mishnah, 257
modern critiques, 233–43
modern debates, 275–77
moral law, 9, 30, 41
Morning Prayer, 124
mortification, 38, 152–154, 158
Mühlen, Karl Heinz zur, 6
Muller, Richard A., 203, 205
Murray, Scott R., xi, xvii, 217, 218, 229
Musculus, Andrew, 218
mysticism, 108

natural law, 9, 17–19, 40, 50, 97, 190
Neander, Michael, 218
Nestingen, James, 221
new commandment, 21
new law, 29, 33, 51, 65, 77, 106
Nicholas of Lyra, 67–68, 80, 109, 164
obedience, 151, 153, 155, 199, 202, 206
office of the Law, 57–58, 69, 70, 79, 108, 112, 118, 128, 141–42, 160, 173, 177, 194, 205. *See also* officium legis; function of the Law.
officium, 57
officium legis, 7, 14, 58, 70, 79, 194. *See also* office of the Law; function of the Law.
only-two-uses consensus, xii, 88, 127, 141, 156, 236, 253
opus legis, 26
Otto, Anton, 218
outward use of the Law, 104
Paris, University of, 55, 59, 66, 67, 68
parish application, 253–54
passivity, 241
pattern, rhetorical. *See* Luther, Martin, rhetoric and dialectic of
Paul III, 209
Paul III, 212
Paul, Apostle, 24–25

Topical Index

Pauline epistles, 26, 36, 39, 41, 43, 237
Peasants' Revolt, 108
pedagogue, 30–31
pedagogical practices, Greek, 31
pedagogical use of the Law, 156
Pelagius, 41–42, 46
persecution, 35
Peter Lombard, 58–59, 62
Petilian, 46
Petrus Aureoli, 66–67
Philo Judaeus, 22–23
Picards, 76
Plato, 17–18
Poach, Andrew, 218
postils, 67, 79, 163–69
power of the Law, 192
Prayer, xi
preaching, 123, 155, 159, 164, 166, 171
Preus, 195
primal experience, 140
promise, 40
prophetic use of the Law, 10, 46, 47, 51, 69, 96, 112, 207
Puritans, 207
questions, historical, xvi, 228–29
Quintilian, 65
Rabanus Maurus, 54–55, 106, 135, 141, 142
Rast, Lawrence R. Jr., 231–232

Reformation theology, xi, 3, 166, 250–52
Regensburg, 209–210
religion, 32
repentance, 37, 38, 142, 152, 158, 172, 204, 238
research strategy, xiv–xv, 13, 36
righteous man's use of the Law, 10, 40, 44, 47, 51, 56–57, 89, 103, 105, 114, 119, 153, 169, 174, 204, 220
righteousness, 143
righteousness, four kinds of, 130
Rodt, Stephan, 1, 65
role of the Law, 38
Roman law, 19
Rorer, 132, 134
salvation, sanative, 4, 31
sanctification, 39, 130
Saxon Mirror legal code, 95, 96
Schaff, Philip, 63
Schenck, Jacob, 218
Schwiebert, E. G., 165
Schloemann, Martin, 99–103, 108
Scholastics, 130
Schurb, Ken, 194, 218, 223
Sedulius Scotus, 37
Seripando, Girolamo, 211–13
Sherman, Franklin, 149
signs, Augustine's teaching about, 44

Silcock, Jeffrey G., xvii
simul justus et peccator, 103, 105, 111, 152, 158, 204, 219, 244, 250–51, 265
Smalcald Articles, 139–145, 209
Solomon, 15
Souter, Alexander, 41
Spirit and the Letter, 102
spontaneous impulse, 123–124
stages of man, 43, 52, 62, 105, 184, 203, 220, 249
status of a Christian, 22, 25, 39, 59, 78, 115, 151, 159
Summa Theologica, 62
Table of Duties, 124
tables of Moses, 83
Ten Commandments, 179, 181
terms, 9–11, 88–89, 197–98, 257–59
Tertullian, 31–34, 51
testaments, relation between, 28, 29, 34, 38, 51, 52
text effect, 136
Theodosian II, 49
theologians, early western, 35–52
theologians, medieval, 53–70
theologians, Reformation era, 73–223
theological schools, 212
theological use of the Law, 10, 46–48, 51, 55, 60, 75, 102, 107, 125, 140–41, 152, 173, 191, 203, 210
theology, central issue of, 139

third office, 112, 113
third use of the Law, 81, 88–89, 100, 218
Thomas Aquinas, 59–62, 109, 220
threefold law, 45
threefold use consensus, xii
threefold use of the Law, 5, 47, 66, 67, 79–81, 92, 166, 169, 193
thunderbolt, Law as, 140–41
torah, meaning of, 15
Torgau meeting, 108
Tosephta, 255
treiben, 117
Trent, Council of, 212–15
Triune God, 45
twofold use of the Law, 67, 80, 112, 154
Tyconius, 37–39, 47, 51
use of the Law, 7, 24, 33, 54, 59, 82, 94, 111, 176, 188, 210, 248. *See also* usefulness of the Law; function of the Law; office of the Law.
use of the Law, biblical basis of, 8, 26, 248
use of the Law, medieval, 249
use of the Law, modern teaching on, 275
use of the Law, terms of, 9
usefulness of the Law, 39, 48, 74–79, 176, 249. *See also* use of the Law; function of the law; office of the Law.

uses of the Law, 10, 46, 51, 93, 105, 154, 202, 220. *See also* use of the Law.
usus didacticus, 10–11, 197, 198
usus elenchticus, 10, 210
usus normaticus, 10–11, 172–74
usus paedagogicus, 10–11, 197, 198
usus politicus, 10, 132, 197
usus legis, 14, 26, **88**, 150
utilitas, 19
utilitas Legis, 48, 52, 68, 70, 75, 79, **88**
Valentinus, 28
Valparaiso theologians, 251
verbs, Luther's, 115–119
Visitation Articles, 193
Vogel, Larry M., xii, 6, 230, 232, 233
Vulgate, 58
Wendel, Francois, 206
Wengert, Timothy, xii, 6, 7, 147, 193, 220
will of God, 9, 221
wisdom, 14–16, 22, 161
Witte, John, Jr., 192, 227
Word of God, 221
work of the Law, 22, 23, 24, 33, 75, 191
World Wars, 140

Peer Reviewed

Concordia Publishing House

Similar to the peer review or "refereed" process used to publish professional and academic journals, the Peer Review process is designed to enable authors to publish book manuscripts through Concordia Publishing House. The Peer Review process is well-suited for smaller projects and textbook publication.

We aim to provide quality resources for congregations, church workers, seminaries, universities, and colleges. Our books are faithful to the Holy Scriptures and the Lutheran Confessions, promoting the rich theological heritage of the historic, creedal Church. Concordia Publishing House (CPH) is the publishing arm of The Lutheran Church—Missouri Synod. We develop, produce, and distribute (1) resources that support pastoral and congregational ministry, and (2) scholarly and professional books in exegetical, historical, dogmatic, and practical theology.

**For more information, visit:
www.cph.org/PeerReview.**

The Church from Age to Age
A History from Galilee to Global Christianity
General Editor Edward A. Engelbrecht

"An outstanding book! ... Combines all the elements that make for a great text."
—Dr. Robert Caldwell, Southwestern Baptist Theological Seminary

The Church from Age to Age examines key historic events from the time of the apostles through today. Informative and clearly written, readers of all ages will find the answers to the who, why, and how behind the current state of Christianity the world over. Maps, readings from primary sources, and an extensive bibliography, index, and timeline make this a complete one-volume resource for the classroom and for home.

Contributors include Robert G. Clouse, Karl H. Dannenfeldt, Edward A. Engelbrecht, Marianka S. Fousek, Walter Oetting, K. Detlev Schulz, Roy A. Suelflow, and Carl A. Volz. (P) 1048 pages. Paperback.

12-4370LBR   **978-0-7586-2646-2**

The Real Luther: A Friar at Erfurt and Wittenberg
Franz Posset

"Students and researchers should read this book as a model for how to do Reformation History."
—Dr. Markus Wriedt, Goethe University Frankfurt/Main and Marquette University

Roman Catholic Scholar, Franz Posset, carefully explores the history of Luther's development in the crucial years of 1501–17 before Luther's views were disputed. Setting aside legends and accusations, Posset clearly presents the facts about Luther as a late medieval friar in an age of reform.

The Real Luther includes: illustrations from Luther's career; a complete, new translation of Philip Melanchthon's memoirs of Luther's life based on actual discussions with Luther; a fresh chronology of Luther's life from 1501–17, based on the latest research; and extensive references to both primary and secondary literature for Luther studies. (P) 224 pages. Paperback.

53-1180LBR   **978-0-7586-2685-1**

www.cph.org • 1-800-325-3040   Concordia Publishing House

The Chief Theological Topics
Loci Praecipui Theologici 1559

Translated by J. A. O. Preus; new foreword by Jacob A. O. Preus III

"One of the several most significant and influential compendia of theology written during the Reformation." —Richard A. Muller, Calvin Theological Seminary

In honor of the 450th anniversary of Philip Melanchthon's death in 1560, a second edition of his Loci Communes ("Commonplaces" or "Common Topics") has been issued. Originally published by CPH in English under the name *Loci Theologici 1543*, this book is actually Melanchthon's last Latin edition, published in 1559. Generations of Lutheran pastors learned theology from this book in the sixteenth and seventeenth centuries. This revised English edition includes several new features: a new translation of Melanchthon's "Definitions of Terms That Have Been Used in the Church," a new historical introduction, cross-references to the original Latin, a Scripture index, and an index of persons. (P) 400 pages. Hardback.

53-1181LBR   978-0-7586-2687-5

The Life, Work, and Influence of
Wilhelm Loehe 1808 – 1872
Erika Geiger; translated by Wolf Knappe

"This first, full-length biography of a key player in Lutheran history is accessible to lay audiences and appreciated by scholars."
—Prof. John T. Pless, Concordia Theological Seminary, Fort Wayne

The latest and best biography of a father of confessional Lutheranism in North America.

Loehe, who never visited the United States, sent missionaries, founded seminaries, established deaconess training, studied doctrine and liturgy, and fought with church officials. Geiger sets forth Loehe's life, and the divided opinions about him, in a compelling and authoritative narrative. (P) 296 pages. Paperback.

53-1176LBR   978-0-7586-2666-0

www.cph.org • 1-800-325-3040   Concordia Publishing House

C. F. W. Walther: Churchman and Theologian
Various Authors

Called "the American Luther," Rev. Dr. C. F. W. Walther is celebrated as a founder of the log cabin college (1839) that became one of the ten largest seminaries in North America: Concordia Seminary, St. Louis. The educational emphasis and precedents Walther set made his theological heirs highly influential in American Christianity.

In 1847, when Walther helped to found The Lutheran Church—Missouri Synod, the church body included only 19 pastors, 30 congregations, and 4,099 baptized members. At the time of his death forty years later, the church body had grown to 931 pastors, 678 member congregations, 746 affiliated congregations, 544 preaching stations, and 459,376 baptized members.

C. F. W. Walther: Churchman and Theologian includes the winning essays from the 2011 Reformation Theology Research Award as well as an extensive Walther bibliography, providing the latest and best research on Walther in commemoration of the 200th anniversary of his birth.

(P) 216 pages. Paperback.

53-1171LBR   **978-0-7586-2560-1**

Law and Gospel: How to Read and Apply the Bible
General Editor Charles P. Schaum; translated by Christian C. Tiews

" . . . the most influential and utilized work bearing the name of C. F. W. Walther."
—from the Foreword by William J. Schmelder

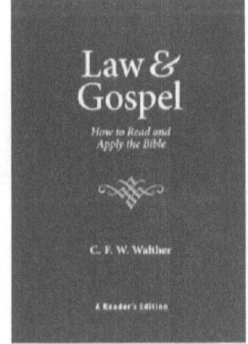

For nearly 100 years, pastors and church workers in the U.S. Lutheran community have read and studied *Law and Gospel* as a classic text on Holy Scripture. This new translation of Walther's 1884–85 evening lectures at Concordia Seminary seeks to communicate in English the passionate and erudite oral delivery of the first president of the LCMS. In addition, readers will find a brief biography of Walther, an overview of Law and Gospel in theological history, maps, photos, and contextual notes that provide a wealth of information on Walther's sources and influences.

(P) 592 pages. Hardback.

53-1166LBR   **978-0-7586-1688-3**

Concordia Publishing House

www.cph.org • 1-800-325-3040

www.ingramcontent.com/pod-product-compliance
Lightning Source LLC
Chambersburg PA
CBHW020639300426
44112CB00007B/171